EDUCATION FINANCE IN THE NEW MILLENNIUM

AEFA 2001 YEARBOOK

Stephen Chaikind
Gallaudet University

William J. Fowler
National Center for
Education Statistics

Editors

EYE ON EDUCATION
6 DEPOT WAY WEST, SUITE 106
LARCHMONT, NY 10538
(914) 833–0551
(914) 833–0761 fax
www.eyeoneducation.com

Library of Congress Cataloging-in-Publication Data

Education finance in the new millenium / edited by Stephen Chaikind and William Fowler, Jr.
    p.   cm. — (Yearbook of the American Education Finance Association ; 2001)
    Includes bibliographical references.
    ISBN 1-930556-16-0
    1. Education—United States—Finance. I. Chaikind, Stephen. II. Fowler, William J., 1945–III. Annual yearbook of the American Education Finance Association ; 2001.

    LB2825 .E253 2001
    379.1′21′0973—dc21

                                                              00-067719

10 9 8 7 6 5 4 3 2 1

Editorial and production services provided by
Richard H. Adin Freelance Editorial Services
52 Oakwood Blvd., Poughkeepsie, NY 12603-4112
(845-471-3566)

Also Available from Eye On Education

**Balancing Local Control and State Responsibility
for K-12 Education: 2000 Yearbook of the American
Education Finance Association**
Edited by Neil D. Theobald and Betty Malen

Money and Schools, Second Edition
by David C. Thompson and R. Craig Wood

Strategies to Help Solve Our School Dropout Problem
by Franklin P. Schargel and Jay Smink

The Emerging Principalship
by Linda Skrla, David Erlandson,
Eileen Reed, and Alfred Wilson

**Data Analysis for Comprehensive
Schoolwide Improvement**
by Victoria L. Bernhardt

**The School Portfolio: A Comprehensive Framework
for School Improvement, 2nd Edition**
by Victoria L. Bernhardt

**The Example School Portfolio:
A Companion to the School Portfolio**
by Victoria L. Bernhardt, et al.

Designing and Using Databases for School Improvement
by Victoria L. Bernhardt

Educating Homeless Students: Promising Practices
Edited by James Stronge and Evelyn Reed-Victor

**Human Resources Administration:
A School-Based Perspective, 2nd ed.**
by Richard E. Smith

Research on Educational Innovations, Third Edition
by Arthur K. Ellis and Jeffery T. Fouts

Resource Allocation: Managing Money and People
by M. Scott Norton and Larry K. Kelly

Urban School Leadership: Issues and Strategies
by Eugene T. W. Sanders

**Working in a Legal and Regulatory Environment:
A Handbook for School Leaders**
by David J. Sperry

DEDICATION

To Hinda, Brian, and Laurie Chaikind,
for their love and patience.

To my 94-year-old father, William J. Fowler,
whose wisdom I hope to attain someday.

CONTRIBUTORS

COEDITORS

Stephen Chaikind is currently Professor of Economics at Gallaudet University in Washington, DC, where he also serves as Chairperson for the Department of Business Administration, Economics, and Finance. A longtime member of the American Education Finance Association, Dr. Chaikind's research interests include the costs of special education, the relationships between health and education, and budgeting and educational administration in higher education. His articles have appeared in various journals, including *Economics of Education Review, Journal of Special Education, Journal of Health Economics, Sign Language Studies*, and *Educational Evaluation and Policy Analysis*. Dr. Chaikind is also a member of the Technical Work Group for the Special Education Expenditure Project, and Book Review Coeditor for the *Journal of Education Finance*.

Previously, Dr. Chaikind was a Principal Analyst at the Congressional Budget Office (CBO), specializing in Social Security and other income security programs, and Chief Economist and Senior Statistical Associate at Decision Resources Corporation, focusing on education finance and the economics of education. He has also served as a Faculty Research Fellow at the National Bureau of Economic Research. Dr. Chaikind received his Ph.D. in Economics from the Graduate School and University Center of the City University of New York in 1978, and also holds a B.B.A. degree from Baruch College and an M.A. degree from City College of New York, both in economics. In 1997, he was named Distinguished University Faculty Member at Gallaudet University.

William J. Fowler, Jr. is the acting program director of the Education Finance Program in the Elementary and Secondary Education and Library Studies Division at the National Center for Education Statistics (NCES), U.S. Department of Education. He specializes in elementary and secondary education finance and education productivity research, and is currently involved with developing and implementing individual student resource measures and issuing a new NCES accounting handbook. In addition, he is also devising a method of reporting education finance in a user-friendly language. His great passion is designing Internet tools for the NCES education finance web site at nces.ed.gov/edfin, as well as graphic displays of quantitative data.

Dr. Fowler previously served as a supervisor of school finance research for the New Jersey Department of Education. He also has taught at Bucknell University and the University of Illinois, served as a senior research associate for the Central Education Midwestern Regional Educational Laboratory (CEMREL) in Chicago and for the New York Department of Education. He received his doctorate in education from Columbia University in 1977. He serves on the editorial boards of the *Journal of Education Finance* and *Educational Evaluation and Policy Analysis,* and on the Board of Leaders of the Council for Excellence in Government. He is also a member of the Governmental Accounting Standards Board Advisory Committee that is charged with developing a *User Guide for Public*

School District Financial Statements. Dr. Fowler received the Outstanding Service Award of the American Education Finance Association in 1997, and served on its Board of Directors from 1992 to 1995.

CONTRIBUTORS

Michael F. Addonizio is Associate Professor of Educational Policy Studies at Wayne State University. His research interests include elementary and secondary school finance and the economics of education. His recent work has focused on nontraditional sources of school revenue, the equity and adequacy effects of school finance reform in Michigan, and the relationship between class size and student achievement. Prior to joining Wayne State University in 1994, Dr. Addonizio served as Assistant Superintendent for Policy and Research for the Michigan Department of Education and as Education Policy Advisor for Governor John Engler of Michigan. He has also taught at the School of Public and Environmental Affairs at Indiana-Purdue University in Fort Wayne. He received the Jean Flanagan Award for the Outstanding Dissertation in Education Finance in 1988 from the American Education Finance Association and served on the Association's Board of Directors from 1987 to 1990. He received his Ph.D. in Economics from Michigan State University in 1988.

Rachel Drown is an Associate in the Research Department of the American Federation of Teachers (AFT). Her research interests include educational reform and school finance issues. Ms. Drown currently is working with the National Charter School Finance Study, a contract to study charter school finance issues funded by the U.S. Department of Education. At the AFT, she also works as a liaison between the AFT and such groups as the Bureau of Labor Statistics, the National Center for Educational Statistics and the Northeast Regional Educational Laboratory at Brown University. Ms. Drown graduated with a bachelor's of science degree in economics from the University of Rhode Island.

David Grissmer is a senior management scientist at RAND. He holds a Ph.D. in physics from Purdue University. His education research includes the study of teacher supply and demand, teacher compensation and attrition patterns, analysis of national test scores to determine the causes of changing trends, analysis of state test scores to determine causes of state differences, and study of the effects of class size reductions. He recently completed a book that analyzes NAEP scores and what these scores indicate about the changing quality of families, communities, and schools, and what educational and social policies work to improve achievement. He was also guest editor for an issue of *Educational Evaluation and Policy Analysis* (EEPA) concerning class size. His current work also includes developing estimates of the number and location of children at educational risk in the United States, and analyzing achievement patterns in central city, suburban, and rural schools.

James W. Guthrie is Professor of Public Policy and Education, Chair of the Department of Leadership and Organizations, and Director of the Peabody Center for Education Policy at Peabody College, Vanderbilt University. He also is chairman of the board of Management Analysis & Planning Inc. (MAP), a private sector management consulting firm that specializes in education finance, management, and litigation support. Previously a professor at the University of California, Berkeley for 27 years, Dr. Guthrie twice has been publicly elected to, and served as president of, the board of education in Berkeley, California. He has been employed by the California and New York state education departments, served as education specialist for the United States Senate, and was a special assistant to the assistant secretary of the federal Department of Health, Education, and Welfare. He holds B.A., M.A., and Ph.D. degrees from Stanford University, undertook postdoctoral study in economics and public finance at Harvard University, and was a Postdoctoral Fellow at Oxford University. He is the author or coauthor of 10 books, and more than 200 professional and scholarly articles.

Mary P. McKeown-Moak is a partner with MGT of America, Inc. a public, governmental and educational consulting firm. Prior to joining MGT, she was the senior financial officer for the Arizona University System. Dr. McKeown-Moak also served as Director of Strategic Planning for Arizona State University, and held various positions for the University of Illinois, the Illinois State Board of Education, the Maryland State Board for Higher Education, Sangamon State University, and Eastern Michigan University. She is a past president of the American Education Finance Association, former chair of the State Higher Education Finance Officers, and past chair of the Fiscal Issues, Policy and Education Finance SIG and Futures Research and Strategic Planning special interest groups of the American Education Research Association. She is the author of four books and numerous articles on education finance and management. Dr. McKeown-Moak received her Ph.D. from the University of Illinois at Urbana-Champaign.

Mary T. Moore is Vice President and Deputy Director of Human Services Research at Mathematica Policy Research, Inc. Her primary research interest is in education. Over a career of 25 years, she has examined policies involving public and private schools, school finance, regular and special education, and the education of disadvantaged youth and adults. Currently, she is the co-principal director of the national evaluation of Upward Bound and the national evaluation of the 21st Century Community Learning Centers. Dr. Moore previously coauthored several congressional reports related to the national assessment of Chapter 1 (Title I), and led the Federal and State Interactions study, a congressionally mandated study sponsored by the U.S. Department of Education that investigated how federal and state education programs and civil rights requirements jointly affect states and localities. She has written numerous reports and articles on topics of educational finance and governance, and twice served on the Board of Directors of the American Education Finance Association.

Ed Muir is Assistant Director of Research for the American Federation of Teachers. A former New York City schoolteacher, Dr. Muir has been an AEFA member since he began working at the AFT in 1996. His responsibilities at AFT include research support for state legislative initiatives, fiscal analysis of school districts in support of bargaining, and managing a program designed to create a network of legislative staff in the various AFT state federations. He is the coauthor of published work on state legislative actions in health care and school finance. Dr. Muir is currently a coinvestigator of the National Charter School

Finance Study funded by the U.S. Department of Education. Muir earned his Ph.D. in Political Science from New York University in 1995.

F. Howard Nelson is Senior Associate Director of Research for the American Federation of Teachers (AFT). He has been a member of AEFA since 1978. Among other responsibilities, he specializes in analyzing budgets, international education data, teacher salary surveys, and analyzing private contracting in public schools. Dr. Nelson is currently the principal investigator of the National Charter School Finance Study funded by the U.S. Department of Education. Prior to joining the AFT, Dr. Nelson taught school finance in the Department of Education Policy Studies at the University of Illinois at Chicago. He has published more than thirty articles in such journals as *American Educational Research Journal, Educational Evaluation and Policy Analysis, Stanford Law and Policy Review, Journal of Education Finance, School Business Affairs, Journal of Labor Research, Journal of Law and Education,* and the *National Tax Journal.* Dr. Nelson was awarded the AEFA outstanding dissertation award in 1980. His master's degree in economics and Ph.D. in educational policy studies are from the University of Wisconsin.

Jennifer King Rice is an Assistant Professor in the Department of Education Policy and Leadership at the University of Maryland. Her research interests include education policy, education productivity, cost analysis applications to education, and educational reforms for at-risk students. Her publications and presentations have precipitated invitations to share her expertise with various organizations, including the U.S. Department of Education, the Maryland State Department of Education, the New York State Board of Regents, the Maryland State Attorney General's Office, the National Center for Education Statistics, and the Society of Government Economists. Prior to joining the faculty at the University of Maryland, Dr. Rice was a researcher at Mathematica Policy Research in Washington DC. She recently completed a term of service on the Board of Directors of the American Education Finance Association. Dr. Rice earned her Ph.D. from Cornell University.

Richard A. Rossmiller is Emeritus Professor of Educational Administration at the University of Wisconsin-Madison. His research deals primarily with the economics and financing of education; he was one of the first researchers to study the deployment and use of resources and their effects in schools and classrooms. Prior to joining the University of Wisconsin faculty in 1961, Dr. Rossmiller served as a teacher, high school principal, and district superintendent. He has also served as a consultant to local, state, national and international organizations and institutions, was Director of the Wisconsin Center for Education Research (1972–1980), Director of the National Center for Effective Schools (1991–1993), and Chair of the Department of Educational Administration at UW-Madison (1982–1990). Dr. Rossmiller was also President of the American Education Finance Association and the University Council for Educational Administration. He has authored or coauthored more than 100 books, monographs, and journal articles, and has testified as an expert witness in more than 20 court cases dealing with state school finance and employment discrimination issues.

Richard Rothstein is a research associate at the Washington, DC-based Economic Policy Institute (EPI), an Adjunct Professor of Public Policy at Occidental

College in Los Angeles, and a senior correspondent for *The American Prospect* magazine. He writes a regular column on education for *The New York Times*. Rothstein's recent publications include *The Way We Were? Myths and Realities of America's Student Achievement* (Century Foundation Press, 1998), *Can Public Schools Learn from Private Schools?* (with Martin Carnoy and Luis Benveniste, Economic Policy Institute, 1999), and *Where's the Money Going? Changes in the Level and Composition of Education Spending* (EPI, 1995 and 1997). He is also the coauthor, with James W. Guthrie, of "Enabling Adequacy to Achieve Reality," in the 1999 National Academy of Sciences volume, *Equity and Adequacy in Education Finance.*

Nancy Van Meter is an Associate Director for the Department of Organization and Field Services for the American Federation of Teachers (AFT). Ms. Van Meter coordinates the AFT's research on the growing role of for-profit companies in providing K-12 instructional services. She has 20 years of experience working with education and health care unions and community organizations. Van Meter received her B.A. degree from Princeton University.

Disclaimer

The chapters in this volume present the views of their respective authors and are intended to promote the exchange of ideas among researchers and policy-makers. The views of the respective authors do not necessarily represent the views of the editors, Gallaudet University, the National Center for Education Statistics, the U.S. Department of Education, or the American Education Finance Association, and no official support is intended or should be inferred.

TABLE OF CONTENTS

THE EDUCATIONAL OUTCOME
CHALLENGE TO EDUCATION FINANCE

PUBLIC AND PRIVATE FUNDS
FOR PUBLIC AND PRIVATE SCHOOLS

CONCLUSION

INTRODUCTION

1

EDUCATION FINANCE IN THE NEW MILLENNIUM: OVERVIEW AND SUMMARY

Stephen Chaikind
Gallaudet University

William J. Fowler, Jr.
National Center for Education Statistics

The genesis of this volume is derived from an idea that, as we peer into the new millennium, the time is ripe for the sometimes provincial field of education finance to reaffirm its bonds with the wider education community. Education finance means many things to many people. The discipline encompasses well articulated topics, of course, such as the design of state funding formulas (which are often dictated through litigation), the achievement of equity in funding, the calculation of future tax revenues from property and other tax sources, and the development of school budgets. And these are important functions. But other questions of a critical nature, such as those involving curricula reform, outcome assessment, accountability, community control, privatization, paying for higher education, and even national economic growth are less frequently addressed as education finance issues.

This American Education Finance Association Yearbook thus assembles a forward looking assessment of the most important education finance policy issues facing the nation as the 21st century begins. The discussions in the chapters that follow are unique in that they examine education finance under the broader rubric of overall education policy. James Guthrie and Richard Rothstein note a wonderfully concise paradigm of this idea at the start of their chapter charting a new era in education finance (Chapter 7). "Old school finance concepts evaluate education in terms of revenue," they note, but "(n)ew finance concepts of adequacy evaluate revenue in terms of education."

Several themes or ideas thought to be closely entwined with the future of education finance emerge with some regularity across the chapters in this volume, including, most notably, those of educational outcomes and accountability. Another common thread concerns how future economic trends and realities will affect education funding. Richard Rossmiller begins his overview of funding in the new millennium (Chapter 2) by reiterating Kirst and Garms's 1980 observation, from the first American Education Finance Association Yearbook, that "The public school system is a dependent variable of larger social and economic forces." He then notes that these very same forces are still at work 20 years later, albeit the dependencies have grown more complex today than ever before.

Clearly, the growth in the number of school-age children will affect education finance decisions in the future. At the start of "Funding in the New Millennium," Rossmiller reviews trends and projections in school enrollment. Stephen Chaikind (Chapter 5) does the same while speculating on the number of future special education students served, and Mary McKeown-Moak (Chapter 6) reviews past and present higher education enrollments. These projections are reasonably well established through current population cohort projections, at least for the total number of students who will be enrolled over the next decade in elementary and secondary schools.

The true challenge in education finance, however, will be to evaluate the financial implications resulting from changes in larger institutional, social, technical, and economic factors that will alter the shape of education for this population. Rossmiller provides, for several population scenarios developed by the National Center for Education Statistics (NCES), what class size and current expenditures might look like in 10 years should basic enrollment trends continue. These measures, and many others, will surely diverge in the coming decades in a variety of ways, as desired goals for improved results, innovative educational processes and programs, technological integration, alternative revenue initiatives, and changing economic conditions, among others, evolve.

Rossmiller continues his overview by discussing how such factors are likely to influence the field of education finance in the future. Both litigation and legislation to ensure equity across school districts will surely continue, as will reforms in the tax structure used to pay for education. Basic changes in educational processes will also affect school finance discussions, especially in terms of technology, class size, and school choice. Although some changes, especially technological innovations, might not increase expenditures, Rossmiller notes that they will nevertheless have financial consequences by changing the budgetary mix.

The planning and assessment of desired education policy goals, of course, cannot occur without timely and accurate data. William Fowler suggests that, although there will be important changes in school and school district financial reporting beginning in 2001, even more improvements are needed to enable better education policy and research. In "Financial Reporting in the New Millennium" (Chapter 3), Fowler proposes three key questions that the public wants to know and, hence, that financial data must address: (1) What is the financial condition of school districts? (2) How has the financial condition of districts changed over time? (3) How is money spent? He addresses these questions through both a review of how data are currently reported at the school district, school, and student levels, and a discussion of changes in finance data reporting necessary to fully answer these key questions.

Although most school finance occurs at the state and local levels, the federal government—in addition to coordinating data efforts—provides funding for a number of educational purposes. The finance of the two largest programs serving at-risk students in the United States are discussed by Mary Moore in "Prospects for Title I in the Early 21st Century: Are Major Changes in Store?" (Chapter 4), and Stephen Chaikind in "Expanding Value Added in Serving Children with Disabilities" (Chapter 5). After summarizing the current funding mechanisms for both of these programs, Moore and Chaikind discuss directions these programs may take in the coming decades. Changes in both will be driven by the congressional reauthorization and administrative regulatory processes, with Title I's reauthorization pending, and important changes occurring in special education as the result of its 1997 reauthorization and 1999 regulations. These programs, serving children who are poor and low-achieving, or who have a disability, appear to be moving towards changes that may, in effect, make them models for education serving the entire population of students, particularly in their use of funds across multiple functions and in their renewed emphasis on outcomes.

In "Financing of Higher Education in the New Century" (Chapter 6), Mary McKeown-Moak discusses future state and federal options in higher education. Higher education finance is related to the costs, or price, of such education, particularly in terms of rising tuition and fees. Federal and state student loan programs, Pell Grants, and other forms of financial aid are also linked to costs. In response to budgetary concerns, state legislators are expected to continue to require more evidence of productivity and accountability as a condition for support for their public colleges and universities. Improved productivity may, in turn, have a moderating effect on higher education costs, especially through potential efficiencies gained in faculty workloads and through the use of technology. However, legislators also wish to see tuition increases moderating, suggesting that more state funding could occur to offset tuition increases.

The demand for improvement, assessment, and accountability in outcomes from the education process is endemic among those who authorize and finance education in the United States. This accelerating focus on outcomes is seen across many of the chapters in this Yearbook. Guthrie and Rothstein suggest an evolution of education finance in three stages in "A New Millennium and A Likely New Era of Education Finance" (Chapter 7), concluding that the future stage will increasingly emphasize outcomes. The first of the stages suggested by Guthrie and Rothstein is one that established a system of schools, the second, ongoing stage is to ensure accessibility and equity, and the third, still evolving stage is the search for adequacy. Guthrie and Rothstein propose a definition of adequacy as "Sufficient resources to ensure students an effective opportunity to acquire appropriately specified levels of knowledge and skills." They also introduce a concurrent concept of "sufficiency," which is a resource level that will provide the opportunity for such outcome expectations to be achieved. They then continue to suggest ways to model and measure adequacy, and pose research questions for the education finance and policy communities to consider when determining adequate resource levels.

Education is a process, of course, where many tangible and intangible factors are combined to achieve a desirable result. The debate for educators begins not in saying that this is in fact true, but by trying to agree on (1) what the desired outcomes should be; (2) what methods or processes should be used to reach these outcomes; (3) how to evaluate both the methods and outcomes selected; and finally, (4) how to pay for them. These ideas have given rise to the concept of education as a production process, and the related, oft-repeated question of "does money matter" in achieving desired educational outcomes. Jennifer King Rice reviews these questions, as well as the history and controversy surrounding education production functions, in "Illuminating the Black Box: The Evolving Role of Education Productivity Research" (Chapter 8). She assesses four overlapping views of the education production process—as a complex configuration of resources, as a multilevel model, as a set of different production processes, and as a dynamic process. Each of these approaches, Rice notes, has its advantages and disadvantages, but, when used judiciously, all can play a role in future education finance policy discussions and in the assessment of ways to improve efficiency.

Another approach to finding answers for key education questions, including those concerning available funding levels and how money spent by schools and districts affects outcomes, is given by David Grissmer in "Research Directions for Understanding the Relationship of Educational Resources to Educational Outcomes" (Chapter 9). Grissmer indicates that experimental research will become an important component in future education finance analysis, both to provide benchmarks for assessment and to further test the results of nonexperimental statistical analysis. Controlled experimentation is probably one of the more difficult forms of education research. Grissmer details a Tennessee experiment on class size during the 1990s as an example of how experimentation can expand measures of outcomes of different education production methodologies and suggest policy alternatives to those derived from sometimes less reliable nonexperimental designs.

The importance of outcomes for education finance appears prominently in other chapters, as well. For Title I programs, for example, Mary Moore (Chapter 4) notes that, while the goal of Title I funding to improve outcomes for underachieving students in poor communities will continue to be supported, opinions differ on how to best achieve this goal. Moore discusses three financial strategies that can be considered to further this goal: (1) transform Title I into a mechanism for broader school reform; (2) consolidate Title I funding to allow autonomy in the use of these funds by states making educational decisions for low-achieving, poor students; and (3) allow Title I funds to be used as part of a broader move towards more privatization and choice for families eligible for these funds. For children with disabilities, Stephen Chaikind (Chapter 5) shows that the 1997 reauthorization and 1999 regulations for the Individuals with Disabilities Education Act explicitly shift the focus of special education towards outcome improvement and assessment. Now, states are required to develop performance goals for students with disabilities, and to include such students in statewide assessments along with regular education students whenever possible. Specific performance indicators have also been developed. Higher education funding, too, is increasingly dictated by performance indicators, and nearly one-half of states have such indicators on their legislative agendas. Mary McKeown-Moak (Chapter 6) cites the National Association of State Budget Officers as saying that "performance based budgeting and funding (is) the most significant trend in state budgeting."

Another general theme that emerges from this 2001 AEFA Yearbook is a cautionary one—that is, that many of the reforms and programmatic changes that will impact outcomes and evaluation are linked to events in the overall economic environment. Many current forces, including the implementation of new technologies, the push for tax reform and tax cuts, the use of vouchers, a movement towards alternative forms of revenues, private management companies in public schools, and the growth of charter schools, among others, depend in part on a strong underlying economy for sustained revenue growth. Although the United States economy showed such growth at the end of the 1990s, the history of business cycles suggests that this expansion will slow in future years—even if the ups and downs in the overall business cycle itself are moderating. The outlook for education finance may change as the economic situation changes, either in terms of the "soft landing" hoped for by current economic policy as the 21st century begins, or in a more pronounced slowdown. However, a slowdown in economic activity will, of course, be followed by other economic expansions during which additional changes in education finance will likely occur.

Despite this expanding economy, Michael Addonizio notes, in "New Revenues for Public Schools: Blurring the Line between Public and Private Finance" (Chapter 10), that "Since 1990,…the growth rate in per pupil expenditures appears to have fallen precipitously." To supplement revenues, many schools and districts have turned to one or more of the new sources of revenues discussed in Addonizio's chapter. These revenues range from the traditional fund raising efforts through sales of candy, gift wrap, or other items, to newer methods such as receiving revenues from tie-ins with internet shopping sites. Whether or not the economy changes—but especially if economic growth slows, pressures to do more with less will ensure that these revenue sources are likely to continue into the future, unless, of course, legislators or the courts question their unequal impacts.

As opposed to receiving private funds to support public education, there is a growing trend into the future to use public money to support more private choice in education. This trend includes hiring private firms to manage public schools, awarding vouchers to families to use in less restricted ways than in neighborhood public schools, and especially increasing the number of charter schools, which are often managed by private concerns, as well. These issues are discussed in detail by Howard Nelson et al. in "Public Money and Privatization in K-12 Education" (Chapter 11). After reviewing these developments, they present a whimsical look at four hypothetical scenarios about what the future of privatization might hold, and conclude that the current trend of growth in the private contracting arena is the scenario most likely to continue.

The health of the economy can affect education finance in other ways too; the authors in the chapters in this Yearbook note many of the following themes. Equity is still an issue before many state courts, and formulas derived to resolve inequitable situations can be affected by the revenue base generated in a strong or weak economy. At the state and local levels, revenue shortfalls from any tax cuts that might be imposed will be linked to the economic situation, as will potential revisions in the property tax basis for K-12 education and in support of public institutions of higher education. At the federal level, issues such as the full funding of special education, the possibility of additional block grant funding for compensatory education, the growth of Pell Grants, the availability of Student Loans for postsecondary students, and other federal initiatives depend on the ability or willingness of Congress to supplement, reduce, or otherwise modify support for these programs. Such support will depend, in part, on surpluses (or deficits) in the federal budget garnered through economic growth.

Technology will affect education finance in several ways, as also indicated across the chapters of this volume. Funding for education stands to benefit from continued economic growth without inflation, brought about by increased productivity due to technological innovation. The implementation of technology at the institutional level will also affect school finance. Costs for enhanced technology may alter the distribution of education spending, as previously noted, although it may also increase funding needs, for example, for capital improvements and training. However, as technologies mature, they may also lead to productivity improvements in education and to cost-savings, and may free additional funds for other processes within the education system. In higher education, McKeown-Moak demonstrates how the use of technology, distance-learning, ubiquitous learning, and other methods raise an extremely complex set of concerns for the finance of higher education and for financial arrangements within institutions.

Finally, there are economic consequences for school finance resulting from the demographic mix in the United States today. We began this overview by observing the effects of changes in the school age population on education finance. But the aging of the entire U.S. population has created an additional competing force for education finance. The costs for publicly supported programs providing services for older individuals, such as Social Security, Medicare, and others, are growing as the population becomes increasingly older, contending with education for a slice of the funding pie. This is less of a problem (or perhaps no problem at all) as long as economic growth continues; however, if growth slows, then education will need to share more limited dollars with these other public programs. And because programs affecting older individuals are funded primarily from federal sources, while education is financed primarily from state and local sources, a shift away from the young towards older individuals will have implications for public finance and taxation as well.

This overview surveys the chapters in this Yearbook. Through the efforts of the authors, the full chapters that follow provide a richness that is only hinted at here. We see this Yearbook as providing education researchers, policy makers, and practitioners with a readily available resource and tool for education finance planning into the coming decades. We believe it will enable additional creative thinking and new ideas as we move into the new millennium. We thank each author for going the extra mile in making this Yearbook a reality.

THE IMPACTS OF EMERGING SOCIAL, ECONOMIC, AND PROGRAMMATIC CHANGE ON EDUCATION FINANCE

2

FUNDING IN THE NEW MILLENNIUM

Richard A. Rossmiller
University of Wisconsin, Madison

The level and the nature of funding for elementary and secondary education in the early years of this new millennium will be the result of economic, social, and political forces that are largely beyond the control of educators.[1] As Kirst and Garms (1980) noted in the first yearbook of the American Education Finance Association, "The public school system is a dependent variable of larger social and economic forces." The forces that will shape school funding in the first decade of the 21st century have, if anything, become more complex than they were at the beginning of the 1980s. The size and age distribution of the population will continue to be an important determinant of educational funding, as will the nation's economic health. In addition, social and political forces are likely to play a more prominent role in determining the level of funding and the way in which funding is allocated to school districts and schools in the next ten years.

One example of these forces is the recent interest in making greater use of market-based systems for delivering schooling to children. This interest has found expression in the adoption of vouchers that may be redeemed at any school—public, private, religious, or secular—in at least three states, and in the establishment of charter schools in a growing number of states. Second, litigation contesting the constitutionality of state school finance programs shows no signs of abating, with greater attention now being devoted to questioning the adequacy of school funding, as well as the equity of funding that characterized the earlier state school finance cases. Third, taxpayers continue to criticize the property tax, the only significant source of tax revenue at the local school district level, and state level policymakers have responded with more limits on local school tax rates or revenues and with higher levels of state funding in an attempt to reduce the reliance on local property taxes. Fourth, critics continue to bemoan the inefficient use of resources in American schools and demand that schools demonstrate greater productivity and accountability. A number of policy makers argue that

---

1 The author expresses appreciation to Allen Odden for his helpful comments and suggestions concerning the content of this chapter.

by providing parents with more choice of schools, the competition inherent in market-based systems would result in greater efficiency and higher student achievement at no greater cost. Given these and other competing forces, predicting future levels of school funding, much less how that funding will be allocated to students and schools, is a daunting undertaking.

PROJECTIONS OF CURRENT EXPENDITURES

Among the factors that influence public school expenditures are pupil enrollments, teacher salaries, and pupil/teacher ratios.[2] The National Center for Education Statistics (NCES) projects that total enrollment in elementary and secondary schools will increase slowly until 2006 and then level off at just over 54 million students (1999a, pp. 3–9), primarily because annual births increased between 1977 and 1990, and are expected to rise again in the first decade of the millennium. Enrollment in public elementary and secondary schools increased by 18 percent between 1984 and 1997 and is expected to increase by an additional 4 percent by 2009. Enrollment in grades K-8 is expected to increase through the 2002–03 school year and then to decline slightly, while enrollment in grades 9–12 is expected to continue to increase throughout the period. Private school enrollment has fluctuated between 5.2 and 5.9 million pupils since the mid-1980s and is projected to increase to about 6 million pupils by 2009. Expansion of private school voucher programs or choice programs during the decade could, of course, alter the distribution of pupils between public and private schools but are not considered in the projections. The NCES enrollment projections are shown in Figure 2.1.

Variables related to school staffing that will influence future expenditures for current operation include teacher/pupil ratios and teacher salaries. Figure 2.2 (pp. 14–15) shows pupil/teacher ratios for the years 1984–1997 and estimated annual average teacher salaries for the years 1984–1998 with three alternative projections for 1998–2009. Pupil/teacher ratios in public elementary schools declined from 19.7 to 18.8 between 1984 and 1992 and then turned upward reaching an estimated 19.4 in 1997. The ratio is predicted to decrease slightly to 19.2 in 2009. The teacher/pupil ratio in public secondary schools dropped from 16.1 to 14.6 between 1984 and 1990, increased to 15.2 in 1992, and declined again to 14.8 in 1997. It is expected to remain quite stable during the projection period—at or near 15.0 until 2009 in the middle alternative projection, at or near 14.8 in the low alternative projection, and to vary between 14.8 and 15.4 in the high alternative projection.

(Text continues on page 16.)

---

2   The projections in this chapter deal almost exclusively with public elementary and secondary schools in the United States. There is no regular collection of common core data from private schools and without reasonably accurate baseline data it is not possible to develop accurate projections for the private elementary and secondary schools in the United States.

FIGURE 2.1 ENROLLMENT (IN THOUSANDS) IN ELEMENTARY AND SECONDARY SCHOOLS WITH PROJECTIONS, FALL 1984 TO FALL 2009

	Total	*Public*		*Private*	
Year	*K-12**	*K-8**	*9–12*	*K-8**	*9–12*
1984	44,908	26,905	12,304	4,300†	1,400†
1985	44,979	27,034	12,388	4,195	1,362
1986	45,205	27,420	12,333	4,116†	1,336†
1987	45,488	27,933	12,076	4,232†	1,247†
1988	45,430	28,501	11,687	4,036‡	1,206‡
1989	45,898	29,152	11,390	4,162‡	1,193‡
1990	46,448	29,878	11,338	4,095‡	1,137‡
1991	47,246	30,506	11,541	4,074‡	1,125‡
1992	48,198	31,088	11,735	4,212‡	1,163‡
1993	48,936	31,504	11,961	4,280§	1,191§
1994	49,707	31,898	12,213	4,360§	1,236§
1995	50,502	32,341	12,500	4,465	1,197
1996	51,375	32,759	12,834	4,486§	1,297§
1997	52,182	33,185	13,137	4,552	1,308
		Projected			
1998	52,768	33,514	13,330	4,597	1,327
1999	53,215	33,701	13,543	4,622	1,348
2000	53,539	33,875	13,658	4,646	1,360
2001	53,821	34,018	13,767	4,666	1,371
2002	54,071	34,075	13,935	4,674	1,387
2003	54,228	34,035	14,119	4,668	1,406
2004	54,369	33,910	14,376	4,651	1,431
2005	54,477	33,723	14,669	4,625	1,461
2006	54,500	33,550	14,868	4,602	1,480
2007	54,435	33,455	14,907	4,589	1,484
2008	54,316	33,421	14,833	4,584	1,477
2009	54,174	33,427	14,699	4,585	1,464

NOTES: * Includes most kindergarten and some nursery school enrollment. † Estimated on the basis of past data. ‡ Estimate is from *Early Estimates* survey. § Projected.

SOURCE: National Center for Education Statistics. (1999). *Projections of education statistics to 2009*, Table 1. NCES 1999-038. Washington, DC: U.S. Department of Education.

FIGURE 2.2 PUPIL TEACHER RATIOS AND ESTIMATED AVERAGE ANNUAL SALARIES OF TEACHERS IN PUBLIC ELEMENTARY AND SECONDARY SCHOOLS WITH ALTERNATIVE PROJECTIONS: 1983–84 to 2008–09

| | *Pupil/Teacher Ratios* | | *Average Teacher Salaries (In 1996–97 Constant Dollars*)* |
	Elementary	*Secondary*	
1984	19.7	16.1	$34,259
1985	19.5	15.8	35,469
1986	19.3	15.7	36,802
1987	19.3	15.2	37,955
1988	19.0	14.9	38,450
1989	19.0	14.6	38,776
1990	18.9	14.6	39,262
1991	18.8	15.0	39,256
1992	18.8	15.2	39,168
1993	18.9	15.1	39,062
1994	19.0	14.8	38,835
1995	19.3	14.4	38,757
1996	18.9	14.4	38,785
1997†	19.4	14.8	38,554
1998	—	—	38,691

Middle Alternative Projections

1998	19.4	14.8	—
1999	19.4	14.8	38,904
2000	19.5	14.8	38,982
2001	19.4	14.9	38,958
2002	19.4	14.9	39,108
2003	19.3	15.0	39,152
2004	19.3	15.0	39,244
2005	19.3	15.1	39,218
2006	19.2	15.2	39,252
2007	19.2	15.2	39,259
2008	19.2	15.1	39,165
2009	19.2	15.0	39,037

| | Pupil/Teacher Ratios | | Average Teacher Salaries (In 1996–97 Constant Dollars*) |
	Elementary	Secondary	
Low Alternative Projections			
1998	19.4	14.8	—
1999	19.4	14.8	38,891
2000	19.4	14.8	38,879
2001	19.2	14.8	38,737
2002	19.1	14.8	38,707
2003	19.1	14.9	38,633
2004	19.1	14.8	38,603
2005	19.0	14.9	38,516
2006	18.9	14.9	38,502
2007	18.8	14.9	38,413
2008	18.8	14.9	38,223
2009	18.7	14.7	38,003
High Alternative Projections			
1998	19.4	14.8	—
1999	19.4	14.8	38,904
2000	19.5	14.8	39,091
2001	19.5	14.9	39,182
2002	19.6	14.9	39,563
2003	19.6	15.1	39,815
2004	19.5	15.2	39,961
2005	19.5	15.3	39,945
2006	19.5	15.4	40,033
2007	19.5	15.4	40,120
2008	19.5	15.4	40,116
2009	19.6	15.3	40,083

NOTES: * Based on Consumer Price Index for all urban consumers, Bureau of Labor Statistics, U.S. Department of Labor. † Projections.

SOURCE: National Center for Education Statistics. (1999). *Projections of education statistics to 2009*, Table 33 and Table 36. NCES 1999-038. Washington, DC: U.S. Department of Education.

Two distinct trends in average teacher salaries (expressed in constant 1996–97 dollars) are evident during the 1984–1998 period. From 1984 to 1990 average teacher salaries showed rapid growth, increasing by over 14 percent from $34,259 to $39,262. This was followed by a decline of 1.5 percent to $38,691 between 1990 and 1998. The average teacher salary is not expected to change a great deal between 1998 and 2009. The middle alternative projection shows a peak of $39,259 in 2007 followed by a decline to $39,037 in 2009; the low alternative projection shows a steady decline to $38,003 in 2009; and the high projection shows an increase to $40,120 in 2007 followed by a decline to $40,083 by 2009. Thus neither average teacher salaries nor pupil teacher ratios are expected to deviate much from the pattern seen in the 1990s.

The National Center for Education Statistics has published projections of current expenditures for public elementary and secondary schools through the 2008–2009 school year (NCES, 1999a). These projections are shown in Figure 2.3. Expenditures for education tend to follow general economic trends quite closely and also track closely with the amount of state aid for education that is provided to local school districts or local governments. The NCES projections are based on a median voter model in which the spending for each public good in the community (in this case elementary and secondary education) reflects the preferences of the median voter, that is, the voter with the median income and the median property value. Thus, "the amount of spending in the community reflects the price of education facing the voter with the median income, as well as his income and tastes" (NCES, 1999a, p. 155). The model used in the projections of educational spending included three types of variables influencing public school expenditures:

1. Measures of the income of the median voter
2. Measures of the intergovernmental aid for education going indirectly to the median voter
3. Measures of the price to the median voter of providing one more dollar of education expenditures per pupil

The three expenditure projections—low, middle, high—reflect different assumed growth paths for these variables and also rest on the assumption that the relationships between these variables and current expenditures for elementary and secondary education will continue throughout the projection period. For example, the effect of decreasing class size, a recent initiative that has attracted considerable support, was not considered in the projections. Similarly, changes in the age distribution of teachers as older teachers retire and are replaced by younger teachers and the potential effects of changes in the way teachers are paid were not considered in the projections. Obviously, any significant changes in these factors will affect the accuracy of the projections. Differences exist among the various states in both the amount of state aid for education they provide to local units of government and in the formulas by which that aid is distributed. Thus, the projections for the nation as a whole cannot be extrapolated to individual states.

(Text continues on page 19.)

FIGURE 2.3 TOTAL CURRENT EXPENDITURES AND EXPENDITURE PER PUPIL IN AVERAGE DAILY ATTENDANCE (ADA) IN PUBLIC ELEMENTARY AND SECONDARY SCHOOLS WITH THREE ALTERNATIVE PROJECTIONS: 1983–84 TO 2008–09

| | | Current Expenditures | | | |
| | | Constant 1996–97 Dollars* | | Current Dollars | |
Year ending	ADA (in thousands)	Total (in billions)	Per pupil in ADA	Total (in billions)	Per pupil in ADA
1984	36,363	$180.2	$4,956	$115.4	$3,173
1986	36,523	200.3	5,485	137.2	3,756
1988	37,051	215.5	5,815	157.1	4,240
1990	37,799	235.6	6,233	188.2	4,980
1992	38,961	242.9	6,234	211.2	5,421
1994	40,146	251.6	6,267	231.5	5,767
1996	41,502	262.3	6,320	255.1	6,146
1997†	42,256	269.5	6,378	269.5	6,378
Middle Alternative Projections					
1998†	42,933	276.8	6,446	281.7	6,562
1999	43,417	282.9	6,516	294.0	6,771
2000	43,787	289.3	6,607	308.8	7,053
2001	44,055	293.0	6,651	321.8	7,305
2002	44,289	299.7	6,767	338.4	7,640
2003	44,497	303.5	6,821	352.7	7,927
2004	44,631	308.3	6,909	—	—
2005	44,753	312.2	6,976	—	—
2006	44,851	316.1	7,048	—	—
2007	44,875	320.1	7,134	—	—
2008	44,824	323.6	7,219	—	—
2009	44,724	326.8	7,306	—	—

(Figure continues on next page.)

Current Expenditures

Year ending	ADA (in thousands)	Constant 1996–97 Dollars*		Current Dollars	
		Total (in billions)	Per pupil in ADA	Total (in billions)	Per pupil in ADA
Low Alternative Projections					
1998†	42,933	276.8	6,446	281.7	6,562
1999	43,417	282.7	6,511	297.1	6,843
2000	43,787	287.6	6,568	315.6	7,209
2001	44,055	289.4	6,568	332.6	7,549
2002	44,289	292.9	6,614	352.4	7,956
2003	44,497	294.7	6,623	371.3	8,344
2004	44,631	297.3	6,662	—	—
2005	44,753	300.0	6,703	—	—
2006	44,851	302.9	6,754	—	—
2007	44,875	305.1	6,798	—	—
2008	44,824	306.6	6,841	—	—
2009	44,724	307.9	6,885	—	—
High Alternative Projections					
1998†	42,933	276.8	6,446	281.7	6,562
1999	43,417	282.9	6,516	291.6	6,717
2000	43,787	291.1	6,648	304.7	6,959
2001	44,055	296.8	6,736	315.8	7,168
2002	44,289	307.4	6,942	332.3	7,504
2003	44,497	315.0	7,079	346.5	7,788
2004	44,631	320.9	7,191	—	—
2005	44,753	325.2	7,266	—	—
2006	44,851	330.2	7,362	—	—
2007	44,875	335.8	7,484	—	—
2008	44,824	341.2	7,612	—	—
2009	44,724	346.4	7,746	—	—

NOTES: * Based on the Consumer Price Index for all urban consumers, Bureau of Labor Statistics, U.S. Department of Labor. † Current expenditures are *Early Estimates,* and average daily attendance is projected.

Projections in current dollars are not shown (marked —) after 2003 due to the uncertain behavior of inflation over the long-term.

SOURCE: National Center for Education Statistics. 1999. *Projections of Education Statistics to 2009*, Table 34. NCES 1999-038. Washington, DC.

Current expenditures for public elementary and secondary schools increased 50 percent between 1983–84 and 1996–97, from $180.2 billion to $269.5 billion in constant 1996–97 dollars. Expenditure per pupil in Average Daily Attendance (ADA) increased from $4,956 in 1983–84 to $6,378 in 1996–97, an increase of 28.7 percent. The percentage of total disposable income devoted to public school expenditures increased slightly between 1983–84 and 1996–97—from 4.4 percent to 4.8 percent (NCES, 1999a, p. 77). Current expenditures per pupil as a percentage of personal income per capita grew from 28.2 percent in 1983–84 to 30.2 percent in 1996–97 (NCES, 1999a, p. 78). These data suggest that public elementary and secondary education is a favored public good, since the percentage of disposable income spent for public education has continued to increase. The U.S. economy has been on a rising growth path in recent years, so it is understandable that total expenditures and expenditures per pupil have increased. It is reasonable to expect that they will continue to increase so long as the U.S. economy continues to grow at a healthy pace.

There has also been an increase in state aid to public schools during this period. From 1982–83 to 1996–97 state aid increased from $402 per capita to $547 per capita in constant 1996–97 dollars, an increase of over 36 percent (NCES, 1999a, p. 177). By 2009 they are expected to rise to $558 per capita in the low projections; in the middle projections they will increase to $590 per capita; and in the high projections they will rise to $625. Disposable personal income per capita (in constant 1996–97 dollars) also has increased—from $17,591 per capita in 1984 to $21,365 in 1997 (NCES, 1999a, p. 176). It is expected to increase to $24,006 in 2009 under the low projections, to $25,398 in 2009 under the middle projections, and $26,799 in 2009 under the high projections.

The low alternative projection of current expenditure per pupil in average daily attendance indicates a slow but steady growth in expenditure per pupil to a peak of $6,885 in the school year 2008–2009. The middle alternative projection also shows a steady increase with expenditure per pupil reaching $7,306 in 2009. The high alternative projection series exhibits a similar pattern with expenditure per pupil in 2009 at $7,746. All three series of projections indicate a period of growing expenditure per pupil but with growth occurring less rapidly in the low and middle series than in the high series. The increase in expenditure per pupil by 2009 under the low projection is about 8 percent (in constant 1996–97 dollars); under the middle series the growth is 14.5 percent, and under the high projection series the growth is over 21 percent. These increases in expenditure per pupil are due primarily to the influence of the three variables noted earlier—increases in income per capita, increasing state aid, and the price to the median voter of increased school spending. Of course, any changes in the trends of these variables will affect the accuracy of the projections.

In summary, it appears from the projections by the National Center for Education Statistics that the first decade of the new millennium will see slowly rising expenditures per pupil, an increase in average daily membership until 2007 followed by a slight decline, stable or slowly rising average teacher salaries, and rather stable teacher/pupil ratios in the neighborhood of 19 pupils per teacher in elementary schools and about 15 pupils per teacher in secondary schools.

EXPENDITURES FOR CAPITAL OUTLAY

A steep decline in the percentage of total expenditures for education that were devoted to capital outlay/debt service since 1959–60 helps explain why it is becoming increasingly evident that there are serious deficiencies in the nation's school plant infrastructure. Why the decline in support for capital outlay and debt service? It may be that, after the explosion of school building projects during the 1950s and early 1960s to provide schools for the children of the post World War II "baby boom," citizens and school policymakers felt very little new capital outlay was needed, or that the school plant infrastructure had been dealt with adequately. Because in most states the burden of financing new school construction or remodeling is borne primarily by the property tax, the decline also may indicate a growing dissatisfaction with the property tax on the part of local taxpayers as reflected in their reluctance to vote in favor of local school bond issues.

Attempting to project future expenditures for capital outlay for public elementary and secondary schools is, at best, a guessing game. Provisions for financing capital outlay vary widely among the 50 states. For example, during the 1993–94 school year 14 states provided no state aid for capital outlay or debt service whereas 8 states funded capital outlay/debt service as part of their basic state aid program, although the specific arrangements varied from state to state (American Education Finance Association, 1995, Table 11). There is growing recognition that the states, and perhaps even the federal government, must become much more involved in providing the revenue to meet the backlog of school building needs—including constructing new schools and retrofitting existing school buildings to take advantage of modern technologies. New Jersey lawmakers, for example, have been debating proposals that could cost up to $11.5 billion over seven years to renovate and build schools in nearly every school district (*Education Week*, Dec. 8, 1999). A *New York Times* headline for an article discussing the various New Jersey proposals captures neatly the dilemma confronting the lawmakers: "Big Plans for New Jersey's Schools, but Where's the Money?" (Nov. 29, 1999, p. B1).

It appears that governors and state legislatures may have to answer the question of where the money comes from because the plaintiffs in state school finance litigation are now questioning the inequities in the school facilities that exist among the districts in a state. The Arizona Supreme Court, for example, in its decision in *Roosevelt Elementary School District v. Bishop* (1994), ordered the state to develop a program of school finance aid that will assure all Arizona school districts have adequate facilities. Similarly, the New Jersey Supreme Court in its 1998 decision in *Abbot v. Burke* ordered the state to pay for the facilities needed in the 28 low-wealth New Jersey school districts that challenged the state's state school aid system.

The extent of the nation's funding shortfall in the school capital outlay area has been quantified in two reports. The General Accounting Office estimated in 1995 that the funds needed to finance new school construction totaled $112 billion. A report by the National Education Association in April of 2000 estimated that $254 billion is needed for new school construction, including remodeling and retrofitting existing schools to utilize new technologies (*Education Week*, April 5, 2000, p. 24).

Some insight into the cause of the capital outlay deficit may be obtained by examining the relationship over time of capital outlay expenditures to total expenditures for public elementary and secondary education. Figure 2.4 summarizes this relationship from 1919–20 to 1994–95. From 1919–20 through 1959–60, expenditures for capital outlay and debt service ranged between 16.58 and 20.18 percent of total expenditures for education. The percentage dropped to 14.33 percent by 1969–70, and then to 8.73 percent in 1979–80. In recent years, it has been in the range of 10 to 11 percent of the total expenditure for elementary and secondary education. A very similar pattern is evident when expenditures for capital outlay/debt service are expressed as a percentage of expenditures for current operation. Between 1919–20 and 1959–60 the percentage ranged from 19.87 to 25.29. It dropped to 16.73 in 1969–70 and to 9.57 in 1979–80, before recovering to around 12 percent in recent years.

FIGURE 2.4 TOTAL EXPENDITURES AND EXPENDITURES FOR CAPITAL OUTLAY (IN THOUSANDS OF DOLLARS) FOR PUBLIC ELEMENTARY AND SECONDARY SCHOOLS, 1919–20 TO 1994–95

School Year (1)	Total expenditures* (2)	Current expenditures* (3)	Capital outlay and debt service expenditures† (4)	Capital outlay and debt service as percent of total expenditures (Col. 4/ Col. 2)	Capital outlay and debt service as percent of current expenditures (Col. 4/Col. 3)
1919–20	$1,036,151	$864,396	$171,755	16.58	19.87
1929–30	2,316,790	1,853,377	463,414	20.00	25.00
1939–40	2,344,049	1,955,166	388,883	16.59	19.89
1949–50	5,837,743	4,722,887	1,114,754	19.10	23.60
1959–60	15,613,255	12,461,955	3,151,300	20.18	25.29
1969–70	40,683,429	34,853,578	5,829,854	14.33	16.73
1979–80	95,961,561	87,581,727	8,379,833	8.73	9.57
1989–90	212,769,564	191,211,902	21,557,663	10.13	11.27
1993–94	265,306,634	236,224,562	29,082,071	10.96	12.31
1994–95	278,965,657	248,993,151	29,972,506	10.74	12.04

NOTES: * All schools. † Prior to 1969–70, excludes capital outlay by state and local school housing authorities.

SOURCE: National Center for Education Statistics. 1998. *Digest of education statistics 1997*, Table 162. NCES 1998-2015. Washington, DC: U.S. Office of Education.

Several of the conditions discussed above (that were not present during the past three or four decades) will exert pressure to increase expenditures for capital outlay/debt service during the coming decade. Based on the middle alternative current expenditure projections shown in Figure 2.3 (pp. 17–18), expenditures for capital outlay/debt service will be about $40 billion in constant 1996–97 dollars by 2009, assuming they continue to be about 12 percent of expenditures for current operation. If the percentage of current expenditures devoted to capital outlay were to increase to 20 percent, as it was during the first half of the 20th century, expenditures for capital outlay/debt service would reach over $65 billion annually by 2009.

POTENTIAL PERTURBATIONS AFFECTING SCHOOL EXPENDITURE PROJECTIONS

The foregoing projections of expenditures for current operation and capital outlay/debt service are based on certain assumptions concerning the economy (per capita income) and the behavior of the political system (state aid for local school governments). Should these assumptions prove to be incorrect, the projections will be inaccurate—although with three sets of projections, one of them is likely to be close to the mark. And even if projections of spending for current operation are close to the mark, it is quite possible that the way in which money is allocated to and within school districts and schools could be altered substantially during the first decade of the millennium. Some sources of potential perturbations—economic, legal, political, or educational policy decisions—that could alter current public school finance arrangements will be discussed in this section.

STATE SCHOOL FINANCE LITIGATION

Litigation challenging the equity and/or the adequacy of existing state aid programs for elementary and secondary education has been going on for more than 30 years and shows no signs of diminishing in the next decade. Already noted are the recent court decisions in Arizona and New Jersey that will require the state to play a much larger role in financing educational facilities, a responsibility that has traditionally rested with local units of government. Most states have had one or more school finance cases, and by the fall of 1999 at least 17 state supreme courts had either held their state's school finance system to be unconstitutional or had upheld lower court decisions that so ruled. In some states where the school finance plan had been upheld in an early case it has been ruled unconstitutional in subsequent actions. Because school finance litigation is usually the result of plaintiffs' frustration with their inability to secure legislative action to improve the equity and adequacy of state school aid programs, one can expect these cases to continue to be filed when legislative efforts to reform the system are unsuccessful.

Substantial differences in expenditure per pupil among the school districts in a state are quite common. These differences result primarily from differences in the local school tax base available to individual school districts, especially in states where a large part of the revenue for current operation is provided by local property taxes. Districts in which the tax base per pupil is small simply cannot raise very much revenue per pupil even if they exert great effort (levy a high tax rate). This poses a conundrum for advocates of local control of education. It is argued that local control of education has little meaning unless the local units of school governance have financial resources sufficient to provide an adequate educational program. But it also is argued that meaningful local control requires that there be a significant local financial contribution. The higher amounts of state aid that are required to neutralize the effect of the large differences among local districts in revenue per pupil that result from large differences in their local tax bases tend to be accompanied by more state mandates and controls, thus diluting local control.

There is ample evidence of the differences in expenditure per pupil within the various states. In fact, it is these differences that give rise to the school finance litigation. Hertert, Busch, and Odden (1994) found large differences within states in both their school revenue and school expenditure statistics in 1989–90. For example, the coefficient of variation for school district revenue per pupil varied from 35.01 percent in Montana to 6.64 percent in West Virginia and the coefficient of variation for school district expenditure per pupil ranged from 43.79 percent in Alaska to 6.79 percent in West Virginia. Per pupil revenue in Alaska at $8,201 was three times greater than that in Mississippi, which had per pupil revenue of $2,618. Average expenditure per pupil ranged from a high of $7,918 in Alaska to a low of $2,606 in Utah.

In a study conducted for the National Center for Education Statistics (1998), Parrish and Hikido also reported substantial interstate differences, noting that "median total revenues differ considerably between the highest revenue state of New Jersey and the lowest revenue state of Utah, both in terms of actual dollars ($9,257 versus $3,185) and in cost- and need-adjusted dollars ($6,721 versus $2,862)" (p. 100). They also found major intrastate differences with a disparity in revenues between students at the 5th and 95th percentiles of more than 2:1 in nine states. Hussar and Sonnenberg (NCES, 2000) examined trends in disparities in per pupil expenditures and concluded that, "For most of the states, a majority of disparity indices for unified districts indicated declining disparity from 1979–80 to 1993–94 (p. v)." They also noted, however, that six of the seven disparity measures they examined showed increasing disparity for the nation as a whole, partly because expenditures per pupil increased at different rates in different parts of the country.

The task of bringing a state's school financial aid program into compliance with its constitutional requirements ultimately rests with the state legislature. A number of remedies are likely to be discussed by legislators in the next few years. Nearly all of them would require altering the program or process by which money is distributed to local school districts or schools. One possibility is to adopt full state funding of all local school districts with no local funding. This would require very large amounts of additional state revenue in most states (and very likely would reduce the overall level of funding per pupil based on California's experience from 1978 to 1998). It also would pose a serious threat to the tradition of local control of American schools. Both of these would work against its adoption. However, other than variations in funding that result from differences among districts due to their varying needs or costs, such a program should result in equal per pupil funding for all districts—although the amount of funding might be equitable but inadequate.

A variation on this theme would be to eliminate the local district and fund each school equally (with necessary adjustments for need or cost differences). If, for example, a state were to adopt a statewide voucher program, it might well choose to fund each school in this way. Another alternative would be to adopt a complete district power equalizing program in which a given local tax rate would be guaranteed to produce a given amount of revenue per pupil and any local revenue above the guaranteed amount would be "recaptured" by the state. Experience has shown that this approach, if not unconstitutional in a given state, is politically difficult or impossible to enact because it takes money raised from the politically unpopular property tax and returns it to the state's coffers. A third alternative would be to adopt an adequate foundation program and to power equalize any optional local tax revenue in excess of the foundation program level. While this approach would not equalize expenditure per pupil in a state's school districts, it has the potential to greatly reduce variations in expenditure per pupil. Adopting any one of these alternatives would require major changes in the process used in funding public elementary and secondary schools in most states.

The attention paid recently to the importance of adequacy as a factor in funding education in a manner that complies with state constitutional mandates also holds important implications for future funding. It is at least conceivable that a state could adopt a school finance program that is statistically equitable but totally inadequate to fund a solid basic educational opportunity for each child. Several state supreme courts, for example those in West Virginia and Kentucky, have attempted to specify the essential components of the educational offering required by their state's constitution. It is entirely possible that decisions based on an adequacy criterion of funding will require higher levels of state/local funding than those based on an equity criterion.

The research cited above shows that very large differences in revenue and expenditure per pupil exist among the states. Even if by some miracle each state was able to adopt a school finance program that provided intrastate equity, significant interstate differences would still exist. Eliminating interstate variations in revenue and expenditure per pupil that are not related to need or cost differences would require action by the federal government. Although not inconceivable, such action does not appear to be of high priority within the next decade given the current political climate in which tax cuts and school choice options have a much higher profile.

TRENDS IN TAXATION

The question of what sources of tax revenue should be used to support public education is one that is likely to be at least as contentious in the future as it has been in the past. From 1919–20 to the mid-1980s there was a consistent trend toward a higher percentage of revenue for public elementary and secondary schools being provided by the state. From about 16.5 percent in 1919–20, the state share of public school revenue increased to 48.9 percent in 1984–85. During this same period the local share of revenue declined from 83.2 percent in 1919–20 to 44.4 percent in 1984–85. In short, there was a clear trend toward increased reliance on state tax revenue and less reliance on revenue from the local property tax to support elementary and secondary schools during this period. Since 1984–85, the state share has declined slightly (to 45.4 percent in 1996–97) and the local share has increased slightly (to 48 percent in 1996–97). The federal share, which reached nearly 10 percent in 1979–80, declined to 6.1 percent in 1989–90 and was 6.6 percent in 1996–97 (NCES, 1997; NCES, 1999b).

The local property tax has been the only significant source of school revenue at the local level. It also is the least popular of the three major sources of tax revenue—income, sales, and property taxes—although none of the three are well-loved as is evident from the tax cutting proposals advanced by politicians of every persuasion during the state and national election campaigns in 2000. Policy initiatives designed to reduce reliance on the property tax as a source of revenue for public schools during the past 80 years have been of two primary types: (1) greater reliance on revenue from state sales and income taxes through increased state aid to local districts, and (2) restricting the use of the property tax by local governments through imposition of tax levy limits, revenue or expenditure limits, supermajority requirements on tax elections, and so on. There is little basis for expecting a sudden increase in the popularity of the property tax and a resumption of the trend toward a higher percentage of state support is quite possible. However, if proposals to roll back either income or sales taxes are successful, state policy makers may find the state does not have sufficient revenue to replace local property tax revenues with additional state aid.

California's experience over the past 25 years is instructive as to the potential adverse effects of higher levels of state aid and limitations on the revenue obtained from local property taxes. The combined effects of the *Serrano v. Priest* (1971) decision, which required that the state distribute its school aid in a manner such that "wealth-related" spending per pupil did not differ by more than $100, and the Proposition 13 initiative, which froze property values and capped local school tax rates, brought about a "leveling down" of expenditure per pupil across the state. Most objective observers agree that one result was deterioration in the quality of education offered in many public schools in California. One may hope that the experience in California will forewarn policy makers in other states to be aware of the potentially adverse consequences of well-intended changes in the way they support public schools.

The current interest in a less steeply graduated income tax rate structure at the federal level, or even a "flat" tax, has important implications for school finance (Rossmiller, 1996). States that levy a tax on income typically use the federal income tax form as a point of departure for calculating an individual's state income tax, so any change in federal income definitions would affect state tax calculations. For example, state and local income and property taxes paid may be claimed as itemized deductions on the federal tax form, thus reducing the taxpayer's federal tax bill and effectively reducing the "bite" taken by state and local income and property taxes. If this deductibility were lost, one could anticipate even more resistance to local property taxes.

TECHNOLOGY

Changes in the technologies employed in delivering instruction will almost certainly occur in the coming decade. Although such changes may have little effect on total expenditures for public elementary and secondary schools, they may have significant effects on the way in which money is allocated to and within schools. For example, rapid changes in communications technology, such as the growth in the amount of fiber-optic cable, the amazing expansion of bandwidth, and the ability to transmit almost infinite amounts of information at enormous speed could transform the delivery of instructional services to learners in ways that have yet to be imagined. Students might receive much of their instruction over the Internet, perhaps at home rather than in a school building. They may have access to the most gifted teachers in a school system or a state for much of their instruction. And the development of wireless communications technology will enable students in small remote communities to access the same gifted teachers and advanced level courses as those in the most exclusive suburban communities.

These opportunities are not without at least some financial consequences. Major investments in renovation and remodeling will be required in many schools to create the infrastructure needed to take advantage of these emerging technologies. This suggests that spending for capital outlay/debt service will need to approximate the level of 20 percent of current expenditures that prevailed prior to 1960 rather than the 12 percent level that has characterized the past 40 years. It also suggests that different kinds of school buildings may be needed in the future.

CLASS SIZE

Reducing the number of students per classroom, especially in the earliest school grades, has become politically popular in many states. Although many people believe intuitively that students will learn more in smaller classes, the results of the Tennessee STAR Project have provided evidence from a controlled experiment that small classes (of 13 to 17 pupils) do result in improved student performance in the elementary grades, and that the improvement persists in subsequent grades (Finn & Achilles, 1999). These results have led several states (at least 19 in 1999) to adopt some type of class size reduction policy. This can be an expensive initiative because implementation of a class size reduction policy on a statewide basis requires more teachers as well as additional classrooms. Brewer, Krop, Gill and Reichardt (1999) have developed estimates of the cost of implementing nationally various policy options concerning class size reductions. They estimated the annual cost (in 1998–99 dollars) of reducing class size in grades 1–3 would be about $2 billion if the maximum class size were 20 pupils, about $5 billion if the maximum class size were 18 pupils, and about $11 billion if the maximum class size were 15 pupils. They questioned whether reducing class size would be the most cost-effective use of the money required to implement such policies. However, given the political popularity of the class-size reduction movement, it is likely to persist in some form and could significantly raise school expenditures in coming years.

TEACHER COMPENSATION

The criteria used in determining teacher compensation may well change in the coming decade and the changes in instructional technology discussed in the preceding section may result in much more differentiation of assignments and responsibilities in the teaching work force. Such changes would have important implications for the procedures and criteria used in allocating resources within school districts and schools, although the total expenditures for public elementary and secondary schools might not change to a significant degree. There has been much discussion during the past few years of the possibility of changing teacher compensation practices to reflect what teachers know and are able to do rather than the long-established practice of basing pay increments for teachers on their years of teaching experience and the number of academic credits or degrees they have accumulated (see, for example, Odden & Kelley, 1997). The success of the National Board for Professional Teaching Standards (NBPTS) in identifying and certifying teachers who meet high and rigorous standards of professional knowledge and practice was an important first step toward basing compensation on a teacher's knowledge and skills. Odden (2000) points out that, "As of April 1999, 17 states (covering 42% of all teachers) had policies that either paid all or a part of the $2,000 fee for teachers to go through the NBPTS assessment procedure or increased their salaries when they earned board certification" (p. 362). Most of the money for school incentive bonuses is "new" money, that is, additional state appropriations earmarked to support this initiative.

The Teacher Union Reform Network (TURN), representing 21 local teacher unions in large urban districts (including both National Education Association and American Federation of Teachers affiliates) has been actively exploring ways in which teacher compensation can be used to support a school's strategic goals and its need to improve student performance (Urbanski & Erskine, 2000). Three new approaches to teacher compensation are currently being explored in the TURN districts. School-based performance award programs that provide an incentive (typically monetary) to a school or to individual teachers that meet specified improvement goals or achieve specified gains in student performance are being explored in more than one-third of the districts. Second, additional compensation tied to NBPTS certification, as well as added responsibilities as lead teachers, mentors, and so on, is available in a majority of the TURN districts. The third approach, knowledge-and skills-based pay systems, which tie additional compensation to demonstrated knowledge, skills, and professional expertise, is being tried in at least nine TURN districts.

The fact that teacher unions are willing to explore various approaches to paying teachers based on their knowledge, skills, and performance represents a tacit, if not explicit, recognition that the single salary schedule approach to teacher compensation has neither encouraged nor rewarded productivity in our elementary and secondary schools. Although a handful of school districts in the United States have tried various merit pay schemes during the 20th century, discussion of merit pay for teachers has been largely an academic exercise. Most merit pay programs have foundered because of the subjectivity involved in determining merit. The new approaches currently being tested, which employ objective criteria and impartial evaluation of performance, hold some promise that during the 21st century we may develop ways of compensating teachers and other educational personnel that recognize and reward them for their success in enhancing their students' achievement. If it can be demonstrated that additional resources intelligently employed can indeed raise school productivity, then policy makers and the public may be willing to support higher levels of spending for public elementary and secondary schools.

SCHOOL CHOICE: IMPLICATIONS
FOR FINANCING EDUCATION

American states typically implemented their constitutional mandate to establish a system of free public school open to all children by establishing local school units (districts) and delegating to these units responsibility for the day-to-day operation of schools.[3] Attention first was focused on establishing "the common school," that is, elementary schools; but by the beginning of the 20th century the system included the high school as part of the public school system. Children generally were expected to attend the school to which they were assigned, usually the one in their neighborhood, and if they or their parents wished to attend some other school, they would need to obtain approval from the local governing board. If they wished to attend school in a district other than the one in which they lived, they would be required to pay tuition to the receiving district as well as to pay school taxes in the district in which they lived.

This organizational scheme has been characterized as a public school monopoly by some critics, who claim that it robs parents of control over the education of their children. They also claim that, because public schools have no competition, administrators and teachers have no incentive to use school resources efficiently. They maintain that the competition inherent in market-based models of schooling would result in greater productivity and efficiency in the use of school resources; that poor schools would be forced to either improve or go out of business as parents and students "voted with their feet" by choosing to attend good schools.

The extent to which school choice exists in the United States varies from state to state and district to district, and it is hard to ascertain the extent to which school choice is available within public school systems. One could argue that the existence of over 15,000 school districts in the United States represents a first level of choice, particularly for those families that can take advantage of the opportunity to reside in a district that matches their educational preferences. The National Center for Education Statistics (1999c) reported that during the 1997–98 school year the public elementary and secondary school system included 82,660 regular schools, 2,068 special schools, 930 vocational schools, and 3,850 alternative schools. Some large districts have for many years maintained specialty schools that are open to students from throughout the school district who possess unique talents in areas such as science, technology, or the performing arts. Some states, for example, Minnesota and Massachusetts, permit students to attend a public school in a district other than the one in which they live. And parents have always been free to send their children to private schools, assuming they are able to pay the tuition. Many children, however, have no realistic opportunity to exercise choice in selecting the school they will attend, either because there is no feasible alternative school in their area, or because they cannot afford to attend any of the alternative schools. The consistently low test scores and high dropout rates

---

3 A discussion of some effects of various approaches to school choice is found in Goldhaber (1999).

found in many schools serving children from low income or ethnic minority families has led to increasing interest in market-based alternatives for providing the free public education required by state constitutions. This is evident in the campaign platforms of some of the candidates for state or federal office in the 2000 elections, who advocated support of school choice programs as a fundamental component of their agenda.

One approach to school choice that has emerged in recent years is charter schools. This might be termed a quasi-market approach, since charter schools are publicly funded just as are regular public schools. Charter schools have been established by a wide variety of individuals and organizations—teachers, administrators, other school personnel, parents, community members, educational entrepreneurs, or other persons. They generally are sponsored by local or state educational organizations, depending on the laws of the state, and are free to decide their own educational goals and objectives and how to organize and manage the school organization. Charter schools are not subject to many of the administrative and bureaucratic controls that constrain regular public schools. In return they are held accountable in two important ways: (1) they are subject to consumer demand and are likely to lose their students if the educational results that were promised are not forthcoming, and (2) their charter is subject to renewal every three to five years and the decision concerning renewal of the charter is based largely on their performance.

From its beginnings with two charter schools in Minnesota in 1992, the charter school movement has grown very rapidly. *The State of Charter Schools Fourth Year Report*, a study by the U.S. Department of Education's Office of Educational Research and Improvement (2000), found more than 1,400 charter schools operating in 27 states in September, 1999, including 421 charter schools that opened for the first time in 1999. During the 1998–99 school year there were over 200,000 students enrolled in the 27 states in which charter schools were open. This represented 0.8 percent of the students enrolled in public schools in the 27 states that had charter schools operating. In California, the 73,905 students enrolled in charter schools represented about 1.3 percent of the total school enrollment in the state. In Arizona, 32,209 students, constituting about 4.0 percent of the state's total school enrollment were attending charter schools. In a recent development, several school districts either have become charter districts, or have moved to have all schools within the district become charter schools (Brockett, 1999).

Because there is a great deal of variation in state laws governing charter schools, it is difficult to generalize about their financing, governance, and organizational arrangements. However, most charter schools are relatively small with a median enrollment of about 137 students, compared to about 475 students in the public schools in the same states. Charter schools are publicly funded, with their funding typically based on enrollment. In most (but not all) states, charter schools receive about the same amount of per pupil funding for current operation that the regular public schools in their community receive and the funding is often provided by the public school district in which the charter school is located. Securing funds for capital outlay and "start up" costs has been one of the largest problems confronting charter schools.

The second major approach to school choice is the school voucher. The basic idea of the voucher approach is to permit families to exercise choice in the schools their children attend by giving them a voucher that can be redeemed at the public or private school of their choice in lieu of paying tuition. Although Milton Friedman (1962) championed the use of vouchers in the 1950s as a way to inject free market competition in the provision of public education, it is only recently that public school voucher programs have been established.

The first state-funded voucher program was established for disadvantaged children in Milwaukee, Wisconsin in 1989. Originally restricted to a limited number of elementary school age children and nonsectarian private schools, the Milwaukee program has since been expanded to include a much larger number of children attending both elementary and secondary schools and now permits the vouchers to be used at sectarian schools. The second state-funded voucher program was established for disadvantaged children in Cleveland, Ohio in 1995. And in 1999, Florida became the first state to enact a statewide voucher program entitling students attending public schools rated as deficient to receive a voucher that may be redeemed at a qualified public or private school of their choice. In addition to the publicly funded voucher programs, privately funded vouchers (scholarships) are available for students to attend private school in at least 30 large cities.

The major legal issue with regard to voucher programs is whether the use of public funds to finance vouchers that are used to defray the cost of tuition in private sectarian schools contravenes the U.S. Constitution's First Amendment by advancing the cause of religion (McCarthy, 2000). The U.S. Supreme Court has not yet ruled on the constitutionality of programs that allow vouchers funded by the state to be used in sectarian schools, but is likely to hear such a case within the foreseeable future. A second issue, which has not yet received a great deal of attention, is whether the unique characteristics that differentiate public and private schools will eventually become so blurred that the two become indistinguishable as a result of the inevitable imposition of rules, regulations, and constraints that accompany public funds.

It is not clear that either charter schools or vouchers will have a significant effect on total expenditures for public elementary and secondary education. Given the hypothesis that school choice will create competition and thus result in greater efficiency in the use of school resources by creating "more bang for the same buck," one could imagine that education funding might decrease if society is satisfied with the output of schools. On the other hand, if schools can demonstrate greater productivity (through higher test scores, fewer dropouts, graduates better qualified to enter college or the work force, etc.), a case can be made that society might be willing to increase its investment in schooling.

Charter schools and voucher programs, at least initially, are most likely to produce changes in the mechanisms through which state financial aid flows to schools. Vouchers can be viewed theoretically as flat grants large enough to cover the cost of providing a student an adequate educational program suited to her/his needs. The same analogy can be applied to charter schools. There is no need for local school districts to serve as intermediaries in this transaction; the money could flow directly to the individual schools. Of course, if the grant is too small to cover the cost of an adequate educational program, the school will be forced to raise money by some other means if it is to compete successfully for students. One can envision citizens besieged by school supporters selling candy, magazines, cookies, and raffle tickets to raise money for their favorite school (and, in fact, this type of activity is common in many areas today). However, it is possible that *if* the flat grant is large enough to fund an adequate education, and *if* the size of the voucher is varied to reflect the additional cost of educating students with special needs, then a voucher program could pass muster on both fiscal equity and fiscal adequacy criteria.

Because private schools receive little or no state aid under existing state aid programs, state adoption of a voucher program would have to increase state expenditures for education to maintain the current level of expenditure per pupil in the public schools, as the money would be spread over as much as a 12 percent increase in students—those now attending private schools. There remain many unanswered questions regarding how a large-scale voucher program would operate—how schools would select students if applications exceed the space available; whether schools would be allowed to charge tuition or fees to supplement voucher funds; and what fiduciary requirements schools would be required to meet. In view of the fact that many candidates for political office are advocates of school choice, we can expect the issues surrounding vouchers and charter schools to be debated extensively in the coming decade.

CONCLUSION

This chapter summarizes the latest available projections of educational statistics as they relate to expenditures for public elementary and secondary schools in the first decade of the millennium. Projections of school enrollments and expenditures require one to assume that the trends that have been witnessed in the recent past will continue into the future. Whether these projections withstand the test of time will depend, in large part, on several emerging trends and factors that may alter in significant ways the amount of money devoted to support public education, and the way in which that money is allocated to districts, schools, and classrooms in coming years. Among these trends and factors are the outcomes of school finance litigation, whether the property tax is reduced or replaced as a source of school revenue, the implementation of new and emerging technologies to deliver educational programs and services, policy initiatives to reduce class size, changes in teacher compensation practices, the growth of charter schools and voucher programs, and almost certainly a number of other factors yet to be identified.

REFERENCES

Abbott v. Burke. 153 N.J. 480, 710 A.2d 450 (1998).

American Education Finance Association & Center for the Study of the States. (1995). *Public school finance programs of the United States and Canada* (vol. 1). Albany, NY: Center for the Study of the States.

Brewer, D. J., Krop, C., Gill, B. P., & Reichardt, R. (1999). Estimating the cost of national class size reductions under different policy alternatives. *Educational Evaluation and Policy Analysis, 21* (2), 179–192.

Brockett, D. (1999, October 26). The charter school movement is spreading to entire districts, *School Board News*, p. 5.

Finn, J. D. & Achilles, C. M. (1999). Tennessee's class size study: Findings, implications, misconceptions. *Educational Evaluation and Policy Analysis. 21*(2), 97–109.

Friedman, M. (1962). *Capitalism and freedom.* Chicago: University of Chicago Press.

Goldhaber, D. D. (1999). School choice: An examination of the empirical evidence on achievement, parental decision making, and equity. *Educational Researcher, 28* (9), 16–25.

Halbfinger, D. M. (1999, November 29). Big plans for New Jersey's schools, but where's the money? *The New York Times*, pp. B1, B8.

Hertert, L., Busch, C. & Odden, A. (1994). School financing inequities among the states: The problem from a national perspective. *Journal of Education Finance, 19*, 231–255.

Johnston, R. C. (1999, December 8). N.J. forging massive school building plan, *Education Week*, pp. 15, 17.

Kirst, M. W. & Garms, W. I. (1980). The political environment of school finance policy in the 1980s. In J. W. Guthrie (Ed.), *School finance policies and practices* (pp. 47–75). Cambridge, MA: Ballinger Publishing Co.

McCarthy, M. M. (2000). What is the verdict on school vouchers? *Phi Delta Kappan, 81*, 371–377.

Odden, A. (2000). New and better forms of teacher compensation are possible, *Phi Delta Kappan. 81*, 361–366.

Odden, A., & Kelley, C. (1997). *Paying teachers for what they know and do: New and smarter compensation strategies to improve schools.* Thousand Oaks, CA: Corwin Press.

Roosevelt Elementary School District No. 66 v. Bishop, 179 Ariz. 233, 877 P.2d 806 (1994).

Rossmiller, R. A. (1996). *The flat tax: Implications for financing public schools.* Arlington, VA: American Association of School Administrators.

Sackett, J. L. (2000, April 5). Momentum building for construction funding, *Education Week*, pp. 23, 24.

Serrano v. Priest, 5 Cal.3d 584, 487 P.2d 1241 (1971).

U.S. Department of Education, National Center for Education Statistics. (1997). *Digest of education statistics 1997.* (NCES 98–015). Washington, DC: U.S. Department of Education.

U.S. Department of Education, National Center for Education Statistics. (1998). *Inequalities in public school district revenues.* (NCES 98–210, by Parrish, T. B. & Hikido, C. S.). Washington, DC: U.S. Department of Education.

U.S. Department of Education, National Center for Education Statistics. (1999a). *Projections of education statistics to 2009.* (NCES 99–038, by Gerald, D. E. & Hussar, W. J.). Washington, DC: U.S. Department of Education.

U.S. Department of Education, National Center for Education Statistics. (1999b). *Revenues and expenditures for elementary and secondary education: School year 1996–97.* Washington, DC: U.S. Department of Education.

U.S. Department of Education, National Center for Education Statistics. (1999c). Overview of public elementary and secondary schools and districts, *Education Statistics Quarterly, 1* (Fall), (NCES 1999–629). Washington, DC: U.S. Department of Education.

U.S. Department of Education, National Center for Education Statistics. (2000). *Trends in disparities in school district level expenditures per pupil.* NCES 2000–020 by Hussar, W. & Sonnenberg, W. Washington, DC: U.S. Department of Education.

U.S. Department of Education, Office of Educational Research and Improvement. (2000). *The state of charter schools 2000—fourth year report.* Washington, DC: U.S. Department of Education.

Urbanski, A. & Erskine, R. (2000). School reform, TURN, and teacher compensation, *Phi Delta Kappan. 81,* 367–370.

3

FINANCIAL REPORTING IN THE NEW MILLENNIUM

William J. Fowler, Jr.
National Center for Education Statistics

INTRODUCTION

Mention school spending to the average citizen, and they will typically think of two things: the average per pupil expenditure in their school district or the average teacher's salary in their school district. Perhaps further reflection will lead them to recall the local school taxes they will pay or the school district budget document they may have received. Curiously, few of these items are typically reported in the "Comprehensive Annual Financial Report" (CAFR), or general purpose financial statement (GPFS), that some CPA has laboriously compiled and filed with the state education agency, and that they have filed, in turn, with the federal government. Nor do these items typically appear in the state audit. How this divergence occurred between the knowledge the public desires compared with the routine financial reporting of school districts requires some explanation.

State agencies generally are charged by state constitutions with providing "a thorough and efficient education," (*Robinson v. Cahill*, 1973) and, in turn, providing state funds to school districts for their operation. School districts also raise funds from local taxes, with some additional funding coming from the federal government. Usually, the state delegates the actual operation of schools to school districts, and conducts audits annually or biannually to assure the proper use of state and local funds.[1] Most of these reports serve an *archival* function:

> Fewer than ten states have statutory or regulatory requirements to *use* the reports of local governments to evaluate their financial condition, the extent of statutory compliance with respect to budgetary allotments, or results of operations.

> For state oversight agencies, dominant uses of the annual financial reports are to gather statewide statistics, provide information to

---

1 Forty-four states regulate the financial reporting of independent school districts, and 30 states require standard report formats (Icerman, 1996, p. 13).

the U.S. Bureau of the Census, and create databases. In addition, finance-related legal and budgetary compliance are verified....[M]ore often than not, these compliance desk reviews are based on the *form* and presentation of the report; *substantive analysis* of the balances is seldom conducted. (Icerman, 1996, p. 16.)

In some 17 states, school districts are required to publish "popular" financial reports, although even then few states mandate what is to be reported, or how. The importance of these findings is to explain why *public* information about school district finances and performance differs so dramatically with available information from states and school districts. Financial reporting by school districts in the millennium promises to be quite different, however, emphasizing more frequently reported "popular" financial information of use in judging school districts' fiscal and outcome performance.

WHAT THE PUBLIC WOULD LIKE TO KNOW

Rather than attempting to understand what is currently reported in school district financial reports, let us turn instead to what people would like to know. Perhaps the first question is:

"What is the true current financial condition of the school district?"

Curiously, the heart of this question is not whether the school district might become bankrupt (the typical concern of those who prepare financial reports). Rather, the public wishes to know if the financial exigencies are so severe that the school district must defer maintenance and renovation, use portable classrooms to alleviate overcrowding, is unable to attract and retain staff, has outdated text and workbooks, is unable to provide safe schools, and/or is not technologically current. These are the financial conditions that no one wishes to permit. However, few current or planned school district financial reports include such information.

The second question people want to know mirrors the first:

"How has the financial condition of the school district changed over time?"

What is desired is the ability to detect changes in the financial condition of a school district that will provide an early warning of problems that could lead to a deterioration of the delivery of educational services. Decreases in spending on instructional functions, technology, or maintenance and repair are all suggestive of untoward changes in the financial condition of a school district. Seldom, however, do current or proposed financial reports contain such information.

A third question speaks further of our ignorance:

"How do we spend money in education?"

Remarkably, despite the collection of extensive information about school district finances, little is known about how money is spent. Primarily, this is because financial information is kept independently of the manner in which schools are operated. For example, if teachers are paid a "signing bonus" when hired, this amount is lumped into "instructional salaries" by the business office when the financial reports are compiled for reporting to the state education agency (SEA) (and by the SEA to the federal government). Consequently, little is known about incentives, or the actual "service delivery system," and the costs of running a school in a particular way. The absence of this information also complicates determining what constitutes practices that are more efficient.

MEANINGFUL FINANCIAL REPORTING IN THE MILLENNIUM

Meaningful financial reporting in the next decades will likely provide greater focus on factors that will lead to improved educational quality and facilitate district, school, and individual level accountability, as well as address the above issues that most concern the general public and the policy makers. Changes in financial reporting will occur at the school district, school, and student levels. These factors are discussed next.

SCHOOL DISTRICT FINANCIAL REPORTING

Shifts in emphasis and data in financial reporting at the school district level might be classified as those that better assess the financial health of school districts, allow benchmarking, foster management and staff analysis, and provide useful trend analysis.

SCHOOL DISTRICT FISCAL HEALTH

What indicates the fiscal health of a school district? Fiscal health, much like a person's health, usually is demonstrated by the absence of constraints. For example, long term health care plans often focus upon the ability of the person to bath, eat, and dress. Similarly, a school district should be able to undertake the education of children without deferring other activities. For this to occur, we would anticipate that a school district would have a unencumbered surplus of about 5 percent or one month's operating costs, whichever is higher. A school district surplus permits the ability to respond to financial emergencies or unexpected costs. Financial emergencies or unexpected costs come in all shapes and sizes, and may be as small as several additional days of operation due to weather cancellations, or as large as severe flooding of a building and the relocation of an entire school.

Perhaps the next most important financial information pertaining to the health of a school district is what is being lessened or deferred because of budget difficulties. Some questions related to such data needs include:

♦ If the school district budget is voted upon, was it rejected by voters, and/or reduced? If the school district depends upon its budget from another governmental unit (city, county), did that unit reduce the budget? What items were reduced?

♦ Were staff salaries (particularly teachers) held only to the increase in inflation (or less)? Were certain deductions (insurance, medical, retirement) increased at staff expense, so that salaries really were decreased? Did raises go to existing staff, while holding starting salaries at a competitive disadvantage? Simultaneously, did the school district superintendent and his or her administrative staff have out-sized raises?

♦ Were maintenance, repairs, and renovations deferred? These defer-ments often stretch on for years, worsening the physical plant and making the learning environment more and more difficult.

♦ Are students being housed in trailers or portable classrooms to relieve overcrowding?

♦ Have substantial investments been made in areas that will not assist students in the learning process? For example, were funds diverted to school safety (metal detectors, armed guards) in order to maintain a learning environment?

Financial reporting that contains these types of information, even for a single point in time, educates the reader about a paucity of funds that may not be appar-ent from data only showing overall spending levels. In this way, financial report-ing speaks to how we use available funds. Economists often speak of such trade-offs, where undertaking one action means another must be limited or forsaken. As Helen Ladd notes:

> In the short run, the existence of long-term contracts and various types of political pressures may make school districts respond differ-ently in the short run than in the long run to changes in their fiscal condition, especially if they expect the change to be temporary. In the short run, districts may not have much choice in how to respond to a deterioration in their fiscal condition; the question in the short run may well be not what would they like to cut, but what can they cut? (Ladd, 1998, p. 47)

Ladd finds that fiscally constrained districts devote more than 1.5 percent more of their operating budgets to instruction than other districts, having less in other areas, particularly plant services (down 2.7 percent) and administrative staff. She also finds that constrained districts have larger pupil-teacher ratios and larger classes; and they use less experienced teachers. Fiscal constraint, she finds, shows up most dramatically in capital outlays for equipment and buildings as well.

BENCHMARKING

Another point-in-time comparison that can be made is to compare similar school districts or schools in how they deploy their financial assets and staff. This is often termed *benchmarking*. For example, one might examine per-pupil spend-ing for different school districts that might be considered *peer* school districts. Peer school districts might be those with similar characteristics in enrollment size, student/teacher ratios, wealth (per-pupil property wealth or median house-hold income), district type (elementary or secondary), and metro status (urbani-city). NCES has such a peer tool on its finance Web page (nces.ed.gov/edfin) that will allow improved benchmarking in the future. Several comparisons are shown in Figures 3.1 and 3.2. In Figure 3.1, the per-pupil current expenditures of dis-tricts are compared. In Figure 3.2, the percentage spent on administration is assessed.

FIGURE 3.1 EXAMPLE OF SCHOOL DISTRICT BENCHMARKS BASED ON CURRENT PER-PUPIL EXPENDITURES

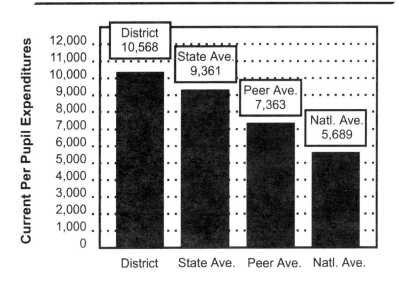

SOURCE: Derived from NCES "Public school district finance peer search," nces.ed.gov/edfin/search/search_intro.asp

FIGURE 3.2 EXAMPLE OF SCHOOL DISTRICT BENCHMARKS BASED ON PERCENTAGE OF EXPENDITURES SPENT ON ADMINISTRATION

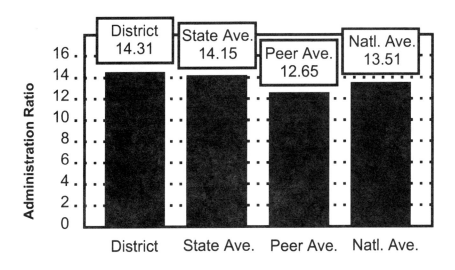

SOURCE: Derived from NCES "Public school district finance peer search," nces.ed.gov/edfin/search/search_intro.asp

Another example of the type of benchmarking that is likely to occur in the future is seen in a comprehensive examination of a school district undertaken by the District of Columbia Financial Authority. The District of Columbia Public Schools (DCPS) were compared to neighboring school districts, as well as those in Baltimore, Chicago, Charlotte-Mecklenburg, Cleveland, Milwaukee, and Newark. DCPS's per-pupil expenditures exceed the national average, and are substantially higher than many comparable urban school districts and neighboring districts. DCPS employed 16 teachers for every central administrator, compared to peers that employed 42 for every administrator. In 1996, DCPS allocated more toward the Office of the Superintendent than the *combined* spending of the school districts of Fairfax County, Montgomery County, and Baltimore. It also spent more than twice as much for the Board of Education than was spent by its neighbors. Because of this peer analysis, the District of Columbia Financial Authority soon closed 11 schools, and replaced 50 roofs (Ladner, 1998). The thorough comparison of the DCPS school system to its peers, neighbors, and comparison districts provides a useful model for how to think about making such benchmarking comparisons.

MANAGEMENT AND STAFF ANALYSIS

Fiscal health is analogous to a person's physical health in that it is most apparent when it is deteriorating and in that a complete yearly examination may not reveal any underlying illness. To extend the analogy, like the patient who first senses something amiss, so often the school or district administration and staff are the first to sense that fiscal conditions are deteriorating. It may be a teacher's need to buy supplies for her students because she cannot obtain them through normal procurement processes. Or it may be that professional development opportunities, or travel, or professional organization memberships are postponed or denied by the school district. None of these examples meet the test of a threshold amount or percent, nor are they large enough to become a "material" item in a financial report, but they are readily apparent to management and staff. If these first inklings of changes in the fiscal health of a school district (or school) could somehow be translated into an "early-warning" system to alert the broader public of impending problems, this would be an invaluable tool for fiscal analysts. So far, Ohio has developed "watch lists" for school districts encountering potential bankruptcy; and the comptroller for the state of Texas has such a list for school districts whose fund balance or percent of instructional budget falls below certain guidelines. In the case of Texas, this has led school districts to implement the comptroller's audit techniques to conduct self-reviews.

However, a new fiscal tool that serves this purpose would be welcomed by all in the new millennium. One possibility discussed below is a Management Discussion and Analysis process that GASB will require of school districts after 2001.

TRENDS

Perhaps nothing is as useful in financial reporting as the past. While benchmarks comparing peer and neighbor districts are useful, changes in the finances of a school district or school over time often are extremely revealing regarding changes in its financial condition. Currently, the best financial measures examining "real" growth include per-pupil spending, teacher salaries, and capital outlay spending. In addition, changes in revenue streams are also indications of changes in financial condition. Economists use the term "real" growth to remove the effects of inflation. Although several measures of inflation may be used to "deflate" expenditures over time, the National Center for Education Statistics uses the Consumer Price Index, which has been shown to be comparable to other deflators (Chambers, 1997).

A slowing in the growth of per-pupil spending, declining teacher salaries, or reductions in the purchases of equipment can be warning signs of impending financial difficulty. Increasing reliance upon state revenues per pupil may also indicate that local revenue sources are insufficient. Figure 3.3 displays an example of these trends for a district whose financials are deteriorating.

FIGURE 3.3. EXAMPLE OF TREND DATA INDICATING DETERIORATING SCHOOL DISTRICT FINANCES

	Years				
	1	2	3	4	5
Real per pupil expenditures	$11,266	$12,393	$13,384	$14,053	$14,615
Percent change		10%	8%	5%	4%
Real average teacher salary	$38,500	$42,350	$44,891	$46,687	$47,621
Percent change		10%	6%	4%	2%

FINANCIAL REPORTING FOR A SCHOOL

Thus far, this chapter has focused upon the financial reporting of a school district. Only recently has financial information at the school, rather than the school district level, been estimated. The reason financial information at the school level is "estimated," rather than reported, is that few school district financial reporting systems—even with computer assistance—can make the necessary prorations to accurately report spending for individual schools. Imagine an itinerant elementary school nurse who spends some of her time in each of three elementary schools. Her salary and benefits (the largest portion of this cost) must be divided between the three elementary schools. Instead of simply dividing by three, we need to know the amount of time that the school nurse spends in each of the three elementary schools. If we are to be really accurate bean counters, maintenance and operations costs should also be similarly computed, including her use of the nurse's office phone to call students' parents and physicians. In addition, her use of medical supplies in each school should also be recorded. The complications of such extensive financial record keeping have previously been called "paralysis by analysis" (Wildavsky, 1984).

Most states that have mandated school-level financial reporting had done so by adopting a simpler method. While there has been little standardization thus far, most school-level reporting has mimicked district-level financial reporting, using the same format and extending downward the existing system of financial reporting to the school. I term this methodology "Downward Accounting Extension" (DAE). Similar to the financial reporting of school districts, these data serve primarily an archival function. DAE seldom illuminates actual spending, nor serves to evaluate a school's financial condition or results of operations.

The public interest in comparing school-level expenditures is immense, however; it may even serve to influence families in selecting a location to purchase a house (Barrow & Rouse, 2000). Certainly any financial reporting system in the future will incorporate reporting at the school level; currently, some 20 states now require the reporting of school-level financial information. Perhaps one of the best of these is exemplified by the New York Board of Education, a sample of which is abstracted in Figure 3.4. Here, for example, extrapolating from school district reported data, the sample school shown is estimated to spend $3,727 per pupil for teachers in classroom instruction, which is 45 percent of per pupil expenditures.

FIGURE 3.4. ABSTRACTED EXAMPLES OF SCHOOL-LEVEL DATA DERIVED FROM SCHOOL DISTRICT DATA

Function	Per Student Amount Spent in School	Percent of Per Student Amount Spent on Function	Total Expended Salary Spent in School	Percent of Total Expended Salary Spent on Function	Total Expended Fringe Benefits Spent in School	Percent of Total Expended Fringe Benefits Spent on Function	Total Expended Other Than Salaries Spent in School	Percent of Total Expended Other Than Salaries Spent on Function
1. Direct Services to Schools	$7,533	90%	$3,451,267	94%	$1,021,596	96%	$1,312,348	78%
A. Classroom Instruction (All Funds)	4,223	50%	2,315,420	63%	710,084	67%	217,455	13%
Teachers	3,727	45%	2,189,928	59%	672,353	63%	0	0%
Education Para-professionals	174	2%	99,357	3%	34,240	3%	0	0%
Text Books	51	1%	0	0%	0	0%	39,128	2%
Librarians and Library Books	3	0%	0	0%	0	0%	2,002	0%
Instructional Supplies and Equipment	122	1%	0	0%	0	0%	93,329	6%
Professional Development	102	1%	19,760	1%	2,970	0%	55,548	3%
Contracted Instructional Services	20	0%	0	0%	0	0%	15,571	1%
Summer and Evening School	24	0%	6,375	0%	521	0%	11,876	1%

SOURCE: Derived from New York City Board of Education Data for a Sample School.

Benchmarking using these data is possible by comparing schools of a similar size, wealth, student composition, and so on. However, it remains difficult to understand why differences in expenditures occur between schools, and typically, this information only can only be obtained through field visits with staff.

However, a far more sophisticated level of financial reporting is possible, using a method of costing staff deployment. This method has been called the "Resource Cost Model" (RCM) and can involve the collection of vast amounts of information on staff and salaries and benefits. Subject expenditures (in math, science, history, etc.) can be portrayed, for example, by teaching assignment, or for special education and remedial teaching assignments. Using this methodology, for example, differences in the costs for special education in two schools can be seen by the way in which the delivery of educational services has been organized, particularly for children with different disabilities. For example, a mainstreamed learning disabled child who remains in the regular classroom might be less costly to educate than a learning disabled child who is removed from the regular classroom and educated for an hour in a separate classroom of a few children with a teacher who is a specialist. The richness of the information that this methodology is able to display can be seen in Figure 3.5. For example, in a typical elementary school, $1,979 is spent per pupil for regular teaching instructional assignments, based on the RCM methodology, while $281 is spent per pupil on a special education teaching assignment. However, in a special needs school, $1,154 would be expended on regular teaching and $4,662 on special education teaching assignments.

The RCM, however, cannot differentiate why professional development expenditures might differ between schools. These and other reallocation issues again require personal in-depth interviews with staff, who may not even be aware of these expenditure differences, and what is driving them.

All of this meaningful reporting of financial information differs quite dramatically from current governmental financial accounting and reporting, and although significant changes are contemplated in the millennium, most of what will be reported will still be quite removed from what most policy makers, researchers, and the public would consider "meaningful."

STUDENT-LEVEL FINANCIAL REPORTING

For at least 30 years, it has been the practice when reporting per-pupil expenditures to report the "average" per-pupil expenditure in a state or school district. This practice is now being extended to the school. Although the "average" expenditure, derived from dividing total operating expenditures by total student counts is informative and illustrative, it seldom represents reality. Students, after all, are in classrooms with teachers who receive different salaries and benefits, and with differing numbers of students. Some students receive supplemental instruction from other teachers (reading, math, speech, federal compensatory program teachers) and are more often involved with guidance counselors, school nurses, principals and their assistants, and coaches. These students may also receive additional school supplies, and have greater or lesser access to PCs. In short, each student receives his or her own level of school resources. To date, no system of estimating resources utilized for each student has been devised, although a nascent system has been developed by NCES (see William J. Fowler, Jr., forthcoming). The development of true "student-level" financial measures of resources is crucial to understand questions of adequacy, equity, and productivity, and will be essential to our emerging view of financial reporting in the millennium.

FIGURE 3.5. ABSTRACTED EXAMPLE OF PERSONNEL BY POSITION: WEIGHTED MEAN VALUE OF ACTUAL PERSONNEL EXPENDITURES PER PUPIL BY POSITION FOR EACH SCHOOL TYPE FOR PUBLIC SCHOOLS IN THE STATE OF OHIO: 1995–96 SCHOOL YEAR

	Weighted Mean of Actual Personnel Expenditures Per Pupil				
Position Descriptions	*Elementary School*	*Middle School*	*High School*	*Special Needs School*	*Vocational School*
Instructional Services					
Regular teaching assignment	$1,979	$2,133	$2,030	$1,154	$1,569
Special education teaching assignment	281	333	206	4,662	226
Vocational education teaching assignment	1	70	341	452	3,813
Educational services teacher	174	165	39	25	0
Special Education supplemental services teacher	1	1	1	0	0
Remedial specialist	79	39	13	27	100
Tutor/small group instructor	42	40	27	119	41
Adult education teacher	0	0	1	38	0
Teaching aide assignment	102	54	47	918	241

SOURCE: Abstracted from Chambers (1999).

THE ROLE OF ACCOUNTING STANDARDS IN FINANCIAL REPORTING

A major surprise to the professional accountants who audit school districts was the Richmond, California school district (now renamed Contra Costa school district), which was bankrupt, but did not appear so to its auditors. In order to appear solvent, the school district used the proceeds from bonds to raise staff salaries and run the school district. In other words, it was running on borrowed funds. How was it possible that the true financial condition of the school district was not clear, even to professionals?

For years, the accounting profession has used differing standards of financial reporting in governmental accounting than for business entities. School districts, as governmental entities, typically did not include the cost of equipment and school construction in the reporting of "operating" expenditures, for example. The reasoning was that equipment and the purchase of land and the building of a school occurred in a single year, even if the repayment costs were spread over many years. Thus, per-pupil expenditures would show a "blip" for the year in which such an event occurred. As a result, these expenditures were kept in a separate group, and did not influence "operating" expenditures.[2] Further, the number of unrecognized liabilities for a school district might be substantial. For example, school districts often did not record the liability that a program to reduce (current) teacher substitute costs might have. The substitute-reduction programs typically pay teachers lump-sum payments upon retirement for their accrued sick leave (future cost). Medical plans for retirees also fell in this category. The use of PCs that may have a useful life of less than three years has exacerbated the exclusion of "nonoperating" expenditures.

As a result of these difficulties, the Governmental Accounting Standards Board (GASB)[3] has decided to adopt an "entity-wide" perspective, which would attempt to portray the true financial condition of a school district. In addition, new standards would require that school districts undertake Management Discussion and Analysis (MD&A) reviews, and the use of "expenses" rather than expenditures. "Expenses" would incorporate a proration of equipment and school construction expenditures, so that the actual cost of operating the school district is known and reported. These changes would go into effect sometime between 2002 and 2005, and suggest that school district financial reporting to state education agencies in the millennium will be superior to current reporting.

GOVERNMENTAL ACCOUNTING FOR SCHOOL SYSTEMS

School system financial reporting is currently a function of state financial reporting requirements for local governments, of which school districts are seen as a subset. Some school districts are fiscally independent components of local governments (such as counties or cities), and the adherence to Generally Accepted Accounting Principles (GAAP) by local governments is often waived. Other school districts are fiscally independent, demonstrated by their ability to set and raise local taxes without permission from another governmental entity. One respondent to a Governmental Accounting Standards Board (GASB) survey concerning small government GAAP reporting stated that most independent school districts (ISDs):

> are reporting on a non-GAAP basis. The most common reasons given are that auditing costs are lower, the public and officials do not understand GAAP based financial statements, and the feeling that information required to be provided in GAAP financial statements is "useless." As a result of these attitudes, we believe that unless mandated

---

2 "The focus of governmental funds is on the flow of *current* financial resources. Accordingly, the balance sheets of governmental funds do not report certain liabilities that are not expected to require the use of currently available resources. Instead, such liabilities are reported in the general long-term debt account group (GLITAG)" (GFOA, 1994, p. 113).

3 "The GASB is the highest source of accounting and financial reporting guidance for state and local governments" (GFOA, 1994, p. 6).

by the federal government, GAAP financial reporting will not become the norm. (Icerman, 1996, p. 19.)

As an example of the latest GASB reporting model, Figure 3.6 displays a portion of a "Sample City School District" financial report. The portion is of a school district that is a component unit of Sample City. Under the Sample City "Statement of Activities," education is simply another function/program line, like public safety or health and sanitation. Even if the Sample City School District has its own, more detailed Statement of Activities (shown in Figure 3.6), "Instructional" is still broken into only "regular," "special," "vocational," "other," and "adult education." It is quickly apparent that even the most recent GASB financial reporting model does not begin to address the questions most people would like to know. (To recap: How severe are the school district's financial exigencies? How has the financial condition of the school district changed over time? How is the school district spending its money?) This is not to make light of the significant advances that the latest GASB financial reporting model makes in governmental accounting. It is simply that governmental accounting is not suited to address the most pressing questions about public educational finance.

To impart a flavor of the beneficial changes that GASB has recently brought to school district and local government financial reporting, though, let us look at several recent innovations.

ENTITY-WIDE PERSPECTIVE

Previously, it was the custom in school district governmental reporting to not include certain activities, including those aspects run like a business (such as food service), activities financed by fees (such as student activities), capital projects, and debt service (such as renovations and school construction). The advent of "entity-wide" or "government-wide" financial reporting will mean fewer such activities that are "off-the-books." This should result in a more accurate reporting of the true financial condition of the school district.

MANAGEMENT DISCUSSION AND ANALYSIS (MD&A)

Although MD&A is a common feature of financial reporting for public corporations, particularly in their annual reports, this is the greatest innovation in the new GASB reporting model, even if it is *required supplementary information* (RSI). The MD&A should introduce the basic financial statements that follow, and provide an analytical overview of the school district's financial activities. It should contain a comparison of the school district's financial condition for this year to last year's, assisting readers in understanding if the financial position has improved or deteriorated. It should also provide an analysis of the significant changes that occurred in funds and in budgets, as well as capital assets and long-term debt activity.

FIGURE 3.6 SAMPLE CITY SCHOOL DISTRICT STATEMENT OF ACTIVITIES FOR THE YEAR ENDED DECEMBER 31, 2002

| | | Program Revenues | | Net (Expense) Revenue and Changes in Net Assets | | |
	Expenses	Charges for Services	Operating Grants	Governmental Activities	Business-type Activities	Total
Instructional:						
Regular instruction	$12,328,240	$147,739	$1,095,297	$(11,085,204)	—	$(11,085,204)
Special instruction	3,346,325	—	1,299,004	(2,047,321)	—	(2,047,321)
Vocational education	819,435	—	51,146	(765,289)	—	(765,289)
Other instructional programs	405,732	—	376,064	(29,668)	—	(29,668)
Adult education	24,589	—	598	(23,991)	—	(23,991)
Support services:						
Pupil services	822,871	—	20,025	(802,846)	—	(802,846)
Instructional services	443,624	—	31,667	(411,957)	—	(411,957)
Administrative services	1,680,317	—	40,891	(1,639,426)	—	(1,639,426)
Health services	311,522	—	88,432	(223,090)	—	(223,090)
Business services	513,064	—	48,431	(464,633)	—	(464,633)
Plant operations and maintenance	2,905,095	300	70.697	(2,834,098)	—	(2,834,098)
Transportation	804,503	—	439,606	(364,897)	—	(364,897)
Other support services	491,563	—	11,962	(479,601)	—	(479,601)
Operation of noninstructional services:						
Athletic programs	497,304	16,343	12,102	(468,859)	—	(468,859)
Community services	117,773	—	2,866	(114,907)	—	(114,907)
Food services	908,263	541,383	344,124	—	(22,756)	(22,756)
Facilities acquisition and construction services:						
Building improvement services	48,136	—	1,171	(46,965)	—	(46,965)
Interest on long-term debt	546,382	—	—	(546,382)	—	(546,382)
Depreciation	4,171,760	—	—	(4,171,760)	—	(4,171,760)
Total	$31,186,498	$705,765	$3,937,083	(26,520,894)	(22,756)	(26,543,650)
General revenues:						
Payment from Sample City				21,893,273	—	21,893,273
Grants and entitlements not restricted to specific programs				6,176,108	—	6,176,108
Unrestricted contributions				285,600	—	285,600
Investment earnings				667,742	6,294	674,036
Miscellaneous				19,950	—	19,950
Total general revenues				29,042,673	6,294	29,048,967
Excess (deficiency) of revenues over expenses				2,521,779	(16,462)	2,505,317
Net assets-beginning				14,209,926	435,506	14,645,432
Net assets-ending				$16,731,705	$419,044	$17,150,749

The totals from these three columns are displayed separately on the reporting entity's statement of activities (B-1).

SOURCE: GASB, 1999.

USER FEES

Schools subsidize many activities, including field trips and athletic programs, by charging user fees. Previously, the funds from these activities simply went into the general fund of the school district, and the net cost of an activity might not be reportable. Under the new GASB reporting model, such activities would have to be shown as net activities.

BUDGETARY CHANGES

Many school district presentations of end-of-the-year financials do not include the changes in the budget that reflect changes in the true financial condition of the school district. The new GASB reporting model would show expenses and revenues that would more fully represent changes from one year to the next, and also indicate the significance of those changes.

DEPRECIATION

Perhaps the most dramatic of the changes in the new GASB reporting model, school districts would now show "user's charges," or depreciation, when governments are reporting their financial statistics. Previously, school districts made distinctions between supplies and equipment. Their "current expenditure per pupil" excluded equipment (and capital outlay) expenditures. The reason for this convention was that equipment, such as school desks and furniture, was often purchased in large quantities. If equipment purchases were included in the current expenditure, it would be much higher in one year than in others. Fiscal experts term such reporting "lumpy." However, when reporting in this way, current expenditures vastly understate actual expenditures per pupil. Costs of building construction and renovation, as well as equipment purchases are excluded, and they can be substantial.

There remain unresolved issues in determining the "threshold" amount of the difference between supplies and equipment. For example, is a hard drive for a PC considered a supply or equipment? States vary dramatically in setting supply/equipment thresholds; for example, Missouri's was recently $500, while Texas's was $5,000. In addition to figuring out what is equipment, one must determine a method of depreciation. There are several techniques for determining depreciation. For example, the IRS considers the useful life of a PC to be five years. Thus, the purchase price might be divided by 5, and that amount would be added to the current expenditures. Finally, many school districts have no notion of the construction or replacement costs for school buildings, so determining the yearly "user's charges" for depreciation of the buildings will require school districts to have their buildings appraised.

EXPENSES PER PUPIL

Once school districts have implemented depreciation, the use of the term "current expenditure per pupil" would be inappropriate, since prorated equipment and capital outlay costs could be included in the per-pupil figure. When these yearly prorations are included in the per-pupil figure, "expenses per pupil" would be the appropriate term. Whether state and federal laws would change their definitions, upon which much financial aid for a school district is determined, is uncertain.

While welcome, these innovations fall far short of the transformation in school district financial reporting that is necessary to satisfy the true needs of the public and the policy makers. These changes do permit the creation of financial ratios to determine the financial position of a school district, its liquidity and solvency, leverage, and coverage ratios. These measures help determine the district's ability to finance services needed by its constituents, but these "ability to pay" measures typically are not widely reported or used, and are neither easily explained nor clearly apparent to the general public or policy makers.

FINANCIAL REPORTING IN THE MILLENNIUM TO MEET PUBLIC NEEDS

Let us return to the heart of this chapter: the contention that current financial reporting by school districts does not now adequately inform the public, researchers, and policy makers of what they most wish to know. The GASB reporting model changes are useful, but may still result in obscure and arcane financial reports. What is needed is financial reporting that is responsive to the interests of the stakeholders described earlier. How do we move from the current *archival* financial reports that are almost never utilized because the information is obscure and arcane, to widely available and informative financial reports on our public schools and school districts?

Pennsylvania may be a trendsetter in this area. The state of Pennsylvania enacted a spending analysis and management project commonly called "Your Schools, Your Money." This new reporting tool is an attempt to provide "user-friendly" education financial information to the public at the district and school levels. As a pilot test, the Pennsylvania Department of Education (PDE) worked in cooperation with over 50 schools and the Pennsylvania Association of School Business Officials for over two years to develop the new reporting system. Starting in December 2001, the PDE will collect expenditures from all districts for three school components: classroom instruction, instructional student support, and facilities and plan management. In December 2002, they will collect subject matter expenditures (math, science, language arts, and social studies) in middle and high schools, and grade-level expenditures in elementary schools. Topical areas, such as special education, noninstructional costs, professional development, technology, and food service will be reported at the district level. While laudable, this new reporting only answers one of the three questions that were posed at the beginning of the chapter that most people would like answered: how do we spend money in education? The true financial condition of the school district and how it has changed over time is still not fully revealed.

Another approach taken over the last decade by the Texas Comptroller of Public Accounts has studied numerous school districts in the Texas School Performance Review (TSPR):

> [The] goal is to direct more of every education dollar into the classroom and to enhance the quality of every student's education. To reach this goal, TSPR auditors visit a school district, review its operations, interview administrators, teachers, parents and students, and recommend ways to cut costs and improve operations. TSPR's evaluation and recommendations are published in a report that is circu-

lated throughout the community. Since its inception, TSPR has reviewed 34 school districts (serving more than 900,000 students) and recommended net savings of $381 million. (Rylander, 1999)

In addition, the Texas comptroller has developed consumer-friendly publications. *Top 10 Ways to Improve Public Schools* (Revised January 2000) and *Food for Thought: Ideas for Improving School Food Service Operations* are two examples.

Perhaps more innovative are the Texas comptroller's school district reports, which include, in one instance, the following cost recommendations (with a 5-year planning horizon):

- Bring all district salaries in line with the market.
- Reduce the statewide average number of noncertified teachers in the next two years.
- Allocate custodial employees to schools using a formula that incorporates demand factors, such as number of teachers, students, or classrooms, as well as cleaning area.
- Implement nonmonetary employee incentives to reduce turnover.
- Eliminate the computer help desk coordinator position and hire a help desk technician.
- Establish a delinquent tax collection policy for the district; and implement regular communication with the county and the attorney responsible for delinquent tax collection.

These examples from a particular school district come much closer to answering the question of "what is the true current financial condition of the school district?" The steps suggested above quickly inform the public that this district's salaries are not comparable to the market, and the amount allocated suggests additional funds are needed to obtain comparability. The district also has more noncertified teachers than the statewide average, has high turnover, has shortages of custodial employees in areas of high need, and has difficulty obtaining delinquent taxes. Were this eloquent picture of the financial condition of the school district combined with how these examples have changed over time, we would have the financial reporting we are seeking.

CONCLUSION

The financial reporting now required of school districts and schools does not serve anyone well. Although many states require school district (and even school) financial reporting, these financial records serve only an archival function. Some states require "popular" financial reports, but these do not address many of the concerns regarding fiscal stringency by a school district or school. The Texas comptroller has made the largest advances in financial reporting, but these have occurred primarily in an effort to reduce spending and to direct spending toward the classroom. Yet all of these nontraditional attempts at changing education finance reporting demonstrate the inadequacy of current financial reporting.

What is needed in the millennium is a truly revolutionary manner of financial reporting, one that will demonstrate, for both districts and schools, where the money goes, how the current financial condition of the school district or school impinges upon its operation, and the degree to which the financial condition has changed over time. Only by meeting these criteria will a financial reporting serve the needs of the public, the education finance research community, and policy makers.

REFERENCES

Barrow, Lisa, & Rouse, Cecilia Elena. (2000). *Using market valuation to assess the importance and efficiency of public school spending.* NBER Working Paper # 438.

Chambers, Jay G. (1999). *Resources in education: From accounting to the resource cost model approach.* National Center for Education Statistics. NCES 199916 (Working Paper). Washington, DC: U.S. Department of Education.

Chambers, Jay G. (1997). *Measuring inflation in public school costs.* National Center for Education Statistics. NCES 9743 (Working Paper). Washington, DC: U.S. Department of Education.

Fowler, William J. Jr., (forthcoming). *What is spent on educating your Kindergarten Child?* Washington, DC: National Center for Education Statistics, Stats in Brief (2000–33).

GFOA (1994). *Governmental accounting, auditing, and financial reporting.* Chicago: Government Finance Officers Association.

GASB. (1999, June). *Basic Financial Statements-and Management's Discussion and Analysis-for State and Local Governments.* Norwalk, CT: Governmental Accounting Standards Board. Statement No. 34.

Icerman, Rhoda C. (1996). *Small government financial reporting.* Norwalk, CT: Governmental Accounting Standards Board.

Ladd, Helen F. (1998). How do school districts respond to fiscal constraint? In William J. Fowler, Jr., *Selected papers in school finance, 1996,* NCES 98-217. Washington, DC: U.S. Department of Education (National Center for Education Statistics).

Ladner, Joyce. (1998). Financing education in the District of Columbia from the perspective of the financial authority. In William J. Fowler, Jr., *Developments in school finance, 1997,* NCES 98-212. Washington, DC: U.S. Department of Education (National Center for Education Statistics).

Robinson v. Cahill, 62 N.J. 473, 303 A.2d 273 (1973).

Rylander, Carol Keeton. (1999, October 14). *Texas comptroller's Texas school performance review wins national "innovations in government" award* (news release).

Wildavsky, Aaron. (1984). *The politics of the budgetary process.* Reading, MA: Addison-Wesley-Educational-Publishers-Incorporated.

4

PROSPECTS FOR TITLE I IN THE EARLY 21ST CENTURY: ARE MAJOR CHANGES IN STORE?

Mary T. Moore
Mathematica Policy Research

For 35 years, Title I, Part A of the Elementary and Secondary Education Act of 1965 (ESEA) has been the largest federal program aiding elementary and secondary education in the United States. Commonly referred to as compensatory education, the program now amounts to over $8 billion in annual support. Approximately 92 percent of all school districts currently use Title I funds to provide extra instructional opportunities and support for 12.5 million students. Youth served by Title I account for 27 percent of all students in the nation, most of whom are in grades K-6.

Successive reauthorizations of Title I have reaffirmed and retained the premise that the federal government has a clear stake in providing funds to improve the educational performance of low-achieving children attending schools in poor communities. Although this central premise has prevailed amidst intensive scrutiny by numerous administrations and Congresses, rival opinions have shaped and continue to shape debates about the most effective means for achieving the program's aims.

OPINIONS SHAPING THE
FUTURE COURSE OF TITLE I

Opinions about how best to carry out the purposes of Title I fall into three main groups. One group of opinions calls for increasing Title I's potency by transforming it into an engine that drives comprehensive school reform. This approach would focus the program almost exclusively on improving Title I schools through requirements for schoolwide instructional models that research can document are effective in significantly increasing achievement. A second group of opinions echoes ideas advanced intermittently in past years—for example, creating a Title I block grant to give greater authority and responsibility to

53

states for addressing the needs of educationally disadvantaged children attending schools in poor neighborhoods. A final body of opinion favors converting Title I to a program that unleashes market forces on behalf of low-income parents by giving impoverished families a direct choice over their child's learning environment.

As we enter the 21st century, Congress once again is poised to reauthorize Title I. Although the final votes have not been taken, the pending reauthorization of Title I seems most likely headed toward maintaining the course set by elected federal officials throughout the 1990s. This course generally emphasizes poverty in the allocation of funds, and ties Title I programs to challenging standards and accountability at the level of the school. Moreover, it seeks to leverage school improvement by promoting whole school reform. Except for matters of scale and research infrastructure, the current approach appears to come closest in structure to that advocated by proponents who favor making Title I a more potent engine of school reform. From a nearer-term perspective, then, these opinions seem to have the edge in shaping the program for the next five years.

Readers should be mindful, however, that the current formulation of Title I also contains certain provisions that align closely with the other two sets of opinions previously described. For example, Title I heavily invokes a state-partnership strategy in linking improvements in student performance to the policies and actions of states. It is plausible that this aspect of Title I may provide the underpinnings for a reconceptualized program based on a block grant that specifically offers strong incentives to the states to improve disadvantaged students' educational performance. In fact, Title I's growing reliance on states' efforts throughout the past decade is noteworthy. For example, the program requires the establishment of demanding state standards of learning for all children, including those from disadvantaged backgrounds. Furthermore, states are responsible for holding Title I districts and schools accountable for progress and stepping in when there is consistent lack of progress. Finally, new federal Ed-Flex legislation transfers to a growing number of states the authority to waive many federal Title I and other requirements in the interests of achieving better student performance.

The current formulation of Title I also contains elements that may provide the basis for refashioning it into a program that gives poor parents a choice over how to escape inferior schools and improve the educational performance of their children. While the program does not provide for individual vouchers for eligible students and their families across the board, amendments in the late 1990s now require districts and states to give to parents of students who attended Title I schools that have repeatedly failed to meet the state's specified standards of progress the option of transferring to better performing public schools in the nearby vicinity.[1] Could these provisions foreshadow a shift toward a more market-driven approach for the Title I program? Many troubling issues surround this

---

1   This provision takes effect in the 2000–2001 school year. It only applies to school districts that have one or more schools identified for improvement and that receive some of the $134 million in funds set aside by Congress in FY2000 to carry out school improvement and corrective action responsibilities under Title I.

approach, not the least of which is the inclusion of private as well as public schools, and of "faith-based" institutions. The point to emphasize here is that the seeds of such a strategy are present and may find fertile ground to grow in the future.

Undoubtedly, the three groups of opinion previously described will be prominent in shaping the future course of Title I during the next decade. Two forces will ensure this. First, Title I's visibility often has made it a target for ideas that gain political momentum and capture the nation's fancy. If they resonate loudly with the public and their elected officials, the devolution of federal authority to state and local governments and the appearance of market concepts based on parental choice are likely to become major considerations in ensuing debates over Title I. Second, since the early years of the program, the lack of unambiguous evidence of the effectiveness of Title I programs in significantly narrowing the achievement gap between disadvantaged and advantaged students has led officials to cast about for alternatives.[2] Certainly the glacial speed with which Title I services and programs change makes it improbable that the next few years will witness a major turnaround in the program's documented effectiveness.

A strong argument can be made that finding compelling evidence of effectiveness is the pivotal issue that will shape Title I's future course. For some time, observers have astutely noted that two fundamental steps must be achieved for the program to demonstrate the desired effects on the learning of children from poor households. As Orland and Stullich (1997) emphasize, Title I's success ultimately depends on optimally orchestrating a sequential process in which adequate resources first reach the intended beneficiaries of the program and secondly are marshaled in ways that elicit substantial gains in learning. The next section examines the current program's progress in accomplishing these steps. With that knowledge as a foundation, the concluding section of this chapter highlights some of the issues surrounding various courses Title I might take in the next decade.

---

2 This chapter will not review the much debated evidence of Title I's effectiveness. The operative adjective to apply to the history of evidence about Title I's effectiveness is "ambiguous." The most recent quasi-experimental evidence from the Prospects study indicates insignificant differences in achievement for students in the program compared to a matched comparison group of students (Puma et al., 1997). By way of contrast, some researchers and the Department of Education have argued that analyses of trend data from the National Assessment of Educational Progress indicate statistically significant levels of improvement, especially among the nine-year-old groups, above and beyond what available factors would explain. These analysts assert that it is highly plausible for Title I and other programs directed at disadvantaged students to have been a factor behind these gains (Grissmer, 1994; U.S. Department of Education, 1999).

PROGRESS ON THE TWO KEY STEPS
FOR MAKING TITLE I EFFECTIVE

Appropriately allocating funds to intended beneficiaries has always been a major challenge for the Title I program. Most federal education programs typically involve considerable state and district targeting, but not the school-level targeting that has come to distinguish Title I. Title I also contains a significant complement of requirements focused on the design and delivery of services, as well as on accountability for progress. These fiscal and program requirements have evolved over a long and sometimes conflictual history during which policy makers contended with pressures for greater local discretion in the distribution of resources, concerns about resource adequacy, and evidence that results were falling far short of the goal of sustained improvement of student achievement. The following sections assess how the current program has attempted to resolve the major challenges of appropriately allocating funds and instituting effective programs.

DISTRIBUTING FEDERAL TITLE I FUNDS

Federal Title I funds flow through two longstanding formulas. In 1997–98, of all Title I dollars, 86 percent flowed through the Basic Grants formula, which calculates each district's allocation based on the number of poor children aged 5–17, using updated census poverty data and adjusting for per-pupil cost in each state. The remaining 14 percent of funds flowed through the Concentration Grants formula, which awards funds to districts with at least 6,500 eligible children or with more than 15 percent of children who are eligible. While Congress has elected not to use a third formula that would distribute funds even more markedly to poorer districts by giving greater weight to districts with higher concentrations of poor children, the basic principle that poorer districts have priority on Title I funding is clearly articulated in the Title I legislation.[3]

Requirements that target funds to higher-poverty schools also underscore the current program's priority on getting sufficient funds to areas with concentrations of poverty. For example:

---

3 This formula is referred to as the Targeted Grants Program and was created by the 1994 reauthorization as the controlling funding arm for funds that exceed the 1995 funding level. However, Congress consistently has overridden this provision when appropriating additional Title I funds. A fourth formula, the Education Finance Incentive Program, also sits unused on the books. This formula allocates funds to states according to the population aged 5–17 multiplied by factors that reward higher levels of fiscal effort and within-state equalization. States would mirror this procedure in making allocations to districts. While the formula may improve interdistrict equities, its effect would be to decrease the proportion of Title I dollars going to the highest-poverty areas. This is largely due to the formula's counting all school-aged children in contrast to other formulas' counting only poor school-aged children.

- Poverty, not low educational achievement, must govern which schools are designated by districts as eligible for Title I funds. In general, schools designated as eligible must meet or exceed the greater of the following: the average district average poverty rate or 35 percent poverty.

- All schools, regardless of grade level, with at least 75 percent poor students must receive first priority by districts for Title I programs.

- District allocations of funds to schools (as distinct from determinations of which schools are eligible to receive funding) must result in higher amounts per low-income pupil for higher-poverty schools than for lower-poverty schools.

- Eligible schools' funding per poor child must amount to at least 125 percent of the district-wide Title I funding per poor child.

The above requirements reflect the current resolution of a historical controversy that has unfolded on two levels. At one level, a debate has pitted groups espousing serving the greatest number of schools and children in need against those who argue that funds must not be spread so thin as to have little chance of making a difference. At another level, the controversy has focused on whether the key problem to be addressed is poverty or low achievement.[4] For now, a moderate consensus appears to have formed around the view that concentrations of poverty are a major contributor to the problem of low achievement in the nation's schools and thus should be an important determinant of funding.[5] Research showing that concentrations of poor children in schools impose additional obstacles to learning that depress the performance of both poor and nonpoor students alike has buttressed this consensus (Anderson et al., 1992; Puma et al., 1997). Moreover, observations of instructional difficulties in higher-poverty schools resulting from higher family mobility, as well as evidence from surveys of school principals indicating that high-poverty schools have teachers with less expertise and fewer parent-supplied extras, also support the current consensus (Chambers et al., 1993). Recent findings showing that low-income students are increasingly situated in high-poverty schools have further reinforced the consensus. The proportion of low-income students who attended schools with 50 percent or more poverty has risen from 51 percent in 1990–91 to 62 percent in 1997–98 (U.S. Department of Education, 1999).

---

4 While poverty status and low achievement are moderately correlated, the relationship is not overwhelming. In fact, the within-district distributions of low achieving students among schools often differs considerably from the distribution of low-income children (Orland & Stullich 1997).

5 The consensus is described as moderate because Congress has been reluctant to shift major portions of Title I appropriations into the Concentration Grants formula or the Targeted Grants Program, which both benefit districts with higher poverty concentrations. In part, this may reflect a reluctance to spend very large sums of new money until more compelling evidence of effectiveness can be obtained. Congress generally is unreceptive to reducing funds to districts.

The emphasis on targeting funds to higher-poverty schools is beginning to realize some of the intended effects, but this is truer for schools than for districts. Overall, 93 percent of districts in the nation continue to receive Title I funds, and the relative shares of funding received by high and low poverty districts have remained basically unchanged since the late 1980s. Significant changes, however, have occurred at the school level. In 1997–98, Title I funds reached 95 percent of schools with poverty concentrations of 75 percent or more, whereas in 1993–94 only 79 percent of these schools were served (Chambers et al., 1999). Moreover, schools with 75 percent poverty concentration accounted for 46 percent of all Title I funds allocated in 1997–98, yet constituted only 27 percent of eligible Title I schools.[6]

It is noteworthy, nonetheless, that interdistrict inequities brought about by state and local funding have remained well entrenched even as recent versions of Title I have attempted to distribute more funds on the basis of poverty concentration. (The Title I changes have made little difference at the district level due to hold harmless requirements and the large majority of funds still moving through the Basic Grants formula.) For example, districts in the highest-poverty quartile are responsible for educating 49 percent of the nation's poor children. Yet, although these districts receive 43 percent of the federal education spending contributed by Title I, they receive only 23 percent of the much larger pool of state and local funds. These disparities are likely to matter in very tangible ways for poor districts. It is plausible that they may help explain why, in 1997–98, schools with low-poverty concentrations (below 35 percent) acquired an average of 12.4 new computers from state and local funds, while schools with the highest concentrations acquired only 4.8 new computers with state and local funds (Chambers et al., 1999).

IMPROVING PERFORMANCE OF DISADVANTAGED STUDENTS

The second of the two steps needed for Title I to effect improved learning, and possibly the most challenging one, is converting funds into instructional programs and services that produce significant achievement gains for poor students. At present (2000), Title I relies on a three-pronged strategy to promote effective services in schools: schoolwide programs, accountability tied to state and local standards, and flexibility to waive various requirements when they are shown to impede delivery of sound services.

Schoolwide programs follow the logic that just as it may "take a village" to rear children effectively, it may take the entire school to significantly increase the educational performance of children from disadvantaged backgrounds. Prior to

---

6   Somewhat less positive evidence of shifts in resources indicates that lower-poverty schools appear to receive higher amounts per child in poverty than do higher-poverty schools. The amount per low-income child, adjusted to 1999–2000 levels and incorporating district-provided instructional services and programs, is $617 for schools with 75 percent or more poverty and $1,001 for schools with 35 percent or less poverty (Chambers et al., 1999).

1988, Title I required schools to target services directly on students who demonstrated the greatest need as defined by low achievement. After 1988, the federal strategy shifted to allowing high-poverty schools to use funds to improve the overall instructional program for all students in the school. Initially, only schools with 75 percent poverty concentration were allowed to implement schoolwide programs, but by the mid-1990s this threshold was lowered to its current level of 50 percent.

A major objective in encouraging schoolwide Title I programs was discouraging the use of pullout instruction. Over the years, local officials came to see pulling students out of regular classrooms as the easiest way to implement targeted assistance and to document that the services provided were supplemental to the regular school program. While sometimes shown to have been effective, pullouts increasingly have been shown to harbor a number of drawbacks to the effective provision of services. Among these are the replacement of a student's instructional time in the regular classroom with time spent on less demanding content, and the stigmatization of children who leave the classroom to receive Title I instruction.

The second component in Title I's current emphasis on improved programs is a strengthened system of accountability to ensure that schools receiving Title I funds realize significant improvement in students' achievement. The current Title I program obligates states to oversee districts and schools to ensure they make continuous and substantial yearly progress towards meeting state performance standards in state-assessed content areas for all children enrolled in Title I programs. States must designate districts and individual schools as needing improvement when those schools fail to make adequate progress against approved state standards for two consecutive years. Once districts and schools are identified for improvement, states must arrange to provide them with assistance and support to remedy inadequacies in their educational programs. Should insufficient progress persist for three or more years following identification for improvement, states must institute various corrective actions, which may include reconstitution of the districts and schools, and opportunities for parents in the failing schools to transfer their children to other, better performing public schools.[7]

Extending flexibility through waivers to states and school districts also has been a thrust of the current Title I program emphasis on coordinating school-level resources so as not to impede improvement and whole school reform. Two types of waiver authorities presently exist. An ESEA waiver authority (which also is repeated through similar provisions in the GOALS 2000 governing statute and the School to Work Opportunities Act) permits state education agencies and school districts to apply to the Secretary of Education for waivers of specific provisions of the ESEA statute or regulations. Furthermore, between 1994 and 1996 the Goals 2000 legislation opened the opportunity for 12 states to participate in

---

7 Corrective actions for persistently low-performing schools will not be effective under Title I until final state assessment systems are in place in the 2000–01 school year.

the Ed-Flex waiver demonstration program.[8] Under this program, the state education agencies in these states can grant waivers of specified federal program provisions to districts within their jurisdiction. Waivers have applied to several provisions of the program, including school eligibility and targeting requirements, the extension of schoolwide programs to additional schools, professional development, and the operation of pilot programs focused on reform (Yu & Taylor, 1999). The essence of the expanded flexibility provided through waivers is to make the first priority for districts and schools of meeting the underlying goals of improving the performance of disadvantaged students; and make blind adherence to specific provisions that are not critical to the program's aims a secondary priority.

The three strategies for school-focused instructional improvement—schoolwide programs, state/local standards-based accountability, and flexibility through waiver authority—have so far exhibited mixed progress. On the positive side, after over a decade of active federal promotion, schoolwide programs have come into wider use. Forty-three percent of Title I schools operated such programs in 1997–98, up from 3 percent in 1990–91 (U.S. Department of Education, 1999). Furthermore, schools operating schoolwide programs in 1997–98 received a clear majority of Title I school-level funds—just over 60 percent. Reliance on pullout services also appears to be declining, although it is still quite prevalent. Seventy-two percent of elementary schools implementing targeted assistance used pullouts in 1997–98 to serve 63 percent of their students; and 48 percent of elementary schools implementing schoolwide approaches served 21 percent of their students through pullouts. Evidence demonstrating the effectiveness of schoolwide programs, however, remains largely inconclusive—most likely because schoolwide programs are highly variable (D'Agostino, 1999).

Progress in instituting a strengthened system of state and local accountability that incorporates Title I has been slow and problematic. Although researchers have reported that Title I provisions are a major stimulus for some urban and rural districts to establish challenging standards, researchers also have found that numerous states and localities are experiencing major obstacles to integrating Title I with state accountability systems (U.S. Department of Education, 1999). Parallel systems of accountability prevailed across many states as the program approached the 2000 target date for full implementation of the state/local accountability system. Further, state and local educational agencies have reported limited capacity to provide the necessary technical assistance to schools identified for improvement and possible corrective action. A recent infusion of $134 million in federal funds is designed to improve this situation in qualifying districts, but substantial gaps in providing assistance are likely to remain. The Title I

---

8   The recently enacted Education Flexibility Partnership Act of 1999 now expands this program beyond its demonstration phase. States can now apply for Ed-Flex under this new program, which is much more closely tied to the standards, accountability, and assessment provisions that are part of Title I. The 12 states in the current Ed-Flex program are Colorado, Illinois, Iowa, Kansas, Maryland, Massachusetts, Michigan, New Mexico, Ohio, Oregon, Texas, and Vermont.

program faces a significant challenge in realizing the envisioned accountability system if major collaboration fails to emerge within the states.

Flexibility linked to the ability to gain waivers has been popular and largely benign in its effects. Initially, waivers tended to grant flexibility for districts to ease into provisions that required them to first fund schools with higher concentrations of poor students. Districts sought to continue serving schools that under new requirements imposed in 1994 would become ineligible. Over time, waivers became more focused on school reform issues such as allowing certain schools below the threshold to operate schoolwide programs and direct more resources to professional development. In addition, many waiver requests were withdrawn or returned simply because they proved unnecessary for the actions districts proposed to take. As one watchful advocacy group cautiously concluded: "To date, the [waiver] process has been administered fairly and waivers do not appear to have contravened the purposes of the law." (Yu & Taylor 1999).

ISSUES IN MOVING FORWARD TO 2010

While proponents of the current approach to Title I may assert that it is too early to judge its payoff, the above assessments do not offer overwhelming confidence that the evidence to establish Title I's incontrovertible impact on learning is close at hand. Inevitably, policy makers are likely to ask whether alternative or bolder courses should be pursued. The three groups of opinions reviewed earlier in this chapter generally frame the alternatives that will be examined. Each raises important issues that must be considered as the future course of Title I is debated.

EXPANDING KNOWLEDGE AND THE INFRASTRUCTURE RELATED TO EFFECTIVE PROGRAM MODELS: MAKING TITLE I AN ENGINE OF SCHOOL REFORM

If Title I is to go beyond trying to ignite school reform and instead become its engine, several observers assert that major enhancements to the existing program are needed. The major challenge will be developing and greatly expanding the infrastructure of research, evaluation, and technical assistance to institute instructional practices that produce impacts on achievement. Slavin (1999) proposes expanding the access of schools to what works through heightened funding of research and development in order to uncover effective instructional approaches. Strategies include investing substantially in local professional development so teachers and administrators can become effective implementers of successful approaches, expanding schools' eligibility to introduce Title I schoolwide programs, and strengthening assessment and accountability procedures to reward successful schools and restructure low-performing schools. Bodilly and Berends (1999) add to these ideas by underscoring the importance of strengthening the role of the district in building school capacity to design and implement schoolwide solutions to problems. They observe that schools will only invest the effort in meaningful reform if the district has indicated sufficient support and a reinforcing climate.

Indeed, looking beyond Title I to several recent instructional programs funded by the federal government, one can see the groundwork for greatly expanding available knowledge about what approaches work and what resources are necessary for their replication in different contexts. The Comprehensive School Reform Demonstration Program, the 21st Century Community Learning Centers which support after-school learning opportunities, New American Schools, and the Reading Excellence Program, all include a significant focus on evaluating how well these approaches work and what supports are important to their successful installation.

Improved knowledge about effective approaches and provision of support to transplant these approaches to an array of local circumstances offers considerable rational appeal. Nevertheless, this expansive strategy for the Title I program contains some drawbacks. First, it will take considerable time to build an adequate infrastructure of knowledge and technical assistance, with simultaneously little short-term results for the elected officials who will have invested substantial funding. Moreover, research methods have improved greatly, but amassing clear and definitive evidence to "prove" one approach is superior to others typically requires many years, as well as adherence to standards of research that generally have not been applied to much educational research. Second, the question of what the federal government will do with so-called "proven" approaches, if found, must be addressed. Although proponents emphasize the importance of voluntary local adoption, unintended pressures may result in mandates to use certain approaches despite limited confidence that they will work in a wide array of situations, or that they are superior to emerging approaches that have not substantiated their success.

UNIFYING FEDERAL, STATE, AND LOCAL EFFORTS TO IMPROVE THE EDUCATION OF POOR CHILDREN: STATE BLOCK GRANT OPTIONS

Interest in a block grant approach to Title I generally has arisen more frequently in legislative circles than among stakeholders and researchers associated with the program. As recently as 1997, for instance, the U.S. Senate passed a bill to establish a Title I block grant to states; the bill ultimately did not survive, but its passage stands as a testament to the idea's appeal in certain quarters. Despite sporadic legislative interest, many researchers tend to dismiss a block grant approach to Title I as seriously flawed, citing past experience with the Chapter 2 education block grant program instituted in 1982, and the historical record of states' and localities' diversions of funds to purposes tangential to the core premise of Title I.[9]

What contemporary analysts may overlook, however, is a growing recognition that the improvements desired under Title I may be largely impossible without the concerted efforts of states in addressing the low educational performance of children in poverty. The current Title I program attempts to build this collabo-

---

9 The Chapter 2 block grant, which was established in 1982 under the Education Consolidation and Improvement Act, included many education programs but excluded Title I (which was renamed as Chapter 1 until 1994). The Chapter 2 legislation greatly restricted states' oversight of local decisions about how to use funds provided by the block grants.

rative effort with states and districts, but so far these efforts have produced uneven results. It is worth considering whether a carefully constructed state block grant program that incorporates major financial and other incentives for states to meet specific achievement benchmarks for students from disadvantaged backgrounds could function more effectively. The 1996 Personal Responsibility and Work Opportunity Reconciliation Act (PRWORA), which created the Temporary Assistance for Needy Families (TANF) block grant and vastly reformed the 61-year-old federal/state welfare structure, may offer instructive lessons for reassessing the wisdom of applying block grants with clear goals and benchmarks to Title I. An approach that relies on states' efforts is not automatically doomed. For example, while many would argue with elements of the TANF welfare program and emphasize that a strong economy has not permitted a full test of it, initial evidence fails to support the dire results that many critics predicted (Pavetti & Wemmerus, 1999).

The largest challenge that a block grant strategy will have to overcome is ensuring that incentives clearly point state actions in appropriate directions. Any workable block grant would have to counteract state and local officials' proclivity to spread resources widely. Furthermore, while states may provide useful laboratories for studying effective strategies to improve the performance of disadvantaged students, they also introduce the prospect of unstable policies in curricular content and student assessment (Orfeld and DeBray, 1999). Whether there are effective safeguards against such instability is an important issue, should Title I take this alternative course. Certainly, the provision of adequate federal resources for research and development that focus on evaluating the consequences of states' approaches would be a critical accompaniment to any proposed block grant.[10]

THE POTENTIAL OF MARKET-DRIVEN REFORM AND INDIVIDUAL CHOICE IN TITLE I

Broad expansion of the small foothold that parental choice currently occupies within the Title I program, while conceivable, is likely to raise issues that are extremely difficult to resolve. It is noteworthy that proposals emanating from the 2000 presidential campaign have called for widening the scope of the public school choice provisions; one proposal, for example, would give poor parents in failing schools a Title I voucher for $1,500 to use for a school of their choosing or to acquire specialized tutoring. Nevertheless, these proposals, depending on their specifics, introduce problems of excessive church-state entanglements that may jeopardize a revamped program's ability to pass legal scrutiny. Individual choice provisions also present a dilemma: while they offer potential benefits for Title I students using the vouchers to transfer to better schools, they can worsen the educational prospects for students who remain because such transfers may increase the concentration of poor students in the students' original schools. This

---

10 PRWORA offers a model in this area with its inclusion of federal resources and requirements for rigorous evaluation of the effects of states' redesigned welfare systems.

is particularly a problem when poorer parents might not be able to supplement the voucher to meet the tuition costs of the transfer school. Institutional capacity issues pose equally significant challenges for individual choice alternatives. Growth of the school-aged population already has placed major demands on available space in many districts, and private or charter schools are unevenly available as options for parents across the country.

These issues, although daunting, probably will not dampen efforts to explore alternative approaches to Title I through the mechanism of parental choice. Focused experimentation may be the initial path that policy makers choose as a temporizing strategy to assess the feasibility and potential effects of a broader choice-based approach to Title I. The first step in such an effort will be careful study of the implementation and effectiveness of the public school transfer options that will be operational for some Title I districts in the 2000–2001 school year.

ARE MAJOR CHANGES IN STORE?

Revolutionary change has not distinguished Title I's 35-year history. Moreover, it is difficult to foresee the issues discussed in this chapter combining to revolutionize the Title I program in the imminent future. The issues posed in this chapter, however, do suggest that a period of transitional change may be quite likely, resulting in reshaping the dominant strategy of the Title I program over the long term. The future structure of the program will turn heavily on the emergence of credible evidence indicating major progress on two key steps that form the foundation for the program to be deemed effective: (1) getting funds to children who are the most at-risk due to poverty and low academic performance, and (2) converting funds into instructional programs and services that produce significant achievement gains for these students. Modest progress is evident on improved targeting of funds to areas of poverty concentration at this time. Much less progress is evident regarding Title I's ability to produce significant achievement gains for poor students. If this picture continues and proponents of alternative approaches, such as incentive-laden state block grants or market-driven choices for parents, can amass plausible evidence that these solutions may lead to greater progress on both steps, then the 2010 emphasis of Title I could be very different.

REFERENCES

Anderson, J., Hollinger, D., and Conaty, J. (1992). *Poverty and achievement: Re-examining the relationship between school poverty and student achievement (An examination of eighth grade student achievement using the national educational longitudinal study of 1988)*. Paper presented at the American Educational Research Association, San Francisco.

Bodilly, S., & Berends, M. (1999). Necessary district support for comprehensive school reform. In G. Orfield, G., & E. H. DeBray E. H. (Eds.), *Hard work for good schools: Facts not fads in Title I reform*. (pp.111–119). Cambridge, MA: The Civil Rights Project, Harvard University.

Chambers, J., Lieberman, J., Parrish, T., Kaleba, D., Van Campen, J., & Stullich, S. (1999, June). *Study of education resources and federal funding: Preliminary report.* Prepared for the U.S. Department of Education, Planning and Evaluation Service. Palo Alto, CA: American Institutes for Research.

Chambers, J., Parrish, T., Goertz M., Marder, C., & Padilla, C. (1993). Translating dollars into services: Chapter 1 resources in the context of state and local resources for education. Washington, DC: U. S. Department of Education, Planning and Evaluation Service.

D'Agostino, J. V. (1999). Teacher roles and student achievement in high-poverty schools. In G. Orfield, G., & Debray, E. H. (Eds.), *Hard work for good schools: Facts not fads in Title I reform.* (pp. 77–85). Cambridge, MA: The Civil Rights Project, Harvard University.

Grissmer, D. W., Kirby, S. N., Berends, M., and & Williamson, S. (1994). *Student achievement and the changing American family.* Santa Monica, CA: RAND, Institute for Education and Training.

Orfield, Gary, & DeBray, E. H. (Eds.). (1999). *Hard work for good schools: Facts not fads in Title I reform.* Cambridge, MA: The Civil Rights Project, Harvard University.

Orland, M., & Stullich, S. (1997). Financing Title I: Meeting the twin goals of effective resource targeting and beneficial program interventions. In Wang, M., & Wong, K. (Eds.), *Implementing school reform: Practice and policy imperatives* (pp. 1–26). Philadelphia: Center for Research in Human Development and Education, Temple University.

Pavetti, L., & Wemmerus, N. (1999). From a welfare check to a paycheck: Creating a new social contract. *Journal of Labor Research, 20*: (4) 517–537.

Puma, M. J., Karweit, N., Price, C., Riccuiti, A., Thompson, W., & Vaden-Kiernan, M. (1997). *Prospects: Final report on student outcomes.* Report prepared for the U. S. Department of Education, Planning, and Evaluation Service. Cambridge, MA: Abt Associates.

Slavin, R. (1999, February). *How Title I can become the engine of reform in America's schools.* Paper prepared for the Office of Educational Research and Improvement, U.S. Department of Education, Baltimore: Johns Hopkins University.

Stullich, S., Donly, B., & Stolzberg, S. (1999). *Targeting schools: Study of Title I allocations within school districts.* Report for the U.S. Department of Education, Office of the Under Secretary, Planning and Evaluation Service. Rockville MD: Westat.

U.S. Department of Education. (2000). *Guidance on the $134 million fiscal year 2000 appropriation for school improvement.* Washington, DC: Office of Elementary and Secondary Education.

U.S. Department of Education. (1999). *Promising results, continuing challenges: The final report of the national assessment of Title I.* Washington, DC: Office of the Under Secretary, Planning and Evaluation Service.

Yu, C. M., & Taylor, W. (Eds.). (1999). *Title I in midstream: The fight to improve schools for poor kids*. Washington, DC: Citizens' Commission on Civil Rights.

5

EXPANDING VALUE ADDED IN SERVING CHILDREN WITH DISABILITIES

Stephen Chaikind
Gallaudet University

SPECIAL EDUCATION FINANCE

The future of special education in the United States is entering a new era of change.[1] Since the passage of PL 94-142, the Education for All Handicapped Children Act in 1975 (renamed in 1990 the Individuals with Disabilities Education Act [IDEA]), special education has matured into the focused set of services that exist today. The ideal of providing public education to children with disabilities is no longer in doubt. Now, discussions concerning the future of special education invoke questions about the processes and methods necessary to achieve the best outcomes for students with disabilities, while at the same time promoting education for all students. Such discussions involve important implications for the finance of special education as well.

IDEA mandates that children with disabilities receive a free appropriate public education, and ensures that related services necessary for the education of these children are also provided. Approximately 6,115,000 students ages 3 through 21 received special education services under IDEA grants to states and preschool programs during the 1998–99 school year, the last year data are available.[2] Another 189,000 infants and toddlers ages 0 to 3 received early intervention services in that year as well.[3] The number of children served has increased from a total of 3,709,000 in the 1976–77 school year, the first year the program was fully

---

1 The author would like to thank Marsha Brauen and Scott Brown for their insightful reviews of this chapter.

2 U.S. Department of Education. Office of Special Education Programs. Data Analysis System (DANS).

3 U.S. Department of Education. Office of Special Education Programs. Data Analysis System (DANS).

functional.[4] Special education students ages 6 through 17 now represent close to 10 percent of all public and private elementary/secondary school students enrolled in the United States in the 1998–99 school year. If the percentage of children ages 3 to 21 served under Part B of IDEA remains at the current level of 8.3 percent of the total population in this age group, then 6,400,000 are likely to be served in the 2005–06 school year, with an additional 100,000 in 2010–11, based on current population projections. However, if there is a growing need for special education services above that resulting only from population growth, as has occurred in recent years, then the number of students receiving special education services would be substantially higher five and ten years into the future.[5]

Total expenditures for special education, however, are more difficult to gauge. An estimated 8 percent of special education expenditures in the United States, until recently, have been funded by the federal government, in the form of grants to states to provide special education in grades K-12, in preschool programs, and in programs for infants and toddlers. These federal grants are contingent upon the adherence of state and local education agencies to federal guidelines on the use of these funds. For 1996–97, federal grants to states totaled approximately $3 billion, with a total of $3.3 billion spent on special education from federal funds in fiscal year 1997.[6] These data indicate that approximately $37 billion was spent on special education and related services nationally by state, local, and federal sources in 1996–97.[7] Federal appropriations and the share of total special education costs supported by these appropriations have increased dramatically in more recent years, however, reflecting a desire for the federal

---

4   U.S. Department of Education, 1995, *Seventeenth annual report to Congress* Table 1.3.

5   This estimate utilized U.S. Census Bureau middle series population projections by age as of July 1 in the year preceding the school year in the estimate. For example, 76.6 million children ages 3 to 21 are projected for July 1, 2005. Hence, if the 8.34 percent of the 3-to-21-year-old age cohort who were served by Part B 1998–99 continues, then 6.4 million students will be served in 2005–06 and 6.5 million in 2010–11. As an upper bound, if the (approximate) average 0.2 percent increase in this percentage that has occurred over the most recent three years continues, then slightly less than 10 percent of this cohort would be served by Part B in 2005–06, and slightly less than 11 percent by 2010–11. Thus, as an upper limit, as many as 7,500,000 to 8,400,000 special education students may be served in 2005–06 and 2010–11 respectively. However, this growth rate may not be sustained, so these estimates might be viewed as a maximum projection for the potential number of students that will be served.

6   Respective estimates are from U.S. Department of Education (1998, Table AG1, p. A-227); and U.S. Census Bureau (1999, Table No. 256, p. 165).

7   This estimate assumes that the $3 billion in federal grants to states was 8 percent of total special education expenditures. This estimate is consistent with other estimates of total costs for special education. Chambers et al. (1998) present calculations for total special education expenditures for 1995–96 using alternative methodologies and data, and estimate spending to be between $30.9 and $34.8 billion in that year.

government to offset a larger percentage of state and local obligations for special education. In fiscal year 1999, $5.1 billion was appropriated for grants to states, and $5.8 billion has been appropriated for fiscal year 2000.

The federal formula authorizing aid to states for most special education appropriations was formerly based on the number of students in each state receiving special education services, up to a maximum of 40 percent of the national average per-pupil expenditure on education. This formula was modified under the 1997 IDEA Amendments, with federal authorizations now based on weighted counts of the school age population for which states mandate special education services and on the number of children living in poverty, subject to certain minimum guarantees. This new formula became effective once appropriations exceeded levels specified in law, which occurred in fiscal year 1998 for preschool grants to states and in fiscal year 2000 for state grants to serve elementary and secondary school students.

Because of limitations on appropriations, full funding has never been achieved, with the federal government never paying more than 12.5 percent of the national average per-pupil expenditure on education toward the excess costs of educating students with disabilities. Recent initiatives in Congress, however, have proposed to fully fund special education programs, with bills introduced in both the House and Senate that variously propose annual federal special education funding levels of $17 billion by 2002 to 2006.[8]

Presently, however, the predominant share of special education and related services continue to be paid by state and local education agencies. States distribute special education funds to local districts through a variety of formulas. The most common reimbursement formula is based on weighted multiples of regular education student costs, with the weights either being uniform across disabilities or varying based on the differences in costs for each disability. Other formulas used include a flat grant method, reimbursement based on resource use, or the reimbursement of a percentage of special education costs.[9]

Continuing debate concerning the future of special education finance, other than the federally determined appropriation amounts, may be summarized into several broad categories. These categorizations are not meant to be to all-inclusive, since there are many complicated and interrelated issues accompanying decisions that will affect students with disabilities. Some of these complexities are indicated in the sections below. Nevertheless, forthcoming special education finance policy will likely be characterized by the following key factors:

- The effects of redoubled emphasis on student outcomes and assessment, and what this means for the finance of special education

- The need to better determine the exact costs for special education

8 More detail on full funding issues for special education can be found in Apling (1999). Examples of recent proposed legislation include S.R. 2341 and H.R. 4090.

9 See Parrish and Wolman (1999) for a more detailed summary of state spending formulas.

- The meaning and financial impacts of "free appropriate public education" in a "least restrictive environment," especially as this relates to increased "inclusion" for students with disabilities

- The ways and means in which related and supplementary services to children with disabilities are provided and financed

- The variations in state special education funding formulas

- The assessment of how other developments in education, including privatization, disciplinary policies, due process and safeguards, parental involvement, and other questions affect special education finance

SPECIAL EDUCATION
FINANCE ISSUES FOR THE FUTURE

This section examines at a global level key policy issues from the perspective of special education finance. These policy questions, such as those related to outcomes, assessment, inclusion, and service provision, for example, vary greatly among states and school districts, of course, based on local practice and needs. The discussion here, though, can help establish a baseline for further special education finance initiatives.

OUTCOMES, ASSESSMENT, AND FUNDING

There is a perceptible shift in the framework for special education into the future toward an increased emphasis on educational outcomes and on the assessment of these outcomes. The culmination of this shift is anchored in the 1997 reauthorization of IDEA (the IDEA Amendments of 1997), and is also specified in other venues as well, including the U.S. Department of Education's response to the Government Performance and Results Act (GPRA) of 1993 and the regulations issued by the Department. While controversy remains about some of the provisions in the 1997 Amendments, as well as in the subsequent regulations, this movement toward what might be viewed as a more student-outcome centered approach to special education can also serve as a potential model for changes in the way other education programs—in addition to those serving children with disabilities—are financed and administered in the future.

More explicit to special education is the obligation for states to establish specific performance goals for students in special education programs, as well as measurable indicators to assess these goals. These goals must, to the extent practicable, link special education outcomes to those in the general education curriculum. Students in special education programs must also be included in regular state assessment programs whenever feasible. Guidance on ways to achieve these outcomes are to be specified in each student's Individualized Education Program (IEP).

The Department of Education has developed a set of performance indicators for special education. These performance standards are summarized in the *Twen-*

tieth Annual Report to Congress by the Office of Special Education Programs (OSEP), in conjunction with the Department's GPRA plans.[10] These standards include, for example, indicators measuring the percentage of children with disabilities in regular classrooms; reading, math and other academic proficiency gains; school completion rates; employment success; disciplinary actions undertaken; parental satisfaction; and many others.

Accomplishing these goals is supported not only through grants for special education and related services, but also through IDEA's funding for a variety of research, professional development, personnel preparation, technical assistance, demonstration, dissemination, and other programs and activities. Part D of the 1997 IDEA Amendments combined funding for 14 formerly disparate programs, and created a new state improvement program, in order to enable more flexible and creative use of these funds toward educational improvement and assessment. OSEP's *Twentieth Annual Report to Congress* notes that the grants to states, combined with state funding of LEAs, along with this discretionary funding, will foster "two quantifiable end outcomes: Improvement of educational results for children with disabilities and greater participation in postsecondary education and employment for youth with disabilities."[11]

Another example of the way future special education funding is linked to the current initiatives for outcomes and assessment is seen in what OSEP is calling "five strategic directions with the greatest potential to improve education results."[12] These directions are based on OSEP-sponsored projects, and may likely serve as indications of what future funding will emphasize. These strategic directions stress a focus on activities and research that will (1) provide support to infants and toddlers, (2) enhance preschool programs that prepare children with disabilities for elementary school success, (3) improve intervention for students with reading or behavior difficulties, (4) improve access to the general education curriculum for students with disabilities, and (5) increase high school graduation rates for students with disabilities.

Further, the recently issued final regulations on IDEA, issued by the U.S. Department of Education in March 1999, also contain provisions that will have longer-term fiscal impacts.[13] In fact, the Center for Special Education Finance has listed scores of regulations that are likely to affect special education costs.[14] These regulations include those ranging from the use of funds by states and LEAs, to the definition of excess costs, funding sources for related services, payment for appeals, use of funds for placement in private schools, treatment of charter schools, and many others. The ultimate intent, of course, of all of these regula-

---

10 See U.S. Department of Education (1998, pp. IV-51 to IV-70).

11 U.S. Department of Education (1998, p. IV-56); a more general discussion of cost implications for standards-based reforms is included in Goertz et al. (1999).

12 To link to this document, go to "Five Strategic Directions" at www.ed.gov/offices/OSERS/IDEA/whatsnew.html.

13 Summaries of these regulations appear in Jones and Apling (1999).

14 The complete list of regulations with fiscal impacts, and interactive links to them, can be found at csef.air.org/idearegs_top.html.

tions is to improve results for children with disabilities. Several of these regulations, however, might be considered more directly focused on enhancing educational outcomes than others, including, for example, those related to graduation success, IEP development, special education service commencement, and the use of extended school years. The magnitude of potential future costs that will result from these regulations will depend on their interpretation and how they are subsequently implemented. For example, one controversial regulation specifies that local districts must not limit extended school year services to students where a student's IEP indicates such extended services will prevent losses of previous educational gains acquired during the regular school year. If this regulation is interpreted to entail an expansion of current extended school year programs, and not simply a codification of current practices, then it has the potential for equally large cost increases for states and local agencies. Other regulations may also have significant potential cost impacts, and several of these are noted in subsequent sections of this chapter where applicable.

COST MEASUREMENT

Policy and accountability measures to provide and demonstrate the most effective outcomes for children with disabilities will, of course, require accurate measures of their costs. Changes in resources needed for various educational environments, for improved IEPs, for assessment, and for related services need to be known with increased precision in order to inform program planning and to ensure adequate funding. While there have been at least three major studies of the costs of special education since IDEA's inception (see Chaikind, Danielson, & Brauen, 1993 for a review of these studies), the most recent of these is presently 15 years old. To fill this void, a new survey of special education costs was commissioned in 1999 by the U.S. Department of Education's Office of Special Education Programs, and is being conducted by the OSEP-funded Center for Special Education Finance (CSEF). This Special Education Expenditure Project (SEEP) began collecting data in early 2000 and is expected to have a final report on this effort by December 2001.[15]

SEEP is designed to be a nationally representative survey, sampling 250 local education agencies, more than 800 schools, approximately 4,000 regular education teachers, and more than 4,000 special education teachers, resource providers, and related service providers. Information concerning 8,000 students will also be gathered. The sample design was developed to ensure each state is represented, although states may opt to supplement their data with an increased sam-

---

[15] The Center for Special Education Finance (CSEF) was established in 1992 to provide research and analysis related to the finance of special education programs and services. While CSEF's mandate in the next several years is primarily focused on conducting, tabulating, and analyzing SEEP information, CSEF will also continue to provide other studies and efforts, as requested by the Department of Education, that will help frame special education finance policy into the next decades. Several extant CSEF analyses also address some of the special education issues noted in this chapter, and are so referenced.

ple size.[16] The sample design also ensures that state and local schools and other agencies established to specifically serve students with primarily low incidence disabilities are adequately represented. Currently available national-level data will be collected as well, and reconciled with the results of these sample data. Data are being collected (by mail and online responses) from a broad range of respondents, including state directors of special education, central office staff, teachers and aides, related service providers, and others. Information derived from this survey will concern resources utilized to provide services to children for each disability classification, placement, and educational setting.[17]

Results from this most recent cost analysis will improve the ability of policy makers and analysts to contrast costs for special education students with those in regular education programs, and will be especially useful in assessing current questions concerning the relative magnitude of special education expenditures on overall public education budgets. These data will also ease the difficulties in calculating total aggregate national special education expenditures that were noted above. While earlier studies have indicated that special education per-pupil costs have consistently been between 1.92 and 2.28 times regular education costs over the past 40 years, with a much narrower range since IDEA was enacted (Chaikind, Danielson, & Brauen, 1993, p. 365), there have been more recent concerns that special education has consumed larger and growing proportions of subsequent public education budgets (see Parrish, 1996). The new cost data developed through the SEEP study will allow a better assessment of such questions.

FINANCIAL ASPECTS OF INCLUSION

Another cornerstone of the recent IDEA Amendments that will affect special education finance into the future is the reinforced emphasis on the meaning of a "free appropriate public education." Currently, this goal is characterized as the need for increased "inclusion" of students with disabilities into regular education programs. Alternatively, this philosophy has been referred to as serving students in the "least restrictive environment" or as "mainstreaming," although these are not purely synonymous concepts. The 1997 IDEA Amendments fostered this approach through several of its finance provisions.[18] First, states must ensure that their funding mechanisms do not result in placements that are restrictive. Second, states are given more leeway in spending special education funds in regular classrooms even if regular education students receive some benefit from

---

16 States have the option in SEEP of contracting with CSEF to extend the sample size for their state, and approximately 9 states have chosen to do so. The additional data from these states will effectively double the sample size. However, while all 50 states will have districts represented in the national sample, only these states with extended data will have sample sizes large enough to allow analysis of state-level special education costs.

17 Continuously updated detail on the status of this study is found on the SEEP web site at www.seep.org.

18 See U.S. Department of Education (1998, pp. I-13 to I-14).

these special education funds. Third, the revision of the federal state grant and preschool grant finance formulas to a weighted count of the school-aged population and the number of children poverty in the state further acts to remove incentives to place students in more restrictive environments in order to increase revenues.[19]

There are many issues that must be resolved when deciding which children are served in classrooms with their nondisabled peers, either full time or for part of the school day.[20] Preeminent among these is whether or not more inclusive school practices are in fact educationally beneficial to students, or if other environments might better serve the needs of many children with disabilities. Often, the debate for inclusion suggests modifications in the way children are placed in the continuum of educational environments, and in the degree of coordination and resource sharing between special education, regular education, and other extant programs for students. Even the potential elimination of some or all special education placement environments has been suggested. Some of these questions are detailed in Fuchs and Fuchs (1998), who maintain that although maximizing educational, social, and postgraduation success calls for as inclusive an environment as possible, not all placements may benefit all children, leading to the necessity to maintain a continuum of placements and services. Currently, the 1999 special education regulations reemphasize the goal for a least restrictive environment, while at the same time maintaining a placement continuum.[21]

Because inclusion is such a critical issue at the heart of many current special education policy decisions, the costs of inclusion will similarly be the focus of much special education finance discussion in the future. And, it is likely that these finance debates will be predicated on what education theory says and on what outcome assessments show are the best practices for students with disabilities. The approach that special education finance alternatives should be derived from policy and educational decisions, rather than policy following finance decisions, is discussed in more detail in Parrish (1995). In practice, some redesign of special education finance based on educational considerations has already occurred, for example, through funding formula modifications in the 1997 Amendments and in certain states. Furthering this idea in future financing debate are issues that might involve enhanced links between regular education and special education funding (see National Association of State Boards of Education, 1994) or more creative departures from the categorical nature of special education financing (McLaughlin, 1995). A precursor of the latter approach might be seen in the 1997 IDEA Amendments' easing of restrictions on commingling of resources

---

19 This link is discussed in more detail in National Association of State Boards of Education (1992) and Center for Special Education Finance (1994).

20 Background and historical perspective on many of these issues is given in Fuchs and Fuchs, (1994).

21 See especially sections 300.550 to 300.556 of the regulations, related to least restrictive environments (www.ideapractices.org/idearegsmain.htm). In addition, an approach toward resolving some of the "tension" between a least restrictive environment and a continuum of service is discussed in Parrish (1995).

that might incidentally benefit regular education students sharing such resources in more inclusive classrooms.

Nevertheless, assuming that the development of each child's IEP predicts educational benefits from a more inclusive environment and that such outcomes are subsequently achieved, then questions turn to the finance of alternative environments. Currently, no a priori statement may be made concerning whether greater levels of inclusion are more or less costly than are less inclusive settings. The need to have both special education and regular education teachers in most inclusive classrooms, as well as the potential need for additional special education aides, however, may mean that inclusive practices are more expensive than, say, greater use of resource rooms or separate classrooms, at least in the short run. There may, in fact, be economies of scale in the latter, less inclusive environment.

Current evidence on the costs of inclusion is still being gathered. An early exploratory study (McLaughlin and Warren, 1994) indicated that the startup costs for inclusion may be expensive relative to current practice (for hiring new instructional personnel or renovating buildings, for example), but may also result in longer-term savings to offset these costs (by economizing on transportation, for example). However, this study was based on interviews in only 12 school districts, and additional detail is needed. One issue raised in this study is that funds for special education must follow students from one educational environment into the newer, inclusive one. It is expected that additional policy discussion and further investigation of the exact costs (and goals) of inclusion will be accentuated in the next several years, especially as data derived from the SEEP survey become available.

RELATED SERVICE PROVISION
AND SOURCES OF FUNDS

In addition to classroom learning, the success of students with disabilities depends on the supplemental and related services they receive while in school. These services may include assessment, health services, psychological counseling, physical therapy, vocational assistance, transportation to school, and others. Estimates show that the costs of related services range from 19 percent to as high as 46 percent of all special education expenditures, depending on whether the costs of regular education were included in the calculations and on the type of placement each student receives, as well as on the data sources analyzed.[22]

The costs for many such related and supplemental services have been assumed by the local or state education agencies over time. Prior to the passage of PL 94-142, though, various state programs existed to assist children with disabilities, with many services provided by public health or vocational agencies. As school systems became more of a focal point for providing services for children with disabilities, some of the responsibility for these types of supplemental services was absorbed by the state or local education agencies, and to their concurrent budgets. This trend might have contributed to a higher observed growth in

---

22 See Chaikind, Danielson, and Brauen (1993, p. 363) for a summary of these costs.

special education budgets than occurred in actual overall spending, since formerly noneducational costs became incorporated as education expenditures. This trend has slowly begun to reverse in recent years, as states increasingly use interagency agreements "to provide more comprehensive, cost-effective, and streamlined services to children with disabilities."[23]

The next decades will see a continuation of this interagency cooperation among service providers, and greater acceptance and cooperation between state agencies is also likely, with related services better linked to the overriding educational goals of special education. Such continued interagency cooperation might shift the financial responsibilities to a more equitable sharing of functions and costs among government agencies. In fact, financial responsibilities among public agencies are specifically spelled out in the new special education regulations, which note that agreements between public agencies must specify which agency supports supplementary and related services, as well as which agency is primarily responsible for such payments, in order to ensure a free appropriate public education.[24]

In addition, there are likely to be future financial impacts emanating from an extended need for supplementary and related services spurred by any increased emphasis on inclusion. For example, the 1997 IDEA Amendments define supplementary aids and services to mean "aids, services, and other supports that are provided in regular education classes or other education-related settings to enable children with disabilities to be educated with nondisabled children to the maximum extent appropriate."[25] Such necessary aids and services must be noted in each student's IEP. In addition, the renewed emphasis on outcomes and employment have led to a strengthened set of transitional services for students about to leave high school, with potential concurrent costs in the need for added interagency cooperation. In fact, the special education regulations specifically refer to a participating agency that will assist with transition services for students as "a state or local agency, other than the public agency responsible for a student's education, that is financially and legally responsible for providing transition services to the student" (§300.340). All of these requirements will have changing implications for the distribution of interagency responsibility for special education finance.

STATE FUNDING FORMULAS

The way states distribute funds to local education agencies has implications for many of the issues discussed in this chapter. As noted above, there is a new permanent formula for federal grants to states and grants for preschool programs that is not linked to placement of students in different disability categories. This funding methodology is sometimes referred to a census-based funding, and it was one of the recommendations by the National Association of State Boards of

---

23 U.S. Department of Education, (1998, p. III-51). See pp. III-51 to III-68 for detailed background on the use of interagency agreements.

24 See section 300.142 of the regulations.

25 U.S. Department of Education (1998, p. I-10).

Education in their report *Winners All* (1994). Claims that the funding formula can in fact result in unwarranted labeling for students and placement in restrictive environments have resulted in several states moving toward census-based funding mechanisms as well.

However, many other criteria also may be used to evaluate state special education funding formulas. Parrish and Wolman (1999) expand work by William T. Hartman to show 14 such criteria for evaluating state formulas, including the need for the funding system to be understandable, equitable, adequate, flexible, accountable, and controllable.[26] Further, the National Association of State Boards of Education has recommended that states should eliminate any links between funding and setting.[27] It is expected that states will continue to discuss revisions in their special education funding formulas over the next decades.

OTHER FUNDING ISSUES

Several general educational trends may also have financial impacts on special education. As detailed elsewhere in this volume, for example, more and more public education reform discussion involves the growth of publicly supported charter schools, as well as issues related to privatizing schools and school systems. Part of the movements to privatization and to charter schools are in essence alternative means of financing education, and these financial formats may have unintended effects on special education, potentially leaving children with disabilities and their families with fewer options and with less protection than currently exists. The IDEA regulations address several issues related to charter schools by requiring such schools in LEAs that receive federal funds maintain the same rights for students with disabilities as in LEA-managed schools.

There are many other funding issues that will occur in the coming decades. Many involve the costs of safeguards, both to specific situations where disputes need to be resolved, as well as protections for future generations of children with disabilities in situations where the nature of public education is changing. For specific disputes, there will always be fiscal issues related to the payment of attorney's fees and fees for other assessments. The special education regulations now strengthen the relationship between the payment of such fees and the process for developing student IEPs, for instance. In this way, the educational needs of the student are moved more toward the front and center of the safeguard question, and disputes concerning form rather than function are likely to become less relevant.

CONCLUSION

Special education continues as one of the two leading federally mandated programs serving children at risk, along with the Title I compensatory education program. This chapter reviews a number of important issues facing special education and discusses their financial implications. The groundwork for the future of special education and its finance has been most recently established in the 1997

---

26 See Parrish and Wolman (1999, Table 9.2, pp. 212–213).

27 See National Association of State Boards of Education (1992).

Amendments and the 1999 regulations, as well as in continuing debate on ways to best serve children with disabilities. The future holds promise as outcome assessment becomes more widespread, as new service delivery methods evolve, and as shifts in the way financing special education occurs. In addition, the Individuals with Disabilities Education Act will ensure that subsequent innovations in education and education finance in the United States over the next decades will continue to benefit children with disabilities.

REFERENCES

Aleman, Steven R. (1997, June 4). *Individuals with disabilities education act reauthorization legislation: An overview.* CRS Report for Congress. Washington, DC: Congressional Research Service.

Apling, Richard N. (1999, March 5). *Individuals with disabilities education act: Full funding of state formula.* CRS Report for Congress. Washington, DC: Congressional Research Service.

Center for Special Education Finance. (1994, Fall). *Finance in an inclusive system: Report from the National Association of State Boards of Education.* (CSEF Brief No. 4). Palo Alto, CA: Author.

Chaikind, Stephen, Danielson, Louis C., & Brauen, Marsha L. (1993). What do we know about the costs of special education: A selected review. *The Journal of Special Education, 26* (4), 344–370.

Chambers, Jay G., Parrish, Thomas B., Lieberman, Joanne C., & Wolman, Jean M. (1998, February). *What are we spending on special education in the U.S.?* (CSEF Brief No. 8). Palo Alto, CA: Center for Special Education Finance, American Institutes for Research.

Fuchs, Douglas, & Fuchs, Lynn S. (1994). Inclusive schools movement and the radicalization of special education reform. *Exceptional Children, 60* (4):294–309.

Fuchs, Douglas & Fuchs, Lynn S. (1998). Competing visions for educating students with disabilities: Inclusion versus full inclusion. *Childhood Education, 75,* 309–316.

Goertz, Margaret E., McLaughlin, Margaret, Roach, Virginia, & Raber, Suzanne M. (1999). What will it take? Including students with disabilities in standards-based reform. In Thomas B. Parrish, Jay G. Chambers, and Cassandra M. Guarino (Eds.), *Funding special education* (pp. 41–62). Thousand Oaks, CA: Corwin Press, Inc.

Jones, Nancy Lee & Apling, Richard N. (1999, March 23). *The individuals with disabilities education act: Department of education final regulations.* CRS Report for Congress. Washington, DC: Congressional Research Service.

McLaughlin, Margaret J., & Warren, Sandra H. (1994, Spring). *Resource implications of inclusion: Impressions of special education administrators at selected sites.* (CSEF Brief No. 3). Palo Alto, CA: Center for Special Education Finance, American Institutes for Research.

National Association of State Boards of Education. (1992, October). *Winners all: A call for inclusive schools.* Alexandria, VA: The National Association of State Boards of Education.

Parrish, Thomas B. (1996). *Special education finance: Past, present, and future.* (Policy Paper No. 8). Palo Alto, CA: Center for Special Education Finance, American Institutes for Research.

Parrish, Thomas B. (1995, Fall). *Fiscal issues related to the inclusion of students with disabilities.* (CSEF Brief No. 7). Palo Alto, CA: Center for Special Education Finance, American Institutes for Research.

Parrish, Thomas B., Chambers, Jay G., & Guarino, Cassandra M. (Eds.). (1999). *Funding special education.* Thousand Oaks, CA: Corwin Press, Inc.

Parrish, Thomas B., & Wolman, Jean. (1999). Trends and new developments in special education funding: What the states report. In Thomas B. Parrish, Jay G. Chambers, & Cassandra M. Guarino (Eds.), *Funding special education.* Thousand Oaks, CA: Corwin Press, Inc. 203–229.

U.S. Census Bureau. (1999). *Statistical Abstract of the United States.* Washington, DC: National Technical Information Service.

U.S. Department of Education. (1998). *Twentieth annual report to congress on the implementation of the individuals with disabilities education act.* Washington, DC: Division of Innovation and Development, Office of Special Education Programs, U.S. Office of Special Education and Rehabilitative Services.

U.S. Department of Education. (1995). *Seventeenth annual report to congress on the implementation of the individuals with disabilities education act.* Washington, DC: Division of Innovation and Development, Office of Special Education Programs, U.S. Office of Special Education and Rehabilitative Services.

6

FINANCING HIGHER EDUCATION IN THE NEW CENTURY

Mary P. McKeown-Moak
MGT of America[1]

At the beginning of the 20th century, 237,592 students and 23,868 faculty "populated" 977 postsecondary education institutions in the United States (U.S. Department of Education, 1999). These institutions spent $35 million to educate students, who were taught in small classes face to face with a professor. In 1900, less than 20 percent of funding for higher education came from public sources (federal, state, or local governments). Families with the means sent their male children off to obtain a higher education, and very little financial aid was available. Performance of institutions was measured only by the success of their students after graduation.

Could those in higher education in 1900 ever have predicted that, at the beginning of the 21st century, their numbers would have swollen to 15 million students, taught by approximately 1 million faculty, at over 4,500 institutions, expending more than $250 billion, about half of which came from public sources (U.S. Department of Education, 1999)? Would they have imagined that the federal government would provide substantial amounts of financial aid to millions of students? Would they have predicted that the performance and productivity of institutions is at the forefront of higher education policy decisions? Can those in higher education in 2000 predict what the shape of postsecondary education will be in 2100? Just as asynchronous learning on the Internet or elsewhere without face-to-face contact with a professor would have been unpredictable in 1900, so, too, the face of higher education in 2100 may be unimaginable.

---

[1] MGT of America is a national consulting firm specializing in higher education management and operational reviews, quantitative and qualitative research, and business evaluations. Dr. Mary P. McKeown-Moak is a principal in MGT's Austin office. MGT's Web site is at www.mgtofamerica.com.

This chapter offers some insights into the shape of higher education in the 21st century, particularly with respect to funding issues. The chapter provides historical perspectives on funding from government and other sources, policy issues, and the impact of policies on educational results. Policy issues likely to be at the forefront in discussions about, and funding for, higher education in the new century are highlighted.

OVERVIEW OF HIGHER EDUCATION FUNDING

Funding for higher education comes from four primary sources:

♦ Students and their families, who pay tuition and fees, which may be subsidized by local, state, federal, and private financial aid

♦ State and local governments, which provide appropriations to support institutions, financial aid, and contracts and grants to carry out specific projects

♦ The federal government, which provides direct appropriations to support the land grant functions of colleges, special grants for specific programs including research funding, and, most importantly, student financial aid

♦ Gifts and endowments from corporations and individual donors

Over the past century, the proportions of total revenues from each of these sources has shifted. In the 1920s, the federal government provided 7 percent of higher education revenues; state and local governments, 31 percent; students, 21 percent; and other sources, 41 percent (see Figure 6.1). By 1950, the percentages shifted, with the federal government providing 22 percent of revenues; state and local governments, 23 percent; and the share students pay dropping to 17 percent. By the end of the century, however, these numbers had once again shifted, with the federal government's share diminishing to 10 percent, state and local governments' growing to 29 percent, and students' to 30 percent. This is quite a significant shift away from government resources to students and their families, reflecting the times. In 1950, the federal government was investing heavily in higher education through grants to colleges for returning servicepersons. In 2000, the federal government's support is reflected in grants directly to students and their families through financial aid, which is counted as part of the students' share of funding.

FIGURE 6.1. SOURCES OF FUNDING FOR HIGHER EDUCATION, 1920–2000

Source of Funds	1920	1950	2000
Students and their families	21%	17%	30%
State and local government	31%	23%	29%
Federal government	7%	22%	10%
Private gifts and other	41%	38%	31%

SOURCE: Calculated from the *Digest of Education Statistics* (1999, Table 335).

Up until the end of World War II, relatively few individuals attended higher education in the United States, and the institutions they attended were state universities, land grant colleges, teachers colleges, or private liberal arts institutions. Students numbered 2.3 million in 1950. At the end of World War II, thousands of returning servicemen started to attend college, and the number and types of colleges changed. Community colleges, regional colleges, and many private institutions began operations to meet the needs of the returning service personnel, and the number of institutions increased from about 1,700 to over 2,500 by 1970, enrolling over 8.5 million students (*Digest of Education Statistics*, 1999). Tuition and fees at public institutions were kept low by increasing state appropriations to the institutions, with tuition making up the rest of revenues needed to operate.

As the scope and mission of public campuses increased and changed (for example, teachers colleges becoming regional universities), so did the complexity of equitably distributing resources among competing campuses. State resources did not keep pace with expanding enrollments, and the competition for state funds increased. State legislators sought methods to distribute available state resources to the campuses, and funding formulas were developed to assist in equitable distributions. By 1984, 36 states were using funding formulas at some point in the funding process for higher education, but that number declined to 30 in 1996, and then rose again to 36 in 2000, when over 15 million students were enrolled (SHEEO/MGT Survey of SHEFOs, 1998 and 1999). In the remaining states, using the prior annual or biennial budget as the base for adjustments, appropriations to higher education usually are made on an incremental or decremental basis to reflect changes in the states' priorities or in clients served.

HIGHER EDUCATION COST ISSUES AT THE BEGINNING OF THE 21ST CENTURY

At the beginning of the 21st century, higher education governing boards consider setting of tuition and fees one of the most difficult and most controversial public policy decisions they must make.[2] Even the popular press devotes considerable attention to the price of higher education. *USA Today* carries stories such as "Paying for college is the new math" (Kelly, 2000, p.1) and *US News and World Report* devotes whole issues to rankings of colleges and "best buys." Such interest would not have occurred at the beginning of the 20th century, when college attendance was limited largely to children of affluent families. Few financial aid programs existed to assist families with the cost of postsecondary education, and issues of access to a higher education, choice of college, and equity in funding were not included in many public policy debates.

In the 1980s and 1990s, the cost or price of higher education was the subject of significant public outcry when tuition levels increased at double-digit rates. Although this was the result of reductions in appropriation levels for public higher education during a time of constrained state budgets, or the result of inflationary pressures in the prices of goods and services that private colleges bought,

---

2 In some states, legislatures or statewide coordinating boards (instead of institutional or segmental governing boards) make tuition and fee policy decisions.

many families perceived that they were being priced out of higher education. Perceptions of the need for postsecondary education had changed from college for the few, to a necessity for the majority. But access to college and choice of college had been made possible in large part by federal financial aid programs.

Public scrutiny of the cost of attendance of higher education reached its peak when Congress appointed the National Commission on the Cost of Higher Education. The Commission released its final report, *Straight Talk About College Costs and Prices* in January 1998. The Commission addressed public anxiety about college prices that rose 400 percent since 1976. Following the release of the report, legislatures in about one-half of the states considered tuition issues during 1998 and 1999 sessions.[3] In addition to heightened interest in state legislatures, the Commission's report is credited with being the impetus for changes in the Higher Education Act, which Congress re-authorized in October 1998. Beginning with academic year 2001, colleges and universities will be required to report data on college costs, using standardized definitions for tuition and fees and the cost of attendance. Additionally, a national longitudinal study of college and university expenditures will provide trend information on tuition and fees compared to the Consumer Price Index and to financial aid.

Undergraduate resident tuition and fees rose 4.7 percent in 1999–2000 at public universities, and room and board charges at four-year public college and universities increased 4.6 percent. Tuition and fees at private colleges and universities rose 3.8 percent. Tuition and fees tend to be higher in the Northeast and Midwest, and lower than average in the South and Southwest. Total cost of attendance at a public four-year college or university typically was $10,909 for an undergraduate in-state student who lived on campus. Average cost of attendance at a private college during 1999–2000 was $21,685 (College Board, 1999a).

Average public four-year in-state tuition rose 98.1 percent in current dollars, or 51 percent in constant dollars, over the fiscal year 1990 to fiscal year 2000 period. In contrast, median family income in constant dollars has risen only 22 percent since 1981, and the average cost of attendance (at public four-year colleges) as a share of family income has increased significantly for low- and middle-income families (College Board, 1999a). For families whose income is in the lowest fifth of the distribution, average cost of attendance has increased from 40 to 62 percent of family income.

Hence, the cost of attendance of higher education continues to receive significant public scrutiny and congressional inquiry. In February 2000, congressional attention focused on the price of higher education as the Senate Committee on Governmental Affairs held a two-day investigative hearing on rising college tuition levels. Senators warned colleges and universities to keep price increases in check or risk federal cost controls (Burd, 2000). During 1999 sessions, state legislatures addressed the issue of rising tuition costs by imposing tuition freezes,

---

3 State Higher Education Executive Officers (SHEEO)/MGT Surveys of State Higher Education Financial Officers (SHEFOs), 1998 and 1999. Data are obtained from a survey of the State Higher Education Financial Officers. This annual survey is conducted as the primary data source for the joint "state of the states" publication of SHEEO and MGT of America, Inc.

reducing tuition levels, placing restrictions on the rate of increase in tuition, and/or by providing appropriations to offset loss of revenues from smaller tuition increases (SHEEO/MGT Survey of SHEFOs).

The level of tuition and fees is especially critical to colleges and universities, whether public or private. Colleges typically balance their budgets by setting tuition and fee levels to fill the gap between what is needed to operate the institution and what is available from other revenue sources like state appropriations, gifts, grants, and contracts. Freezes on tuition levels, or limitations on their rate of increase, therefore, can negatively impact expenditure levels, leading to spending freezes, layoffs, and reduction in the level of services offered.

FINANCIAL AID

At the beginning of the 21st century, the issues of cost and financial aid are tightly linked, because almost all federal financial aid, and most state financial aid, is related to the cost of higher education. Two general types of student financial aid are available: need-based and non-need based. Complex formulas are used to determine how much aid a student is "entitled" to based on financial need. Of course, some aid is distributed based on student characteristics other than need (e.g., "ability," whether it be athletic ability, musical ability, or academic ability), and this aid is called non-need based.

In academic year 1998–99, an estimated total of $64.1 billion in student financial aid was awarded to students attending postsecondary institutions, an increase of 4 percent over academic year 1997–98 after adjusting for inflation. The federal government provided about 72 percent of total annual aid, and over 55 percent of total aid was awarded as loans (College Board, 1999b). Not included in the totals are student wages that are not a part of work-study programs, nor any of the federal tuition credits created by the Taxpayer Relief Act of 1997. These benefits took effect for tax year 1998, and it has been estimated that this will provide $12 to $15 billion in credits each year when fully phased-in by 2002. Total student financial aid exceeded state appropriations for higher education.

Over the last ten years, financial aid increased about 85 percent in constant dollars although increases in loan programs accounted for over 67 percent of the increase. Loans from all sources totaled 58 percent of all aid, compared to 47 percent in 1992–93 and 41 percent in 1980–81. The greatest increases have occurred in the unsubsidized loan program that comprises 45 percent of all federal student loans. State grant funding increased by over 65 percent in constant dollars over the past ten years, but still comprises only 5.5 percent of total student aid. Although institutional aid has more than doubled since 1989, available grant aid has not offset relative declines in federal grants, nor has total aid increased as fast as increases in the cost of attendance. Consequently, the cost of attendance consumes a greater share of personal income, as mentioned earlier.

FEDERAL AID TRENDS

The federal government entered the student financial aid business with the passage of the GI Bill (the Servicemen's Readjustment Act) at the end of World War II. Aid was given to returning servicemen and servicewomen in the form of tuition assistance and subsistence funds; aid went directly to students after verification of enrollment by a university and was conceived of as an "entitlement." These returning service personnel were given access to postsecondary education based on particular characteristics (service) rather than on financial need.

Contemporary federal student financial aid programs began with the passage of the National Defense Education Act in 1958 (Moore, 1983, p. 28). This act created the National Defense Student Loan program, later called National Direct Student Loans, and currently called Perkins Student Loans. By 1964, federal student financial aid totaled about $100 million (Gillespie & Carlson, 1983) and was directed to colleges and universities to lend to needy students. During this time, the federal government funded aid as a matter of national security. The legislation specifically addressed the issue of opportunity to a higher education: "no student of ability will be denied an opportunity for higher education because of financial need" (Public Law 85-864, 1958, p. 1), but the program was not perceived to be an entitlement like the GI Bill.

In the post-Sputnik era, the federal government also became concerned with the supply of scientists and engineers, and allocated approximately $30 million to fund 8,000 graduate fellowships and traineeships. Support was allocated to institutions to fund students who met specific criteria, in keeping with the apparent federal philosophy of access, delivered through institutions. Graduate aid reached its highest point during 1968–69, when 51,400 fellowships and traineeships totaling $270 million were awarded to institutions for graduate financial aid (Carnegie Council on Policy Studies in Higher Education, 1975, p. 18). Such funding has declined significantly since 1970, as federal priorities have shifted.

In 1965, Congress passed the landmark Higher Education Act (HEA). The Higher Education Act Title IV authorized the programs that comprise the foundation of federal financial aid today: the Stafford Guaranteed Student Loan (GSL), Educational Opportunity Grant (EOG), and College-Work-Study programs. The HEA of 1965 also reauthorized the NDSL program. Each of these aid programs provided aid to institutions for distribution to needy students, primarily through loans. Entitlements were not a component of Title IV aid; rather, aid was delivered through institutions to the "needy." Nevertheless, each of the aid programs were intended to promote access to a higher education (Gladieux & Wolanin, 1976). Over the next eight years, federal student aid grew by 900 percent (Hearn, 1993).

In 1972, Congress reauthorized the Higher Education Act, making minor adjustments to existing programs and adding the State Student Incentive Grant (SSIG) and the Basic Education Opportunity Grant (BEOG, now called Pell Grant) programs. The SSIG program provided federal funds on a one-to-one match with state dollars to create additional aid for needy students within that state. SSIG can be perceived to have been a continuation and expansion of the apparent federal policy of granting need-based aid to students that would be delivered through existing institutions or agencies. The creation of the Pell Grant program, on the other hand, signaled a major change in federal student financial aid policy.

BEOGs, or Pell Grants, were, at their conception, entitlements for needy students that replaced, or at least were designed to mitigate, the need for loans. Intended to be the base for packaging aid to needy students, Pell Grants would not have to be repaid and would follow the student to whichever institution the student chose (Fenske & Gregory, 1993). Because Pell Grants are an entitlement program, Congress annually appropriates funds sufficient to cover program costs determined by formula. Pell Grants were a program that focused on student choice, not access, since the aid was directed to the student and the institution of his or her choice. Thus, the 1972 Reauthorization of the Higher Education Act altered the federal role in student aid from a policy focus on access, to focus on access and choice, with aid delivered through a combination of grants, loans, and work from institutions. Federal appropriations for student financial aid increased over 50 percent during the next five years.

The 1978 Reauthorization of the Higher Education Act ushered in a new era of federal student financial aid. Congress passed the Middle Income Student Assistance Act of 1978, greatly expanding eligibility for Pell Grants and Guaranteed Student Loans to students from middle- and upper-income families. Removal of the income cap from the GSL program, increases in college enrollments and costs, and inflation contributed to significant increases in federally funded student aid. Between 1978 and 1981, aid grew 114 percent from $1.6 billion to $4.8 billion (U.S. Department of Education, 1988, pp. 2–4). Aid, predominately in the form of loans delivered to students instead of through institutions, became focused on middle- and upper-income students, moving away from low-income or needy students. The huge cost of GSLs shifted funds away from the entitlement program (Pell Grants) that was to have been the federal government's primary student aid vehicle. By 1981–82, only 24 percent of the combined Pell and GSL funding came through Pell Grants (College Board, 1991). During the 1980s, the federal government retreated from the policies that made nearly every student eligible for GSLs by placing restrictions on the program. The focus of aid continued to be loans directly to students; however, the concept of attendance at any college of choice was undermined for low income students who were less likely to attend a university than a community college or proprietary school.

During the 1980s, several entitlement programs were eliminated or severely restricted. As the majority of Vietnam War veterans completed college, veteran's educational benefits were phased down. Social security survivor's benefits for college were eliminated. Thus, the focus of federal student financial aid moved away from entitlement programs and grant programs for the needy to loans with expanded eligibility.

FUTURE FEDERAL ISSUES IN HIGHER EDUCATION FINANCIAL AID

The recent enactment of the Taxpayer Relief Act of 1997 (TRA97) provided new federal "student aid" through the use of income tax credits, savings incentives, and limited deductibility for interest paid on student loans. These programs are projected to cost about as much as all other existing federal financial aid programs combined, and represent a significant shift in how the federal government provides funding for higher education (Conklin, 1998). The new credits are not need-based, represent revenue foregone rather than expenditures, and will benefit primarily middle- and upper-middle-income students and their families. Lower-income students who owe no federal taxes will not benefit, and those students whose family tax bill is less than the credit will receive partial benefits.

Federal tax expenditures (such as the Hope and Lifetime Learning Credits) that represent foregone income are estimated to total about $13.8 billion in fiscal year 2000, compared to about $7.2 billion for Pell Grants (Rayburn & Setter, 1999). Some provisions of federal law related to tax treatment of some "financial aid" were amended in 1999 tax changes. Continued expansion of tax expenditures instead of increased traditional financial aid implies that the goal of access to higher education has changed.

The Taxpayer Relief Act, including the Hope Scholarship and Life Long Learning Tax Credits, appears to have contributed to the debate over tuition increases. State legislators question whether the tax credits and increases in federal financial aid created incentives for public colleges and universities to raise tuition and fees, or reduce the need for increased state financial aid (AASCU, 1999c). During 1998 and 1999 legislative sessions, about 50 percent of the states discussed reducing state costs by lowering appropriations, increasing tuition, or reducing student financial aid to capture the revenues from the tax credits. Continued debate is likely as the revenue implications (on state budgets) of TRA97 become clearer.

STATE APPROPRIATIONS AND FUNDING

In 1920, the first year for which detailed information on sources of funds is available, state governments appropriated $52 million to higher education. State appropriations to higher education reached $56.7 billion in fiscal year 2000, a thousandfold increase over 1920. State appropriations in fiscal year 2000 increased 7.0 percent over fiscal year 1999 (Hines, 2000) and represent the largest total ever appropriated by states for higher education. Total state general fund appropriations for all government services increased by 5.5 percent over fiscal year 1999, and increases in appropriations for higher education outpaced the increase in total state general fund appropriations. Total state appropriations to higher education reached 13 percent of state budgets in fiscal year 2000, the second year in a row of increases in higher education's share of state general fund budgets, following a decade of decreases.[4] For the first time in 15 years, during fiscal year 1999, no state reported reductions in state appropriations for higher education from one year to the next, and only Wyoming, which is in the second year of a biennial budget, reported no increase. Between fiscal year 1999 and fiscal year 2000, total state budgets decreased in Alaska, Hawaii, Missouri, Nevada, and Vermont, but higher education budgets did not. In 32 states, increases in appropriations to higher education outpaced increases in the total state budget.

STATE FINANCIAL AID TRENDS

A significant trend in financial aid is state scholarship or grant programs based on merit, without regard to need. In 1997, Georgia started this trend by passing the Hope Scholarship, entitling students with at least a B average in high school to free tuition. During 1998 legislative sessions, 12 states adopted some merit based scholarship program, copying the Georgia program in most cases.

---

4 Calculated by author from NASBO/NGA state budget reports.

Despite negative press related to the Georgia Hope Scholarship program (Selingo, 1999), the focus on affordability of higher education continued in 1999 legislative sessions, as 17 states enacted new financial aid programs or extended the provisions of existing programs.

Another significant shift in financial aid programs has been the creation of college savings or prepaid tuition programs. Under a college savings program, families can put funds into an IRA-type account to be used for the tuition and other college costs of a family member. Interest earned on the savings is exempt from state and federal income taxes. In a prepaid tuition program, families invest funds for the future college costs of a child. The amount invested is dependent upon the child's age, and on the type of college the child will attend. The state guarantees that the investment will cover the tuition and fees at the type of institution chosen by the student. In the prepaid plan, the state (and colleges) assume the risk of return on investment not keeping pace with increased tuition costs. Families who participate in these programs tend to be upper-middle- to upper-income, with very few families in the lower-income brackets participating.

At least half the states now have prepaid and/or savings account plans (Florida and Virginia have both). All of the prepaid college tuition or college savings programs, and the federal Hope and Lifetime Learning programs, represent tax expenditures, or foregone revenues, to federal and state governments. Significant questions have been raised about the trend of governments subsidizing the clients of higher education (students and their families), as opposed to subsidizing institutions. The impact of these programs on access and equity issues is unclear (AASCU, 1999a). The biggest concerns relate to the idea that benefits of tax expenditure "aid" go mostly to upper-middle and upper-income families, rather than to the "neediest" of students. In tight budget times in the 21st century, will these programs replace need-based financial aid programs?

Since 1981, current fund revenues of public higher education institutions have experienced a shift in the proportions of revenues from state appropriations and tuition, as was mentioned earlier. It appears that universities, and especially research universities, are becoming state-aided instead of state-funded. The trend of placing more of the financial burden for the costs of higher education on students instead of on the state as the main provider of funds is troubling. The increasing reliance on unsubsidized loans as the main form of student financial aid even for the most needy students, and the shift to tax expenditures as additional "financial aid" that benefits primarily middle- and upper-middle-income families, portend a shift in which individuals will be likely to attend college. Questions on commitment to access to a higher education for all are raised by these shifts.

There is no clear evidence yet on how the tying of state appropriation increases to freezes or reductions in the rate of tuition increases will impact on institutional revenues. Over half of the states reported that colleges and universities are constrained by state policy to limited increases in tuition. In some states, tuition increases cannot exceed the increase in the CPI or Higher Education Price Index (HEPI) (AASCU, 2000). In the short run, institutional budgets should not be negatively impacted; however, when the economy experiences a downturn, freezes on tuition increases coupled with little or no increase in state appropriations will require reductions in services or quality or an increase in productivity.

Indeed, the University of North Carolina system's board sharply increased tuition for the next two years at its flagship campuses in response to the prospect of reductions in state appropriations (*Chronicle of Higher Education*, 2000). In this case, financial realities appear to have taken precedence over keeping tuition more affordable.

CURRENT AND FUTURE STATE FINANCING ISSUES

The 1999 state legislative sessions were marked by limitations on tuition increases coupled with designated appropriations to offset any decline in college and university revenues, and increases in the use of performance measures and other accountability requirements. Affordability, workforce preparation, accountability, performance-based funding, and reform of teacher preparation programs have been called the top issues facing higher education on state legislative agendas in 2000 (Schmidt et al., 2000. p. A28; see also SHEEO, 1999). Legislators appear to be concerned about increasing competition for state resources, especially from health care programs, about the quality of educational programs and services, and about tuition reduction and the affordability of higher education. Indeed, among the nation's governors, improving the quality of education is the number one priority and figures largely in gubernatorial budget proposals for FY2001 (National Governors' Association).

Many states earmarked increases in appropriations in order to moderate tuition increases, economic development activities, student financial aid, community colleges, and one-time expenditures such as construction, deferred maintenance, and technology initiatives. The focus on one-time spending increases may reflect a desire to avoid overcommitment of resources that led to reversions and budget cuts during the 1980s and early 1990s (AASCU, 1999a).

During 1999 legislative sessions, several states discussed additional flexibility as a tradeoff to performance indicators or funding. The National Association of State Budget Officers has called performance-based budgeting and funding the most significant trend in state budgeting (National Association of State Budget Officers, 1999). In 1998, 34 states either had adopted performance budgeting or performance funding for public institutions (Burke, 1998). South Carolina is the only state where the majority of state appropriations are supposed to be allocated by performance funding; in most other states, no more than 5 percent of the appropriation is allocated by performance indicators. Burke and Serban (1998) contend that these funding programs represent a significant shift in funding priorities from what states should do for higher education, to what higher education should do for the state and its citizens.

Higher education officials note that the increase in the number of the states using funding formulas in the resource allocation process for higher education has increased because of the use of performance indicators (SHEEO/MGT Survey of SHEFOs). States that abandoned the use of funding formulas during the 1990s (e.g., Virginia, Arkansas, Maryland) had used the formulas for more than 25 years to ensure equity in the distribution of state resources. In the 1990s, when budgets were declining, protection of base budgets became more important than equity. Now that state budgets are flush and higher education is receiving larger shares of the budget, equity is again an issue. However, state legislatures appear unwilling to appropriate more to higher education institutions without some measure of outcomes or performance. Consequently, Virginia, Arkansas, and Maryland all are using funding formulas again, but the formulas are tied to performance indicators. At least ten other states have modified their funding formulas, so that an equitable and adequate amount of revenues are calculated by the formula. However, institutions do not receive the full formula amount unless they reach the level of performance specified in their plans.

ADDITIONAL EMERGING
ISSUES IN THE 21ST CENTURY

As the national economy continues to boom, there appears to be optimism among higher education officials that funding will increase and greater autonomy will result from legislative sessions. Higher education leaders had expected that fiscal year 2000 appropriations for higher education would increase over 12 percent on average at four-year institutions and over 21 percent at two-year colleges.[5] However increases in appropriations averaged much less. Few state appropriation increases matched leaders' expectations. For the senior colleges and universities, leaders had predicted that increases for fiscal year 2000 would average 12.8 percent, while actual percentage increases for four-year colleges and universities averaged 6.3 percent. For community colleges, average increases were 7.6 percent, compared to 21.4 percent projected. Despite this poor record, leaders continue to predict that increases for 2001 will exceed 10 percent.

Moreover, the economy appears to be slowing as the rate of growth in the Gross Domestic Product (GDP) has moderated. Inflation likely will continue to be in check, which may put pressure on unemployment rates (AASCU, 1999a). Tax cuts are likely to continue, although states may have reached the limit of tax decreases. States continue to maintain high budget balances (albeit smaller balances that represent less than 5 weeks of expenditures) to protect against downturns in the economy and midyear reversions or reductions of the kind that occurred in the 1980s and early 1990s.

Higher education leaders in a third of the states foresee continuing interest in limitations on tuition increases and/or increased appropriations to offset freezes or reductions in the rate of increase in tuition and fees (SHEEO/MGT Survey of SHEFOs). Competition from elementary/secondary education and health care components of state budgets are likely to place pressures on continued increases in appropriations for higher education, not only in the first part of the 21st century, but throughout the first half.

Performance funding and accountability issues are likely to be one locus of public policy debates in the 21st century. Over half the states are studying some form of performance measurement, and 21 states report that performance funding or accountability measures will be on legislative agendas (SHEEO/MGT Survey of SHEFOs). Another one-third of the states are examining workload and productivity as a means of improving learning outcomes or decreasing expenditures. Of course, faculty productivity will continue to be an issue in the 21st cen-

---

5 Calculated from data in Schmidt & Selingo (1999).

tury as it was in the 20th. Since the majority of expenditures in higher education are for faculty salaries, the focus of legislative interest appears to be on ways to make faculty more productive.

Hardly a legislative session in any state goes by without requests for faculty workload studies. In a faculty workload study, faculty members report how many hours per week they spend in "scholarly pursuits," which include activities related to teaching, research, and public service (the three missions of most universities). Since 1900, no matter which college or university's faculty is surveyed, faculty members spend 50 to 60 hours per week "on the job" (Layzell & McKeown-Moak, 2000). Legislators appear to find this hard to believe, and consequently, ask for faculty workload studies.

Measures of faculty productivity are likely to be one of the most hotly debated policy issues in the 21st century, not only because faculty are such a high cost item in college and university budgets. In the new century, asynchronous learning, and how to pay for that learning, is likely to be the subject of many public policy debates. "Asynchronous learning" refers to learning at different times and different places, and refers most commonly to classes taught on the Internet, by television, or on other media. In 2000, the public policy debates on distance learning, as asynchronous learning often is called, revolve around who should pay how much to whom when (Bowes, 2000). Colleges and universities believe that only they should offer courses in their service area. But how are service areas measured when anyone can hook up to the Internet and download courses from universities all over the world?

How should states "pay" for distance learning at public institutions? Should the state pay for the costs of development of the courses that are offered? Should the credit hours generated be included in the funding formula? If students at institution A take a course offered by a professor at institution B, which institution gets "credit" for the credit hours? If a student in Australia "takes" a course offered on the Internet by a university in South Carolina, should the student pay out of state tuition for the course? If a professor at institution Y develops a course offered by the institution on the Internet, does the professor get royalties or maintain a copyright on the course materials? These are only a few of the questions that must be answered as Earth moves to the technological society.

These issues were highlighted in the recent *New York Times* article "Boola, Boola: E-Commerce Comes to the Quad" (Steinberg & Wyatt, 2000). Entrepreneurial faculty members are coming to loggerheads with their universities over who owns the rights to faculty products such as course materials and syllabi. Colleges and universities appeared to have little interest in the royalties when faculty wrote books, although patented products developed on campus were a different matter. Many companies, such as UPI, Inc. sprung up to handle the offshoots of products developed by faculty members that might have commercial viability. For example, toothpaste was developed at the University of Illinois, and continues to bring significant revenues into the university's endowment, just as Gatorade does for the University of Florida.

But, from the university's perspective, the income-generating potential from Internet courses or learning materials is yet untapped. The *New York Times* declares that professors and their schools are "elbowing each other in pursuit of the same pot of gold" (Steinberg & Wyatt, 2000). Will this competition tear apart the academy, or will this source of revenue be an offset to state appropriations in the 21st century?

Funding for the technology that powers the Internet and asynchronous learning, or other issues related to technology and distance learning, has been cited as an interest of legislators in over 60 percent of the states (SHEEO/MGT Survey of SHEFOs). This interest continues as legislators respond to employers who seek workers trained in technological applications. The response of higher education to these demands is another area that is likely to be debated heavily throughout the first part of the new millennium. And the next waves of the Internet are likely to tax the campuses heavily.

How will campuses throughout the world react and respond to "nomadic computing," which is hailed as the next big thing to the Internet (Olsen, 2000)? Nomadic computing, and the next innovation beyond that, ubiquitous computing, are the future, and higher education is unprepared. Nomadic computing refers to the idea that people will be able to gain access to information over the Internet through a variety of handheld devices from virtually anywhere in the world. Ubiquitous computing refers to the Internet being available everywhere and always being on, through sensors connected to items within a room (as seen in the science fiction adventures of *Star Trek: The Next Generation*). Research will be instantly available on any topic. Does nomadic or ubiquitous computing render today's campus obsolete? Will libraries continue to exist? Should states fund new or larger buildings for campuses? Clearly, these issues are too complex to resolve here.

CONCLUSION

Although the U.S. economy remains strong, some signs of stress are beginning to appear. Growth rate in the Gross Domestic Product has slowed and personal savings rates continue to fall. If the past can be used to predict the future, higher education is unlikely to achieve increases projected by higher education officials for state appropriations in this new century. If a recession occurs in the near future, a number of states will face significant budget pressures that may be compounded by transfers of health care programs from the federal to state governments.

Higher education is one of the few discretionary items in state budgets, and always is vulnerable to funding reductions. When coupled with the trend to fund students and their families from tax expenditures, institutions may be facing actual budget reductions in the next ten years. Pushes to incorporate asynchronous learning based on technology also will tax university budget makers, at the same time as traditional institutions are competing for students with e-commerce companies such as Concord, an online law school; Unext.com, a startup company that plans to offer a full range of college courses over the Internet; and for-profit Web sites offering online liberal arts education. Perhaps implementation of alternative delivery mechanisms and funding sources, such as worldwide sales of courses over the Internet may be the 21st century way to balance higher education budgets.

In *State Spending for Higher Education in the Next Decade* (1999), Harold Hovey points out that this may not be higher education's turn for any increases in appropriations. The fiscal forecast for state spending indicates that even with normal economic growth over the next decade, states likely will face significant fiscal deficits. Higher education will not see significant expansion for any program unless expansion is funded by cuts in other higher education programs, and so the challenge will be to maintain current service levels to an expanding client population. That certainly gives higher education officials a challenge and opportunity during the 21st century.

REFERENCES

American Association of State Universities and Colleges. (2000, January). *State Issues Survey*. Washington, DC: AASCU.

American Association of State Universities and Colleges. (1999a, August). *State Fiscal Conditions*. Washington, DC: AASCU (available at www.aascu.org).

American Association of State Universities and Colleges. (1999b, September). *State Fiscal Conditions*. Washington, DC: AASCU.

American Association of State Universities and Colleges. (1999c, August). *Student Charges, A Special Report*. Washington, DC: AASCU.

Bowes, William. (2000, March). Distance learning and funding alternatives in the University System of Georgia. Paper presented to the Georgia Board of Regents.

Burd, Stephen. (2000, February 10). Rising cost of college could leave many americans behind, senators warn. *Chronicle of Higher Education*.

Burke, Joseph, & Serban, Andrea. (1998). *Current status and future prospects of performance funding and performance budgeting for public higher education: The second survey*. Albany, NY: Nelson A. Rockefeller Institute of Government.

Carnegie Council on Policy Studies in Higher Education. (1975). *The federal role in postsecondary education*. San Francisco: Jossey-Bass.

Chronicle of Higher Education. (2000, February 14).

College Board. (1999a). *Trends in college pricing, 1999*. New York: Author.

College Board. (1999b). *Trends in student aid 1999*. New York: Author.

College Board. (1991). *Trends in student aid: 1981 to 1991*. Washington, DC: Author.

Conklin, Kristin D. (1999). *Federal tuition tax credits and state higher education policy*. Washington, DC: National Center for Public Policy and Higher Education. 1998.

Fenske, Robert H., & Gregory, Brian D. (1993, October). *The dream denied: evaluating the impact of student financial aid on low income/ minority students*. Paper presented at the annual meeting of the National Association of Financial Aid Administrators, Washington.

Gillespie, D. A., & Carlson, N. (1983). *Trends in Student Aid: 1963 to 1983*. Washington, DC: College Board.

Gladieux, L. E., & Wolanin, T. R. (1976). *Congress and the colleges: The national politics of higher education*. Lexington, MA: Lexington Books.

Hearn, James C. (1993). The paradox of growth in federal aid for college students, 1965–1990. In *Higher Education: Handbook of theory and research* (vol. 9). New York: Agathon Press.

Hines, Edward. (2000). *Grapevine*. Bloomington, IL: Illinois State University (www.coe.ilstu.edu/grapevine).

Hovey, Harold A. (1999, July). *State spending for higher education in the next decade: the battle to sustain current support*. Washington, DC: National Center for Public Policy and Higher Education.

Kelly, Dennis. (2000, February 16). Paying for college is the new math. *USA Today*, p. 1.

Layzell, Daniel, & McKeown-Moak, Mary. (2000, January). *Issues in faculty productivity*. Paper provided as part of a study for the Pennsylvania State System of Higher Education.

Moore, James W. (1983). Purposes and provisions of federal programs. In Fenske, Huff, and Associates, *Handbook of Student Financial Aid*. San Francisco: Jossey-Bass.

National Association of State Budget Officers. (1999, December). *Fiscal survey of the states*. Washington, DC: Author.

National Commission on the Cost of Higher Education. (1998, January). *Straight talk about college costs and prices*. Washington, DC: National Commission (also available at www.nasulgc.nche.edu/Pub_CostCommPT2Jan98.htm).

National Governors' Association. Nation's governors committed to excellence in education. www.nga.org

Olsen, Florence. (2000, February 18A UCLA professor and net pioneer paves the way for the next big thing." *Chronicle of Higher Education*.

Public Law 85–864, September 2, 1958, p. 1.

Rayburn, Jack, & Setter, Gerald. (1999, August). *Tax issues and postsecondary education*. Paper presented at the State Higher Education Finance Officers Professional Development Seminar, Breckinridge, CO.

Schmidt, Peter, Selingo, Jeffrey, & Hebel, Sara. (2000, January 27As legislatures convene, colleges push their spending priorities. *Chronicle of Higher Education*, p. A28.

Selingo, Jeffrey. (1999, April 20). Many freshmen lose eligibility for Georgia's HOPE scholarship, report says. *Chronicle of Higher Education*.

State Higher Education Executive Officers (SHEEO)/MGT Surveys of State Higher Education Financial Officers (SHEFOs). (1998 and 1999).

Steinberg, Jacques, & Wyatt, Edward. (2000, February 13). Boola, boola: E-commerce comes to the quad. *New York Times*.

U.S. Department of Education, National Center for Education Statistics. (1999). *Digest of Education Statistics*. Washington, DC: U.S. Government Printing Office (also available on line at www.nces.ed.gov).

U.S. Department of Education. (1988). *A self-instruction course in student financial aid administration*. Washington, DC: Office of Student Financial Assistant, Department of Education.

THE EDUCATIONAL OUTCOME CHALLENGE TO EDUCATION FINANCE

7

A NEW MILLENNIUM AND A LIKELY NEW ERA OF EDUCATION FINANCE

James W. Guthrie
Vanderbilt University

Richard Rothstein
Economic Policy Institute

Old school finance concepts evaluate education in terms of revenue. New finance concepts of adequacy evaluate revenue in terms of education.

PROLOGUE

American education finance may be entering a new era characterized by the challenging concept of adequacy.[1] This concept directly links financial distributions with education arrangements, and thereby propels education finance from the periphery to the center of policy debate. Equity issues, the dominant education finance challenge for the last portion of the 20th century, focus attention on resource inputs, and take as measures of success esoteric indicators of distributional fairness. Adequacy, even if inartfully defined, forcefully links resource levels and their allocation to societal expectations for the performance of students and schools, the means of instruction, individual needs of pupils, and the effective performance of the system. Still, adequacy as a concept may fail to fulfill its productive potential if it cannot be more precisely defined and if means cannot be determined for more accurately discerning the instructional needs of students usually at risk of failure.

---

1 This chapter further develops an account that previously appeared in Guthrie and Rothstein (1999). The authors gratefully acknowledge the substantial intellectual contributions to this material made by their colleagues Gerald C. Hayward and James R. Smith in the development of the Wyoming school adequacy model described in this chapter.

99

HISTORIC OVERVIEW

Prodded by judicial decisions and parallel policy developments, the once technically pedestrian and professionally esoteric field of education finance is about to play a more central role in the organization of schooling than ever before.

The principal challenge facing education policy makers in the 19th and early 20th centuries was fashioning a system of common schooling that could contribute to and sustain a democracy. State statutes mandating the formation of school districts, and pupil attendance incentives, had their intended effects—by the early 1900s, there were 129,000 local school districts, enrolling 80 percent of the nation's school-age children.

This phase (we label it Stage One of education finance history) was dominated by those who strove for implementation of a system of financial mandates and inducements. In this era, flat grants or state subsidies enabled local districts to establish schools. By the conclusion of the 19th and beginning of the 20th centuries, under the leadership of Ellwood Patterson Cubberley, Paul R. Mort, and George D. Strayer, distribution formulas were developed that combined local property tax revenues with state subsidies, establishing financial incentives for localities to extend education offerings.

Stage Two was initiated in the late 20th century when the principal policy challenge was to ensure that this state-by-state system of public education was accessible and fair. The original system of common schools, however well intended, had bypassed or shortchanged important population groups. Disadvantaged racial and ethnic minorities, those with disabilities, the indigent, immigrants who did not speak English, and students who resided in property-poor locations became major targets for school improvement in the decades following the end of World War II.

Beginning in the 1960s, education finance theorists contributed to a national effort to achieve greater equity with attempts to apply the federal constitution's Fourteenth Amendment equal protection clause to finance distribution and taxpayer participation. Conceptual efforts of John E. Coons, Stephen D. Sugarman, and William H. Clune (1970) and of Arthur Wise (1970) were landmarks. They prompted three decades of litigation and legislative efforts intended to provide greater equity in the generation and distribution of education revenues.

Stage Two is yet incomplete; full equity has not yet been achieved. After the U.S. Supreme Court rejected the federal constitution's equal protection challenge (in *San Antonio Independent School District v. Rodriguez*, 1973), advocates turned their attention to similar provisions in state constitutions, and to those constitutions' education clauses, as well. Even if these state challenges had been fully successful, however, they could not have addressed interstate inequalities in education finance, and thus could not remedy the fact that some states, despite taxing themselves fully, are unable to generate per-pupil revenues comparable to those generated in wealthier states. There also remain important intrastate per-pupil revenue disparities (Hussar and Sonnenberg, 2000), and these are linked in an unsettling manner to differences in local district property wealth. There are still educationally unsound intradistrict per-pupil spending differences embedded in outmoded budgeting, salary, and personnel assignment practices. Still, even with this unfinished reform agenda, three conditions are worth noting.

First, the American policy system responds to ideas. Coons, Clune, and Sugarman, and Wise, arrived at their education finance concepts through different experiences.[2] Still, their books and articles, and those patterned after them, triggered Stage Two reform. James A. Kelly's creative application of Ford Foundation funding to the establishment of a network of sophisticated attorneys and analysts capable of participating in litigation and designing state legislative remedies was also a signal contribution. These seminal scholars launched a movement the end results of which, while not yet complete, are dramatic examples of the power of the pen.

Second, while intrastate inequities persist, they have been reduced. States with equal protection court decisions have, on balance, reduced interdistrict spending disparities while increasing overall per-pupil revenues by approximately 10 percent in comparison to states without such decisions, and these changes have not come at the expense of reductions in other public sector service levels (Murray, Evans, & Schwab, 1998).

Third, the concept of adequacy appears to be gaining in application, both judicially and legislatively. Whereas distributional equity has not, and probably will not, soon disappear as an issue, it may be overtaken by adequacy as a finance reform challenge.

A quest for adequacy may represent Stage Three in America's education finance evolution.

EDUCATION FINANCE'S EVOLVING STAGE THREE: THE CONCEPT OF ADEQUACY

A growing number of state court decisions suggest that the concept of an adequate education is challenging equity as the standard to which state school revenue distribution plans should be held (Minorini & Sugarman, 1999). Parallel developments in states without such court mandates also suggest that a commitment to provide an adequate education to all students may be defining a broader national consensus.

School spending has been increasing in every state. There is no claim here that it is a concern for adequacy alone that has propelled this change. A national pattern of growing elementary and secondary expenditures in states with or

---

2 Arthur Wise was a University of Chicago doctoral student taking graduate courses in school finance and school law when it occurred to him that the distributional consequences of state finance plans might violate equal protection guarantees. He proceeded to hone the idea and devoted his dissertation to the challenge of applying equal protection theory to education finance. Initially independent of Wise, Coons was a professor, and Clune and Sugarman his students, at the Northwestern University Law School, engaged in research for the federal Equality of Educational Opportunity investigation (the "Coleman Report") when they came to understand that the Illinois distribution formula might deny students equal protection.

without a history of equity or adequacy litigation is apparent. All states have increased average per-pupil spending in the last quarter century, and most have increased it dramatically.[3] In some states without litigation, spending has increased to avoid litigation. In other states where courts have upheld previous financing schemes, spending has still increased at rates similar to, or nearly similar to, those where litigation had an opposite result. Thus, the national adequacy debate can be seen, in part, as an effort to evaluate whether this spending growth has been sufficient and to ensure that new money is distributed within states in a fashion intended to produce desired outcomes.

The Stage Two concept of equity is itself more complex than it first appears, because nominal equity takes account neither of differences in student need nor of geographic differences in costs. Such complexity aside, the Stage Three concept of adequacy adds an additional complication, requiring a link between cost calculations and decisions about appropriate resource input levels and measures of school outcomes. While defining equity is essentially a technical and mathematical enterprise, moving to adequacy requires policy and value judgments about which achieving consensus, ultimately, may be even more difficult.

HISTORIC "ADEQUACY": POLITICALLY DETERMINED INPUTS

Despite recent renewed interest, adequacy is not a new concept in school finance. Charles Benson (1978) was one of the first to explain it. And Kirst and Garms (1980) explored it in the very first yearbook published by the American Education Finance Association.

But although the term "adequacy" has been used for 20 years, the concept has had a practical school finance meaning for much longer, because many states have politically determined adequate levels of inputs to support the schooling process. The roots of the concept of adequacy are deep, having been part of the thinking that motivated Stage One experts (such as Cubberley, 1919a, 1919b; Mort, Reusser, & Polley, 1960; and Johns, Morphet, & Alexander, 1983) to develop the notion of the foundation plan that had "adequate" as an assumed condition. The foundation amount was, and in most states still is, a per-pupil dollar floor below which a state does not permit a district's spending to fall.

However, this historic attention to adequacy seldom resulted in a rationally determined level of per-pupil revenue. Original practical expressions of a foundation, or a floor below which per-pupil spending would not sink, were more politically than rationally determined. In practice, state officials defined a per-pupil revenue foundation after having previously determined politically acceptable tax rates and the revenues they would generate. Knowing what revenue was available, they decided how much of it to distribute to schools. In effect, they

---

3 Until recently, California was a likely exception to this statement. Now, however, it is likely that California, with state coffers full in the economic recovery of the late 1990s, is catching up with a national trend toward higher elementary and secondary school expenditures.

backed their way into foundation amounts from prior agreements regarding revenue amounts and taxation levels.

In most states today, governors and legislatures still define an adequate foundation amount by determining how much state revenue is available, or how much additionally they are willing to generate through added taxation. As Minorini and Sugarman note, "almost nowhere could it plausibly be shown that the actual minimum foundation plan level…had been determined as a result of a genuine statewide appraisal" [of what is actually necessary to fund an 'adequate' education] (1999, p. 190). Some states, however, have relied on alternative definitions of adequate inputs, such as teacher certification requirements, state textbook selection, and acceptable class sizes or pupil-teacher ratios. Each of these alternate conceptions of a foundation has been intended to prevent systematic underinvestment in schooling within a state.

Foundation-related per-pupil revenue levels have been questioned politically and legally for three decades, but it was initially a foundation program's statewide per-pupil revenue distributional equity that came under scrutiny, not the adequacy of that spending level. The legal assaults of the last three decades were mostly intended to ensure that state-authorized spending levels, be they adequate or inadequate, were at least equally accessible to local school districts. But recently, the focus has broadened.

The more modern and still evolving concept of adequacy suggests that something beyond equity is at issue. The "something else" is a notion of sufficiency, a per-pupil resource amount sufficient to achieve some performance objective. Thus, adequacy is increasingly being defined by the outcomes produced by school inputs, not by the inputs alone. Clune contends that as the nation increasingly debates means for obtaining higher levels of student academic performance, the policy debate is shifting from "equity" and toward means of ensuring that students receive resources offering them an expanded opportunity to learn to higher standards.

Thus, adequacy deliberations sometimes are bundled with quests for "opportunity to learn standards" (Porter, 1993). "Delivery standards" is another related idea, asserting that pupils and schools cannot fairly be held accountable for performance unless there is first an assurance that levels of available resources are adequate and that students are appropriately exposed to the knowledge they are expected to master.

A Modern, Rational, and More Outcome-Oriented Concept of "Adequacy"

Here we suggest a more modern definition of adequate financing:

Sufficient resources to ensure students an effective opportunity to acquire appropriately specified levels of knowledge and skills.

The operant terms here are "effective opportunity" and "appropriately specified." The first, "effective opportunity," suggests that resources adequate to provide nominal exposure of students to academic content may still be insufficient in cases where, because of social or economic disadvantage or physical, emotional, or, in some cases, cognitive disability, students have not been prepared to take full advantage of this exposure. Thus, to be truly adequate, required resources may be greater for students facing greater social or economic challenges, or disabilities. The second, "appropriately specified," assists in separating modern concepts of adequate from previously promoted foundation plans. In today's definition, a level of revenue must be linked to an expected level of student knowledge and skill acquisition.

These ideas are summarized as follows: Whereas old concepts of foundation and equity evaluated education in terms of revenue, new finance concepts of adequacy evaluate revenue in terms of education. Does this mean that politics can somehow now be divorced from education? With adequacy in ascendance, does politics descend? Do education technicians now replace elected officials as principal decision makers regarding education? No, adequacy calculations do not take politics out of education, nor should they. However, a quest for adequacy does offer the prospect of altering the role of elected officials and the political system. Under an adequacy model, the appropriate point of political intervention should be the definition and shaping of the polity's expectations for educational outcomes. Thereafter, if political leaders find that delivery of these outcomes are too expensive to afford, they can then reduce their educational expectations.

This is no different, for example, than how we expect the president and Congress to set defense policy. They cooperate to define the levels of security they desire, and are then informed by technical and analytic staff of associated costs. If particular weapon systems are subsequently seen as too expensive, then expectations are altered until costs are brought into line with preferences for spending. In this manner, elected officials still maintain control over both expectations for levels of security and overall costs. However, they are not rationally free, generally, to reduce costs and simultaneously preserve previously specified performance expectations. In practice, this model does not work so neatly, as weapons manufacturers and other lobbying groups advocate resource levels and deployments from the perspective of private interests, not security objectives, although the arguments from private interests are generally couched as security concerns. It can be no different in education policy.

CONSTRUCTING A PRACTICAL MODEL OF ADEQUACY

If adequate is to have a meaning beyond what is assigned to it via a set of political decisions about revenue availability, then a judgment has to be made about expected ends to be achieved, some level of accomplishment or performance. Adequate to do what? Adequate how? Adequate for what purpose?

Thus, the determination of adequate funding levels necessitates a twofold policy judgment about (1) learning or performance levels to be attained (the outcomes) and (2) resource levels likely to permit schools to accomplish these learning levels with students (the educational technology). Only by specifying what students should know and be able to do, and what resources are necessary to generate such outcomes, can calculations of the cost of sufficient resource levels be undertaken.

Anchoring "Adequacy" in Expectations

Specifying learning is difficult, more difficult than it first appears. While we have an apparent national consensus that student outcomes are currently inadequate, this consensus extends only to the vaguest of generalities when it comes to specifying the extent to which this is the case.

Consider one of the early attempts by a state court to define adequate outcomes, that of the West Virginia Supreme Court in *Pauley v. Kelley* in 1979. The Court required the legislature to fund a school system that would develop the following capacities "in every child":

- ♦ Literacy
- ♦ Ability to add, subtract, multiply, and divide numbers
- ♦ Knowledge of government to the extent that the child will be equipped as a citizen to make informed choices among persons and issues that affect his own governance
- ♦ Self-knowledge and knowledge of his or her total environment to allow the child to intelligently choose life work—to know his or her options
- ♦ Work-training and advanced academic training as the child may intelligently choose
- ♦ Recreational pursuits
- ♦ Interests in all creative arts, such as music, theater, literature, and the visual arts
- ♦ Social ethics, both behavioral and abstract, to facilitate compatibility with others in this society

Other state courts and legislatures have required funding adequate to develop similar collections of competencies. In at least one case (Kentucky, in *Rose v. Council for Better Education*, 1989) an additional, relative capacity was added: "sufficient levels of academic or vocational skills to enable public school students to compete favorably with their counterparts in surrounding states."

The Wyoming Supreme Court (in *Campbell County v. The State of Wyoming*, 1995) required resources sufficient to provide each student with a "proper education," and the legislature subsequently defined a basket of education services that comprise such a proper ("adequate") education. The "basket" consisted of some 30 courses and kinds of knowledge, designed to achieve a group of broader outcomes similar to those specified in West Virginia, Kentucky, and other states. Subsequently, this "Basket of Education Expectations" was modified in 1997 by the Wyoming legislature; an example of some of these changes is shown in Figure 7.1. This legislative action illustrates the new role of political actors in an adequacy system. In this case, state legislators intervened to modify, in surprising detail, the outcomes that the state would require of its education system. Technical experts were then charged with responsibility for calculating the cost of delivering these specific outcomes.

**FIGURE 7.1. WYOMING LEGISLATIVE 1997 MODIFICATIONS
TO THE STATE'S BASKET OF EDUCATION EXPECTATIONS**

♦ Common Core of Knowledge
  • Changed "Language Arts" to "Reading/language arts," and required that reading writing and mathematics be emphasized in grades 1 through 8.
  • Changed "Career Options" to "Career/Vocational Education."
  • Added "Government and Civics (including state and federal constitutions)."
♦ Common Core of Skills
  • Changed "Life Skills, including Cardiopulmonary Resuscitation (CPR) Training" to "Life Skills, including personal financial management skills."
♦ Graduation Requirements [High School] Added
  • Four school years of English
  • Three school years of Mathematics
  • Three school years of Science
  • Three school years of Social Studies (including history, American government and economic systems and institutions)
  • Mastery of the common core of knowledge and skills

SOURCE: Catchpole (1996).

A study of these modifications leads quickly to the conclusion that a precise calculation of adequacy for Wyoming schools is dependent upon the particular policy judgments made by the state regarding outcomes. For example, are the same resources required to deliver a "career options" course of study as would be necessary to deliver a "career/vocational education" curriculum? Further, even a cursory review of such outcome goals suggests that few can be measured by standardized reading and math tests of the kind generally called for when discussing school finance. Whether, for example, the same resources that produce mathematical competency also, without augmentation, produce the adequate performance in creative arts required by the West Virginia Supreme Court is a question which analyses of finance adequacy cannot ignore, but which has yet barely been addressed by education finance theorists.

KNOWING WHAT TO
SPEND TO OBTAIN ADEQUACY

Designing a state school finance system, even one oriented toward adequacy, inevitably creates a tension between the dictates of a system design and the characteristics of individual students. State policy makers cannot easily prescribe the nature of instruction and the levels of resources for each of a state's thousands or millions of individual students. Hence, the necessity of designing a "system." Such a system should attempt to provide local school districts, local schools, and even classroom teachers with resources and inducements to tailor instruction to the characteristics of students.

However, ultimately, state-level policy makers must design a school finance system and cannot design a resource allocation program for each individual student.[4] Because presently available policy tools are often clumsy, the needs of a system may sometimes prove blunt when measured against the needs of individual students. Tailoring school finance to individual student characteristics is a research frontier where yet far more knowledge is needed. It can be approximated in steps, by summarizing the characteristics of like groups of students, but even here, our understanding is today far from accurate. Researchers, for example, may determine that low-income students, on average, require different resources than students generally, but there is more variation within these groups than between them.

Notwithstanding these complexities, policy analysts and researchers have been pioneering four approaches to calculating the costs of adequacy: (1) inferring costs from outcomes by statistical analysis of statewide databases, usually including test scores, spending levels, demographic characteristics, and other variables; (2) inferring costs from outcomes by empirical observation of districts that seem to generate adequate outcomes; (3) inferring costs from the actual price of whole school reform designs; and (4) inferring costs from professional judgment about the resource requirements of specific outcomes.[5]

The first and second of these approaches usually depend upon states having sophisticated student achievement testing systems that provide standardized statewide measures of student performance, with data linking this performance to student background characteristics.[6] In states where such testing systems do not exist, then the third and fourth approaches, whole school design prices and professional judgment, seem to be the only alternatives, where "getting to adequate" necessitates building an instructional resource model to which costs can

---

4 There is a significant exception, already, to this assertion. The 1975 Education for All Handicapped Children Act, and its subsequent elaborations, require that schools engage with professional experts and parents to design an Individualized Education Program (IEP) for each student with a disability covered by the legislation. This strategy, while still far from perfect, is a significant step in resolving a tension between the practical necessity for a statewide system of school finance and the widely varying characteristics of individual students.

5 Space prohibits a full explanation of these four approaches. For greater detail about, and a critique of, each approach, see Guthrie and Rothstein (1999).

6 However, as we note below, the second approach has been utilized in some states without controls for student background characteristics. And one statistical analysis illustrative of the first approach (Duncombe & Yinger, 1999) utilizes a "voter preference/tax price" model to estimate adequate outcomes, without reference to tests or other measures of student performance.

subsequently be assigned. These methods need not be considered mutually exclusive. There are circumstances in which they can be used in tandem.

Each of these four alternatives results in an estimate of the cost of an adequate education for a presumed or hypothetical student type. Having made this calculation, each alternative must then adjust the costs (or perhaps redefine the goal of adequate outcomes) for students in different socioeconomic circumstances and locations. With these results—estimates of the costs of an adequate education for each category and location of students in a state—policy makers must then determine how to distribute an adequate level of funds to districts and whether districts should be required to spend the funds in a particular manner likely to produce the adequate outcomes being sought.

Even when an adequate amount of funding has been determined by pricing a specific collection of resources expected to produce adequate outcomes (approaches 3 and 4), a state need not require all districts and schools to spend their funds on the precise resource collection used as the basis for the calculations. If a state meets its obligation to provide funds to districts and schools in sufficient amount to generate adequate outcomes, it may still leave to local discretion whether to generate those outcomes in the modeled fashion, or whether to experiment with the production of outcomes utilizing different resource types from those used by the state to estimate the funding amounts. The state may permit such discretion either from a desire to encourage local control and decision making, or from a belief that continued experimentation with resource strategies by districts may lead to the discovery of new efficiencies in the technology of education.

INFERRING COSTS FROM OUTCOMES
BY STATISTICAL ANALYSIS

While the statistical methods are complex, the principle behind them is relatively simple.[7] With a sufficiently large database, each factor contributing to school costs can be examined and its unique relationship to another factor determined, distinct from the influence of other factors. If, for example, one desires to know how much more it costs to hire a teacher in an urban community than in a nonurban one, if there exist sufficient data on teacher salaries and community characteristics, it is possible to separate the common relationship between salary and urbanicity in all communities from factors that may vary from community to community—from, for example, teachers' experience or training, community climate, community housing costs, and the like. The result is the statistical generation of an abstract urban community in which teacher salaries are uninfluenced

---

7 This statistical approach to estimating adequacy has won increasing favor among academic econometricians in recent years. The methodology has recently been applied by William Duncombe and John Yinger (1999) to New York data, and by Andrew Reschovsky and Jennifer Imazeki (1998) to Wisconsin and Texas data. Ladd and Yinger (1994) and Downes and Pogue (1994) have made important theoretical contributions on which the New York, Wisconsin, and Texas studies build.

by variations in these other costs, or by the choices districts may make in the type of teacher they hire.

If adopted as a basis for policy, this correlational strategy would derive a unit cost (per classroom or per pupil) amount found to be associated with adequate levels of pupil academic achievement and recommend allocation of such resource levels to school districts or other operational agencies. This approach could include statistical controls for social and economic characteristics of students. How available revenues were translated into an instructional delivery system would be of no policy consequence in such a "black box" approach. Presumably, districts or schools would be free to undertake whatever operational translation they desired, knowing that assigned per-pupil revenue amounts had been found sufficient to elevate their mix of pupils to the specified level of performance.

In this "black box," or raw correlational approach, the policy system, after determining an acceptable level of pupil performance or proficiency, then determines a delivery system dollar amount associated with it. This strategy bypasses any effort to construct or deduce a desired instructional delivery system. Such a bypass also obviates the need to determine costs of instructional components. Under this correlational approach, the cost of attaining adequacy is whatever agencies that achieve adequate outcomes happen to spend, after accounting for any identifiable inefficiencies in these agencies' operations.

INFERRING COSTS FROM EMPIRICAL SEARCHES FOR INSTRUCTIONAL ADEQUACY

This strategy determines a level of acceptable pupil performance or proficiency specified as adequate, and then identifies school districts or schools that achieve the desired goals.[8] The level of resources expended by such school districts is then deemed to be adequate. "The underlying assumption is that any district should be able to accomplish what some districts do accomplish" (Augenblick, 1997, p. 4).

Skeptics may contend that such deductive strategies are based upon past and existing expenditure patterns that may themselves be products of unfair and perhaps unconstitutional school finance plans, and thus these strategies lead to inadequate funding recommendations. However, the actual spending levels determined by research to be associated with desired levels of pupil performance seem to achieve the goal in mind. In effect, what successful districts spend, however unconstitutional or inadequate they may appear when examined without reference to outcomes, have sufficed to obtain the performance ends desired. Hence, these dollar amounts must be presumed to be "adequate," provided their derivation has fully controlled for the nonschool resource factors (like student family background characteristics) that are also known to affect academic achievement.

---

8 The empirical approach is described in detail in a description of the investigation undertaken by John Augenblick, Kern Alexander, and James Guthrie (1995) for the State of Ohio, and then revised in a report by Augenblick (1997).

In reality, as with the statistical model discussed above, this strategy runs a greater danger of leading to overfunding of education, because it relies on data from all districts that produce adequate outcomes, including those that produce them inefficiently.[9]

INFERRING COSTS FROM MARKET MODULES

The last decade has witnessed the development of "whole school reform" models and a host of privately supplied incremental components. These are off-the-shelf school blueprints intended for adoption in their entirety by schools (Odden, 1997; Odden & Busch, 1998). The New American Schools organization, for example, has adopted several designs for promotion to schools, including Roots and Wings (Success for All) developed by Robert Slavin's team at Johns Hopkins University, Atlas Communities based primarily on the School Development Program (SDP) developed by James Comer, the Audrey Cohen College System developed at the college of that name in New York City, Co-NECT, a school design developed by a Cambridge (Massachusetts) consulting firm, the Expeditionary Learning program affiliated with Outward Bound, the Modern Red Schoolhouse designed by the Hudson Institute, and the National Alliance for Restructuring Education that cooperates with schools (e.g., in Kentucky) to restructure their resources to meet higher academic standards. Other whole school design models are those of the Edison Project, the E. D. Hirsch Core Knowledge Curriculum, Accelerated Schools developed by Henry Levin at Stanford University, and the CMCD (Consistency Management and Cooperative Discipline) program now being disseminated in Texas, Chicago and Norfolk (Fashola & Slavin, 1998).

None of the above-listed designs can yet be said to be firmly established by research, in the sense that the achievement of students in schools following these models has been proven superior in replicated controlled empirical or experimental studies. However, many education policy makers are impressed with anecdotal evidence concerning the success of some or all of these programs, and with some limited empirical data that tend to confirm them. These designs will become more formidable if research continues to accumulate regarding their effectiveness. The resources specified by each of these designs (with the exception of the National Alliance for Restructuring Education, which does not promote a single design as such, but tailors its recommendations to individual affiliated schools) could be priced, and the result might be considered the cost, at the school level, of an adequate education. One preliminary effort to estimate the costs of some of these programs was undertaken by Jennifer King (1994).

---

9 This methodology, based on an empirical search for districts with adequate outcomes, is the implicit theory of the New Jersey Supreme Court in *Abbott v. Burke* (1990), in many ways the most radical of state court adequacy decisions. The Court's reasoning suggested a requirement that (poor) districts with low outcomes (including test scores) must be able to achieve high outcomes by spending what (rich) districts with high outcomes spend.

These new models and modules are sold on the market to local school districts. Their proponents have priced-out the delivery of services and products, and, hence, have an idea of what is adequate, based on market experience. However, in cases where entire school designs, not merely add-on components, have been sold to school districts, it has often been the case that the cost to districts and the cost of operation may not be the same. In some cases (for example, the Edison schools), the proprietor supplements district fees with foundation grants or outside investments. Without data on the actual cost of operation, these whole school designs cannot yet be the basis for conclusions about adequacy.

INFERRING COSTS FROM PROFESSIONAL JUDGMENT

Another strategy (presently favored by the authors) for determining the cost of the instructional components undergirding an adequate education is to rely upon professional judgment to construct an ideal delivery system, without either statistical or empirical inference from actual measured outcomes. The components of such a system can then be identified and costs assigned to them. While, at first glance, such an approach may seem unscientific, the approximations inherent in professional judgment may be no less precise than those embedded, though more hidden, in statistical, empirical, or market methods. Professional judgment, if carefully exercised, may be better able to adjust for the vast multitude of factors involved than a statistical or empirical approach.

A professional judgment approach that utilizes consultation with local experts was first implemented by Jay Chambers and Thomas Parrish (1994) in proposals they made for funding adequate education systems in Illinois in 1992 and in Alaska two years later. An elaboration of this method, supplementing panels of local experts with reliance on national research and whole school designs, was adopted in 1996 by a group led by James W. Guthrie to calculate an adequate level of resources to be distributed to Wyoming school districts (Guthrie et. al., 1997).

Guthrie et al. adopted the professional judgment approach (as opposed to Augenblick's Ohio approach of inferring resources from observed adequate outcomes) not only because of concerns, described above, about poorly specified outcome measures in education generally, but also because Wyoming did not utilize a standardized achievement test like that in Ohio, even for narrowly defined academic outcomes. Thus, even poorly specified outcome data were not available. In many states without adequate assessments, the professional judgment method may be the only alternative available, without resorting to the sorts of indirect voter preference models suggested by Duncombe and Yinger (1999).

The utility of the professional judgment approach does not necessarily stem from its greater precision than the statistical or inferential methods. Indeed, the conclusions of professional judgment may, in some cases, be less precise than those statistically derived. Rather, the professional judgment approach is useful because its imprecision is more transparent. When one econometric model finds a great difference in cost between two districts, while another model finds a much smaller difference, policy makers are at a loss to understand what assumptions inside the "black box" create these conflicting results. However, when prototypical resource models of adequacy have different costs, it is clear what the reasons for this difference are—one professional judgment model may propose a third grade class size of 15 students, for example, while another may propose a class size of 20. Policy makers, educators, and voters can then enter this debate, exercising their own best judgments about whether the research evidence on the benefits of smaller class sizes in the early grades is sufficiently persuasive to justify the additional cost. As this research evidence advances, the professional judgment method will be able to improve the precision of its results.

For now, the professional judgment method makes explicit what statistical methodologies tend, unwittingly, to hide. And it makes easier the substitution of new modular prices as views about resource effectiveness evolve. As the Rhode Island Supreme Court stated in a recent adequacy decision, "what constitutes an 'equal, adequate, and meaningful' [education] is 'not likely to be divined for all time even by the scholars who now so earnestly debate the issues'" (quoted in Minorini & Sugarman, 1999).

Nevertheless, whatever its advantage by way of understandability, the professional judgment approach is itself far from being fully developed. It suffers from the possibility of not being reliable. Will duplicate panels arrive at similar conclusions when provided with similar information? When Guthrie et al. utilized this approach in Wyoming, two panels, operating six months apart, did arrive at similar judgments. However, there is no guarantee this will in fact occur in other applications of the method.

CRUCIAL RESEARCH CHALLENGES
REGARDLESS OF THE APPROACH UTILIZED

Space does not permit a full explanation of the many research-related questions that must be answered before the concept of adequacy can realize its full policy potential. However, in the paragraphs that follow, a few of the more significant challenges are described.

- ♦ What outcomes do we truly desire?

  With regard to outcomes, the professional judgment approach does not submerge a discussion of outcomes in obscure statistical formulas. For example, if, in addition to math and reading competency, we want schools to generate outcomes in the areas of fine arts and physical well-being, then a prototypical model of adequate schools may have to provide for music, art, or physical education teachers. Other methods that statistically control only for standardized test scores, or that cite marketed programs solely designed to improve math and reading proficiency, will not account for these outcomes.

- ♦ What resources and resource configurations contribute most forcefully to pupil achievement?

  Adequacy forcefully elevates questions of efficiency, and little is known regarding the tradeoffs contained in instructional circumstances. What are the advantages of smaller classes relative to better prepared teachers? Is staff development a wise investment or would financial incentives for schools and teachers be a better use of the money? One could pose a nearly endless number of such tradeoff questions, but the point would be the same. Our knowledge regarding the processes of producing performance is slender, and our knowledge of the costs involved is even less.

♦ How should exceptional pupils' needs be translated into adequacy?

Our knowledge of what is necessary to educate a student from low-income circumstances, or to assist one who has a disability or limited in his capacity to speak English, is embarrassingly slender. There probably is no more pressing need in school finance research than to come to a better understanding of the costs associated with instructing categories of exceptional students. To reach this understanding, policy makers must confront an issue that has consistently been suppressed in these debates: Should all categories of students be funded to achieve the same outcomes, on average, or should all categories of students be funded only to achieve a minimally acceptable proficiency?

♦ What is a qualified teacher, and how does his or her cost compare to contemporary teacher compensation?

Scholars' understanding of the teacher labor market is very primitive, and there is great disagreement regarding the formal characteristics of teachers capable of generating the outcomes states increasingly demand. Should teachers be hired from other professional fields, with minimal specific pedagogical training? Should districts require new teachers to have master's degrees in education, or should districts instead seek college graduates without specific teacher training but who have strong records in an academic major? Once these decisions are made, what salary levels are necessary to attract such teachers, and how do these compare with salaries presently paid to teachers who may have different qualifications? These issues become part of adequacy calculations.

For example, while there is a nationwide teacher shortage, there are some states, particularly in the upper Midwest, where there is a large teacher surplus, and districts receive scores of qualified applications for each opening. In this case, an adequacy model based on professional judgment could posit a teacher salary considerably below that presently paid, because the present salary is apparently in excess of what is required to attract qualified teachers (at least as districts in these states presently define "qualified"). In contrast, the New York City Board of Education last year offered a 15 percent salary bonus to experienced teachers who would voluntarily accept assignment to the city's most poverty-stricken low scoring schools. But this bonus was not sufficient to fill the positions. In this case, if other instructional and organizational decisions were unmodified, a professional judgment adequacy model, based on the outcomes sought in this case by the Board of Education, might posit a teacher salary considerably above that presently paid—one higher than 15 percent above that presently paid to experienced teachers.

♦ How should special education be financed?

There is growing interest in census-based special education finance programs. In these programs, districts are funded for an expected incidence of special education children, not on a cost-reimbursement basis. If districts identify more than the expected incidence of disabilities, the districts themselves are at risk for the additional expense. An adequacy model utilizing the professional judgment approach must take a position on this development, as prototypes must include resources for special education that will vary depending on how many special education children can be funded on a census basis. Most special education finance experts conclude that census-based financing is appropriate for high-incidence and/or low-cost disabilities, but not for low-incidence and/or high-cost disabilities (Rothstein, 1998). However, there is no distinct line between these categories, and a professional judgment prototype must make a decision about where to draw it. Similarly, there is a feedback relationship between census-based funding required for high-incidence and/or low-cost disabilities and the resources included in a regular education prototype. For example, fewer children may be formally identified as learning disabled, and require special services, in regular classes of 15, than in regular classes of 25. In the former, regular teachers, properly trained, can provide the necessary services. In the latter, this may not be possible.

♦ How should components of education be financed when it is not practical to average their costs?

Some elements of adequacy may not be amenable to analysis by the professional judgment approach. Pupil transportation is one example. It is difficult to imagine how transportation could be included in a prototype. Transportation costs are a function, in part, of the unique geography of a school district. It is one thing to say that a district should, to deliver an adequate education, ideally construct elementary schools to house 360 pupils. It is quite another to say that, to receive an adequate education, children should, on average, live a given number of blocks or miles from that school. Such conditions vary in practice, and are beyond the practical control of school districts, and so there is no way to fund districts for a typical transportation cost.

Similarly, there may be no standardized summary of economies of scale that appropriately characterizes small districts and small schools. We certainly know from experience and observation that small schools and small school districts are more expensive to operate than their larger counterparts. However, we have little understanding of how much more in resources is needed, or of the relationship of scale to economy. And, as in the case of transportation, how small an isolated rural district or school should be is often a function as much of geography as of educational desirability.

These are only a few of the unresolved challenges facing adequacy calculations utilizing the professional judgment method. There are many more. In addition, it is important to note that there are two issues that must generally be confronted by any adequacy approach, not only that utilizing professional judgment.

♦ Adjusting for geographic cost variation

The costs of education vary greatly in some diverse states that include metropolitan, resort, and rural communities. It may at first appear that metropolitan and resort communities have higher education costs, but in some respects the opposite may be true. In fact, it may require higher salaries to attract highly qualified teachers to communities considered less desirable by educated professionals. Only six states currently adjust school finance distributions for regional cost differences. In each case, the apparatus for doing so is clumsy and inadequate. A principal problem is that greater accuracy carries greater information costs. A state can spend substantial sums to develop an intrastate education cost index, but then these are funds no longer available for pupils' education.

♦ Adjusting for changes in costs over time

Policy makers cannot design an adequacy protocol or prototype that is adequate for all time. By what mechanism should periodic examinations of the system and its costs take place? Even if a professional judgment approach to adequacy perfectly captured the current state of research on the relationship of inputs to outcomes, improved educational technologies or improved understanding of educational technology will soon render some elements of an adequacy model obsolete. Further, a state's determination of its educational goals will evolve over time. How frequently should an adequacy calculation be updated? And even if the model itself is not modified, should there be an automatic multiplier by which a state's entire system is ratcheted upward by some measure of inflation in education? Legislators will resist such automatic spending arrangements on grounds that doing so usurps their authority. On the other hand, it is clear that costs of inputs do escalate and a system that fails to acknowledge these changes can deteriorate to inadequacy in short order.

ADEQUACY'S EFFECTS ON
EDUCATION POLICY DISCUSSIONS

Adequacy, as a policy objective, will likely change the hierarchy of various components in deliberations on education policy. For example, when adequacy is the policy objective, the following ascend in significance:

♦ The role of the state

An equity-based school finance plan need not lead to greater state control. Power equalizing or guaranteed yield schemes could preserve local district discretion over per-pupil spending levels. However, in reality, practical solutions to equal protection controversies pursued by most states have increased state control. Regardless, whatever a state's existing levels of authority, adequacy almost assuredly reinforces the state role even more greatly. In a finance plan concentrated on providing adequate resources, the state becomes the prime actor in determining "adequate for what?" Certainly, local districts and schools can add to whatever expectations a state agency promulgates, but the state's view of what should be learned will likely drive assessment systems, accountability provisions, and levels of financing.

♦ Schooling purposes and pupil performance

Conventional equity can be satisfied by the elimination or dampening of input disparities. Pupil performance need never be a factor in the analyses. Conversely, in an adequacy-based system, low pupil performance becomes an alarm for the prospect of inadequate resources.

♦ Pupil, classroom, school, and district characteristics

A determination of adequacy necessitates calibration regarding the characteristics of individual pupils, schools, and, in some instances, school districts. For example, students who speak little or no English, geographically remote schools, or districts located in unusually high-cost areas may all need adjustments to their resource levels, or an otherwise rationally determined level of resources may prove inadequate.

♦ Measurement of outcomes, performance feedback, and consequences

An adequacy finance model depends for its ultimate legitimacy upon a rational link between resources and student performance. Consequently, whereas one may initially design adequacy systems by one or a combination of the four strategies specified in the previous section, eventually, adequacy must be empirically linked to performance.

Furthermore, when adequacy is the policy objective, the following descend in significance:

♦ Local school district discretion

If great care is not taken, this long standing conventional element of American education can be seriously attenuated. Local control suffers if a state, in a quest for adequacy, specifies what students are expected to learn, then allocates resources rationally determined to be sufficient to achieve such levels of performance, and takes further steps to limit local spending in excess of such a per-pupil amount. If the state should go further and direct that local districts actually spend resources in specified ways, then the necessity of having local school districts at all is seriously brought into question.

♦ Sources of revenue

In an equity-oriented system, consideration is usually given to property tax rates and the impact of reform on property tax payers. An adequacy-based school finance system is virtually oblivious to the sources of revenues. In practice, an adequacy system may result in a statewide property tax or something quite close to it. However, for the rational purpose of building a school finance system, the source of revenues is of little concern. All that matters is the level of spending and the means by which it is determined.

♦ Issues of distributional equity

If a system is oriented toward adequacy, and the needs of pupils, schools, and districts have been rationally determined, per-pupil disparities will of necessity exist. Of course, such spending differences should now have a rational explanation. They should not be a function of wealth, other than the wealth of the state as a whole. Deployment of conventional per-pupil equity measures is of no consequence.

CONCLUSION

This chapter ends where it began. Adequacy as a concept holds the promise of rendering education less dismal and more rational. It holds the promise of elevating debate about education to a consideration of what ought to be learned, how it ought to be taught, and how we should measure the outcomes. It holds the potential for elevating debate about the purposes of schooling and taking attention away from the sources, as opposed to the levels, of revenue. It also holds the prospect of helping improve the learning lives of millions of students. To fulfill this potential, however, adequacy must be provided with a far more solid research base than now exists.

REFERENCES

Augenblick, J. (1997). *Recommendations for a base figure and pupil-weighted adjustments to the base figure for use in a new school finance system in ohio.* School Funding Task Force, Ohio Department of Education, July 17.

Augenblick, J., Alexander, K., & Guthrie, J. W. (1995, June). *Report of the panel of experts: Proposals for the elimination of wealth based disparities in education.* Submitted by Ohio Chief State School Officer Theodore Sanders to the Ohio State Legislature.

Benson, C. (1978). *The economics of public education.* Boston: Houghton Mifflin.

Catchpole, J. (1996, September). *Accreditation guide, November 1995. (Revised.)* Cheyenne, WY: Wyoming Department of Education.

Chambers, J., & Parrish, T. (1994). State level education finance. In Barnett, W. S. (Ed.), *Advances in educational productivity.* Vol. 4: *Cost analysis for education decisions: Methods and examples.* Greenwich, CT: JAI Press.

Coons, J. E., Sugarman, S. D., & Clune, W. H. (1970). *Private wealth and public educa-tion*. Cambridge, MA: Harvard University Press

Cubberley, E. P. (1919a). *Public education in the United States: A study and interpreta-tion of American educational history; an introductory textbook dealing with the larger problems of present-day education in the light of their historical development*. New York: Houghton Mifflin.

Cubberley, E. P. (1919b). *State and county school administration*. New York: The Macmillan Company.

Downes, T. A., & Pogue, T. F. (1994, March). Adjusting school aid formulas for the higher cost of educating disadvantaged students. *National Tax Journal, 47* (1), 89–110.

Duncombe, W., & Yinger, J. (1999). Performance standards and educational cost indexes: You can't have one without the other. In Ladd, Helen, Rosemary Chalk, and Janet Hansen (Eds.), *Equity and adequacy in education finance*. Com-mittee on Education Finance of the National Research Council, National Academy Press.

Fashola, O. S., & Slavin, R. E. (1998, January). Schoolwide reform models: What works? *Phi Delta Kappan*, 370–79.

Guthrie, J. W., & Rothstein, R. (1999). Enabling "adequacy" to achieve reality: Translating adequacy into state school finance distribution arrangements. In Helen Ladd, Rosemary Chalk, and Janet Hansen (Eds.), *Equity and adequacy in education finance*. Washington, DC: Committee on Education Finance of the National Research Council, National Academy Press.

Guthrie, J. W., et al. (1997, May). *A proposed cost-based block grant model for Wyo-ming school finance*. Sacramento, CA: Management Analysis & Planning Asso-ciates, L.L.C.

Hussar, W., & Sonnenberg, W. (2000). *Trends in disparities in school district level expenditures per pupil*. Washington DC: National Center for Education Statis-tics, Office of Education Research and Improvement, U.S. Department of Edu-cation, NCES 2000-020.

Imazeki, J., & Reschovsky, A. (1998, November). *Measuring the cost of providing an adequate education in texas*. Austin, TX: National Tax Association Proceedings.

Johns, R. L., Morphet, E. L., & Alexander, K. (1983). *The economics and financing of education*. Englewood Cliffs, NJ: Prentice Hall.

King, J. A. (1994, Spring). Meeting the educational needs of at-risk students: A cost analysis of three models. *Educational Evaluation and Policy Analysis, 16*(1).

Kirst, M., & Garms, W. I. (1980). The political environment of school finance pol-icy in the 1980s. In *School finance policies and practices: The 1980's, a decade of con-flict* (pp. 47–78). Yearbook, American Education Finance Association. Cam-bridge, MA: Ballinger.

Ladd, H. F., & Yinger, J. (1994, March). The case for equalizing aid. *National Tax Journal, 47*, 211–224.

Minorini, P., & Sugarman, S. D. (1999). Educational adequacy and the courts: The promise and problems of moving to a new paradigm. In Ladd, Helen, Rosemary Chalk, and Janet Hansen (Eds.), *Equity and adequacy in education finance*. Washington, DC: Committee on Education Finance of the National Research Council, National Academy Press.

Mort, P. R., Reusser, W. C., & Polley, J. W. (1960). *Public school finance: It's background, structure and operation*. New York: McGraw-Hill.

Murray, S. E., Evans, W. N., & Schwab, R. M. (1998, September). Education finance reform and the distribution of education resources. *American Economic Review, 88* (4), 789–812.

Odden, A. (1997). How to rethink school budgets to support school transformation. *Getting Better by Design* (vol. 3). Arlington, VA: New American Schools.

Odden, A., & Busch, C. (1998). *Financing schools for high performance: Strategies for improving the use of educational resources*. San Francisco: Jossey-Bass.

Porter, A. C. (1993). Defining and measuring opportunity to learn. In S. I. Traiman (Ed.), *The debate on opportunity to learn standards: Supporting works*. (pp. 33–72). Washington, DC: National Governors Association.

Reschovsky, A., & Imazeki, J. (1998, July). The development of school finance formulas to guarantee the provision of adequate education to low income students. *Developments in school finance 1997*. Washington, DC: National Center for Education Statistics, U.S. Department of Education, NCES 98-212.

Rothstein, R. (1998, May 20).Wyoming education finance issues report: An analysis of the modified census based special education program. Sacramento, CA: Management Analysis & Planning Associates, L.L.C.

Wise, A. R. (1970). *Rich schools: Poor schools*. Chicago: University of Chicago Press.

8

ILLUMINATING THE BLACK BOX: THE EVOLVING ROLE OF EDUCATION PRODUCTIVITY RESEARCH

Jennifer King Rice
University of Maryland

Over the past several decades, the attention of both education research and policy-making communities has gravitated toward the notion of education outcomes; the resulting research and policy agendas now focus on how to produce desirable outcomes more effectively, efficiently, and equitably.[1] This emphasis on outcomes is evident in the current call for adequacy, the preoccupation with accountability, the promulgation of "performance-based" rewards and punishments, and the intensification of efforts to measure and track educational outcomes, primarily though testing. Information on the level and distribution of fiscal resources across districts and schools is no longer sufficient grounds for making decisions about the relative desirability of different financing strategies. The spotlight now focuses on the complex processes through which these inputs translate into sought-after educational outcomes. Reaching a clearer understanding of this production process holds great promise for advancing progress toward efficiency, equity, and adequacy goals in education.

Unfortunately, the education production process has been exceedingly difficult to define and interpret. Some have even characterized it as a mysterious "black box" into which resources are deposited and from which outcomes emerge. Others have struggled to demystify this black box by empirically linking

---

1 The author gratefully acknowledges Betty Malen and Steve Klees for their insightful input and constructive comments on earlier versions of this chapter.

inputs and outcomes in systematic ways with the goal of defining at least some of the properties of this complex production process While many disciplines, including sociology, anthropology, and psychology, have contributed to our understanding of the relationships between educational inputs and outcomes, the economic concept of a production function has played an important role in framing empirical studies of these relationships. Knowledge of a production function sheds light on the ways in which inputs into a production process are systematically transformed into desired outcomes. Since a production function indicates the maximum level of outcome possible for various combinations of inputs, education productivity research could play a critical role in a policy environment emphasizing accountability for both resources and outcomes. Even though not all education inputs and outputs can be understood through productivity research, the approach can be very instructive in defining salient properties that are well-defined, measurable, and predictable.

While the application of the production function concept to education holds potential, the role of the education production function has been contested terrain at three levels. First, much debate centers on whether a production function for the education process exists at all. Second, among those who agree that production function methodology is valid, the inconclusive and inconsistent findings of this body of research have resulted in controversy surrounding the nature of that production function. Third, the absence of normative criteria limits the power of this tool for decision making. The utility of production function research in the future depends on the ability of analysts to recognize and address these concerns.

This chapter takes the position that the production function is a potentially fruitful tool for understanding the educational process and informing current and future policy directions. The chapter begins by defining the production function and describing the controversy that has surrounded it, and contends that, despite the controversy, it is prudent to pursue this line of inquiry. Such prudence is warranted given the current policy environment that often presumes that knowledge of the education production process is, in fact, available to those being held accountable for results. The section that follows recommends that, rather than abandoning this line of research, efforts should be made to further strengthen this work. The final section appraises the future utility of education productivity research, and argues that, despite its inherent limitations, productivity findings can and should be used alongside other types of information to guide education policy decisions.

THE CONCEPT AND THE CONTROVERSY

The education production function describes the systematic relationship between educational inputs and outcomes. Information about the productivities of various inputs can be combined with data on prices to reveal the marginal returns to different types of educational investments (e.g., smaller classes versus higher teacher salaries). This line of research recognizes the multiplicity of competing policy alternatives and identifies those with the highest productivities relative to cost as the most preferable on economic grounds. Further, to the degree that inefficiencies exist in the education sector, productivity studies have the potential to improve current resource allocation practices.

In simplest terms, specification of the production function involves three steps: (1) identifying the inputs, (2) identifying the outcomes, and (3) specifying the function that transforms inputs into outcomes. Levin (1976) describes a common general form of the education production function as the following:

$A_{it} = g(F_{i(t)}, S_{i(t)}, P_{i(t)}, O_{i(t)}, I_{it})$, where

> A_{it} = a vector of educational outcomes for the ith student at time t.
>
> $F_{i(t)}$ = a vector of individual and family background characteristics cumulative to time t.
>
> $S_{i(t)}$ = a vector of school inputs relevant to the ith student cumulative to time t.
>
> $P_{i(t)}$ = a vector of peer or fellow-student characteristics cumulative to time t.
>
> $O_{i(t)}$ = a vector of other external influences (e.g., community) relevant to the ith student cumulative to time t.
>
> I_{it} = a vector of initial or innate endowments of the ith student at time t.

This formulation is conceptually quite comprehensive in that it includes a wide array of possible inputs (school, community, family, peer, and individual across time) and outcomes (achievement, attitudes, performance, as well as other less quantitative types of outcomes such as civic competencies and cultural tolerance). The actual specification of the model to be tested is left to the analyst who faces serious constraints with respect to the available data and methods.

While productivity findings could be of great use to education policy makers, much controversy has surrounded this approach to describing and analyzing the educational process. As noted in the introduction to this chapter, the application of the production function model to education has been critiqued at three levels. First, there is no consensus on the degree to which the education process is subject to an identifiable production function; critics here argue that the production function is not a valid tool for thinking about education phenomena. A production function assumes a systematic relationship between inputs and outputs, and some have maintained that no such systematic relationship exists between educational inputs and outputs.[2] According to these critics, sometimes education activities simply work, and sometimes they don't; there are no identifiable factors that can promote success or explain failure. In other words, the education process is not predictable and cannot be modeled as a function; the fundamental idiosyncratic nature of the education process undermines the whole notion of an education production function.

A second level of criticism concerns the fact that productivity research has been plagued by results that are neither fully consistent nor statistically signifi-

---

2 For a discussion of the existence of an education production function, see David H. Monk (1990).

cant (Hanushek, 1986; Monk, 1992; and Murnane, 1981). Consequently, even among those who agree that the production function is a valid tool for thinking about education, there is a conspicuous lack of agreement about its nature. Despite volumes of research, there is no clear consensus or clean, undisputed description of the attributes that characterize productive teachers, ideal class sizes, or efficient groupings of students in schools and classrooms. This realization has led some researchers to turn away from the promise of systematic, predictable relationships to champion alternative approaches to improving productivity, such as performance incentives, that depend less on a broad-scale, predefined production process (Hanushek et al., 1994; and Hanushek, 1996). Others argue that the inability of empirical research to demonstrate the existence of systematic relationships speaks to the complexity of the educational process. The response, they argue, is not to abandon the approach but to improve it: "What is needed is the willingness to take small and tentative steps, to consolidate knowledge of past success and failures, and to continually refine both the instruments and the processes" (Cohn & Geske, 1990, p. 196). Researchers, they say, should focus their efforts on developing methods that are more sophisticated, acquiring better data, and reaching a greater understanding of which aspects of education can be modeled and which cannot.

A third level of criticism about the education production function focuses on the inability of this analytic tool to consider normative issues. Education policy making is a value-laden process that can pose serious dilemmas for decision makers who must balance competing goods. Malen, Theobald, and Bardzell (2000) argue that efficiency has surfaced as a dominant social value, over other priorities such as equity and autonomy. The emphasis of productivity research on efficiency makes it a good fit with a policy environment that prizes this social value above others. However, information about the marginal productivities and costs of various education policy options must be considered alongside other types of analyses that recognize normative issues. For example, acting exclusively on findings from productivity research that identify certain student grouping policies or resource allocations as ways to promote student achievement could result in serious compromises of other important societal values such as equity and liberty, as well as of other outcomes such as civic responsibility and tolerance for diversity. We must ask, efficiency at what expense or whose expense? While productivity research has not typically been associated with the goal of equity, it is central to the current policy emphasis on adequacy, which requires a very refined and contextualized understanding of the education production process. The absence of normative criteria is not unique to production function research; all empirical analyses must be considered in light of the normative tradeoffs they imply. Yet the inability of production function research to address normative issues remains problematic.

Despite these sources of controversy, this chapter argues that education productivity research can and should play a role in education policy making, particularly with respect to improving efficiency, a major concern evident in the current policy context that is likely to persist. One characteristic of this policy environment is the expanding range of potentially effective policy alternatives coupled with the public's growing demand for greater accountability for resources. These pressures place education decision makers in a position where they must choose among policy alternatives (e.g., class size reductions versus additional time in the school day and/or school year) while controlling costs. Analyses that shed light on the relationships between investments in policy options and the outcomes they promise could help to inform these difficult decisions.

Many prominent education policies assume that an education production function exists and that essential properties of this production function can be known. For instance, many high-stakes accountability systems reflect a belief in the existence of an education production function that can guide both practitioners and policy makers to a more optimal use of education resources. These policies rest on the premise that we either have this knowledge or could readily procure it at site, district, or state levels. Advocates argue that more robust incentives and stringent sanctions to procure that knowledge and put it to use are required. Likewise, state takeover plans and many market-based reform strategies (e.g., contracting with private for-profit companies) assume that knowledge of the education production process is not being effectively used. By introducing competition, these policies force schools to apply the knowledge they have or to acquire the knowledge they need to use resources more efficiently. Finally, the current adequacy movement assumes a highly sophisticated and contextualized understanding of the basic properties of the education production process (e.g., class size, facilities, instructional resources). At minimum, success of this movement hinges on the ability to specify outcome standards expected of all students, identify the critical inputs needed to produce those outcomes, determine the costs of the inputs, and develop financing strategies to ensure that all students across a range of contexts have access to an adequate education. Because these sorts of policies are prevalent in the current education policy landscape and are likely to persist into the future, education productivity research may be even more important now than in the past.

In sum, knowledge of the education production function can be very valuable, particularly for some issues. Consequently, rather than abandon this genre of research altogether, this chapter advocates a concerted effort to identify and seriously attend to the shortcomings that have pervaded education productivity research. The next section describes four issues that, if effectively addressed, might strengthen this research tradition.

STRENGTHENING EDUCATION PRODUCTION FUNCTION RESEARCH: NEW DIRECTIONS FOR THE NEW MILLENNIUM

The inconclusive and inconsistent results of education production function research suggest that formulating and estimating the education production function is a complex task. A decade ago, Monk (1990) identified a series of major challenges that have complicated the study of the education production function: identifying and specifying inputs and outcomes, selecting the functional form, choosing the level of analysis, weighing longitudinal versus cross-sectional data, attending to the role played by intelligence, and dealing with an array of other methodological issues including limited variation, simultaneity, and selection effects. Many of these issues will continue to undermine education production function research in the 21st century. This section presents four broad themes that hold promise for strengthening this tradition of research. Each implies a different way of conceptualizing the education production process. These are (1) the education production process as a complex configuration of resources, (2) the education production process as a multilevel phenomenon, (3) the existence of multiple education production processes, and (4) the education production process as dynamic and time-bound.

Although these issues are reviewed here individually, they give rise to overlapping problems for production function analysts. In what follows, the conceptual distinctions are maintained but with the recognition of instances where the boundaries presented are blurred. This discussion of conceptual issues gives rise to methodological challenges for the education productivity researcher. Some of these are noted throughout; others require the acceptance of methods that are not traditionally recognized as productivity research but contribute to our understanding of the relationships between inputs and outcomes (e.g., case studies, experimental designs). Finally, these themes are not new. Researchers have begun to view the educational process in these ways, and this discussion highlights instances where exemplary research is occurring and shows how that research provides evidence that attention to these matters bolsters the quality of education productivity research.

CONFIGURATIONS OF RESOURCES

Education is a complex process. Educational inputs from a variety of sources combine to form the total package of resources available to a student. In the context of the general production function model presented above, the educational outcome for each student is determined by innate traits as well as by the resources offered to him/her by family, school, peers, and community. The greater the investment of productive resources from each of these sources, the higher the output (Levin, 1976).

However, the relations among inputs and outcomes are interactive. The productivity of one input can be affected by the amount and quality of another. Thus, the many discrete inputs combine in complex ways to form a "package" or configuration of resources available to the student. Conventional production function studies give little attention to these complex interactions among resources.[3]

Several examples may help to clarify how inputs from various sources interact with one another. Title I funding is increasingly linked to the adoption of comprehensive school reform (CSR) models as promising alternatives for schools serving large concentrations of at-risk students.[4] These models combine a variety of resources in ways that are expected to affect the entire educational experience of students during their elementary school years. For instance, the Success for All

---

3 This point is argued by Monk (1992) and Richard J. Murnane (1981). However, Anita A. Summers and Barbara L. Wolfe (1977) provide a noteworthy exception.

4 For a brief description of the Comprehensive School Demonstration Reform program, see Education Commission of the States (1998).

model involves a specific curriculum, an eight-week assessment program, and a reading tutor component for students experiencing difficulties.[5] These program components may be inextricably linked with one another in producing effective results. Consequently, studying the productivities of each as individual, independent inputs could yield misleading results. It is the "package" of resources that make up this model that should be studied.

Another CSR model is the Accelerated Schools program (Levin, 1987). The full implementation of the program is heavily dependent upon the availability of productive community and parental resources (King, 1994). In a community where these resources are not available or productive, the program has little chance of succeeding, regardless of the amount of school-level resources invested. Conversely, consider a community where parents have a great deal of spare time (a slack resource) that they would like to invest in the education of their children.[6] Assume that this time is a potentially productive resource. The productivity of this parent time is dependent on the way in which the school utilizes it. A community that adopts the Accelerated Schools program may make much more productive use of parent time than a community that limits parent involvement to more conventional educational support in the home (e.g., assistance with homework). The Accelerated Schools presumably offer institutional resources that interact with those from the home to increase the productivity of each.

A final example of the importance of the interactions among various educational inputs is class size reduction, a policy alternative that is currently receiving a great deal of attention. Research has shown that the effectiveness of class size reduction policies depends on the availability of other resources, such as a sufficient pool of qualified teachers and adequate classroom space to house the additional classes (Bohrnstad, Stecher, & Wiley, 2000). Further, some have argued that the impact of class size reduction policies depends on the availability of professional development opportunities to teach teachers instructional methods that take advantage of smaller classes (Bahrnstad et al., 2000; Geary, 1988; and Rice, 1999). These sorts of interactions are essential to consider when studying the productivity of reduced class size.

As we move into the 21st century, education productivity research must acknowledge the multiple types of resources that interact with one another to comprise the total package available to each student. This is not to say that analysts must study everything at once in order to make progress. On the contrary, much progress has been made by researchers conducting value-added productivity analyses where the goal is to gain insight into the impact of one or more variables rather than to estimate the complete education production function.[7]

---

5   For an overview of the Success for All model see Ross et al. (1997) and Center for Research on Effective Schooling for Disadvantaged Students (1992).

6   For a discussion of the productivity of time, see Gary S. Becker (1976).

7   In fact, this chapter questions the existence of a complete education production function that is able to explain all of the variance in educational outcomes. Instead, it focuses on discovering the scope of what can be known through this

Whatever the emphasis, care must be taken to look at how the many pieces of the production function interact to systematically produce desired educational outcomes.[8]

MULTILEVEL ASPECTS OF EDUCATION PRODUCTIVITY

An ongoing issue in productivity research has focused on which level of analysis is most appropriate to assess the effectiveness of resource allocation practices.[9] Over the years, studies have shifted from designs using highly aggregated data at centralized levels of analysis[10] to approaches focused on productivity at more micro-levels of analysis[11] to investigations tracing resource flows to individual students (see Brown & Saks, 1986, 1987; and Kiesling 1984). Amidst this "level of analysis" debate, Burstein and Miller (1986, p. 196) argue, "To think of multilevel analyses simply as problems in the choice of a unit of analysis is inadequate." Studies of the effects of schooling must address its multilevel nature.

Productivity researchers have begun to recognize that the complexity of schooling is manifest in the nested nature of its production function. The educational process is a function of student and family characteristics as well as policies and practices at multiple organizational levels: students are nested in classrooms, classrooms are nested in schools, schools in districts, and so forth. These influences are all operating simultaneously to create the whole educational experience for each pupil. Productivity research must address the various levels of the process and aim to disentangle their effects on pupil outcomes.

The multilevel nested nature of the educational process has been recognized by numerous researchers employing hierarchical linear modeling (see Bryk & Raudenbush, 1992). William Fowler (1993, p. 2) explains, "Hierarchical linear modeling (HLM) is a statistical modeling approach…that implements a multilevel technique that avoids the problems of the aggregation and desegregation methods, remains statistically correct, and does not waste information. In addition, HLM yields greater understanding of the relations and variance within each level, and across levels." For these reasons, throughout the past decade HLM has become a common approach to analyzing the effects of education inputs on student outcomes.

Applications of HLM tend to fall into two categories: (1) organizational studies, and (2) developmental studies. Applications of HLM in organizational

---

approach.

8 This goal may require the use of methods from a variety of disciplines to understand the relationships between packages of inputs and outcomes (e.g., case studies, experimental designs).

9 For a more complete discussion of levels of analysis in education productivity research, see Monk (1992).

10 See, for examples, Hanushek (1972), and Burkhead, Fox, and Holland (1967).

11 Examples include Hanushek (1971), Murnane (1975), and Summers and Wolfe (1977).

research generally include the specification of a person-level model (level 1) where the outcome is represented as a function of individual characteristics, and an organization-level model (level 2) where each level 1 regression coefficient can be conceived as an outcome variable that depends on organization level variables (e.g., classrooms, schools, and districts). HLM allows the analyst to simultaneously model relationships at the individual and organizational level. For example, a study by Lee and Bryk (1989) used HLM to explore the impact of a number of secondary school characteristics on the achievement of students from a variety of different backgrounds. Student characteristics included each student's academic background, minority status, and socioeconomic status. School level predictor variables included measures of the social and academic composition of the schools, perceived quality of instruction and of teacher interest in students, disciplinary climate of the school, academic pressure of the school, and curricular structure.

Applications of HLM in developmental research (the study of individual change) also involve at least two levels. Level 1 is the repeated observations model where an individual's observed status at a particular point in time is a function of a systematic growth trajectory plus random error. Level 2 is a person-level model, which reflects the assumption that the parameters specified in level 1 vary across individuals and can be explained by person-level variables. Finally, a third level could be included where institutional-level variables model level 1 and level 2 coefficients to explain variance across organizations (Bryk & Raudenbush, 1992, 1987). A study of the influences on children's early vocabulary growth by Huttenlocher et al. (1991) is an example of a multilevel growth model. These examples illustrate the ways that hierarchical modeling is emerging as a promising tool to enable analysts to study the multilevel nature of the education production process.

MULTIPLE PRODUCTION FUNCTIONS

A third way to strengthen education productivity research is to recognize that a single production function may not "hold true" for all groups of students, subjects, grade levels, or schools, and to seriously explore the possibility of multiple production functions. One could identify different functions that describe the production process for different groups of students. These different functions may involve different combinations of a set of resources or different resources altogether. Although attention to different student groups might lead to more accurate production functions, there are drawbacks to positing different production functions for different types of students. Stratifying by different student characteristics can become so disaggregated and narrowly defined that there exists a unique set of production functions for each individual student (Monk, 1990). As this happens, the policy relevance of the research diminishes. The analyst's job is to identify clusters of students (e.g., by background, grade level, subject area, type of school) that share common production processes.

Many studies estimate the relationships between inputs and outputs across a broadly-defined aggregate sample, evidencing the assumption that all students profit similarly from a given set of resources (e.g., the impact of class size or teacher experience on the academic achievement of American public high school students). However, the possibility of multiple production functions has been entertained through research that has focused on input-output relationships for specific subject areas (Jones, 1988; Rice & Roellke, 1998; Monk, 1994) and levels of education (Educational Research Service, Inc., 1983; Kohut, 1988; and Rice, 1995). Further, most education production function studies include at least some consideration of student background characteristics (e.g., measures of socioeconomic status). To move closer to identifying the kinds of factors that account for different production processes, these efforts need to be extended to fully explore such indicators as risk of educational failure and student culture. To illustrate, several studies have identified educational practices that are particularly important for the educational success of at-risk students. Examples include smaller class size (Wehlage, 1991), preschool programs, and counseling and parent involvement programs (Taylor & Piche, 1991). In addition, a number of studies have examined how culture affects achievement in mathematics and science (Stigler & Barnes, 1988; and Lancy, 1983).

As discussed above, in response to the growing concern for at-risk students, policy makers have advocated the use of a number of alternative school-level programs tailored to meet the specific educational needs of this student population (e.g., Accelerated Schools, Success for All Schools). Such initiatives imply that at-risk students benefit from different resources or different uses of the same resources than students not at risk. In other words, these models reflect the assumption that there exists a unique education production function for this population. Unfortunately, many of these programs lack sufficient convincing evidence to verify their effectiveness[12]—and consequently to support the proposition of multiple production functions. In order to examine the possibility of multiple production functions, analysts must draw on a variety of research methods (e.g., case studies, experimental designs) to systematically study the impact of various resource configurations and resource patterns for different student populations over time.

EDUCATION AS A DYNAMIC PROCESS

Education is a process of continuous development; its status at any point in time depends on the cumulative effect of a variety of inputs.[13] Studies of the productivity of the educational process, then, should measure effectiveness in terms of change or growth over time rather than status at a particular point in time. However, research questions on learning and development that naturally lend themselves to a longitudinal investigation are too frequently analyzed using a cross-sectional design (Willett, 1988). Such an approach measures current status rather than change or growth.

Productivity research that does involve data at more than one point in time often divides the education process into discrete years marked by two measurement points ("pre" and "post") to examine the relationships between inputs and

---

12 For an overview of the work evaluating various schoolwide models, see the recent study by the American Institutes for Research (1999).

13 See the conceptual formulation of the education production function presented earlier in this chapter.

outputs. This "gain score" approach does consider growth and provides insight into the value added by a particular resource or set of resources. However, important information is lost when mapping an individual's growth trajectory with only two points, especially when the two points are widely spaced.

Consider Figure 8.1, which maps the achievement growth trajectories over time for two individuals—ABD and ACD. For both individuals, point A is the starting point, representing the level of achievement at time 1, and point D is the final status at time 3. The line mapping AD is the trajectory for both individuals based on only two observation points at times 1 and 3; in contrast, ABD and ACD include an intermediate observation at time 2. The dotted lines, x and y, are the best-fit lines for trajectories ABD and ACD. There are at least two concerns with relying on model AD based on only two observation points. First, the regression line of an individual's growth trajectory based on only two data points yields no residual term (Willett, 1988). Any empirical measurement of an individual's status is afflicted by error, which acts to disturb the observation. In other words, true status equals observed status plus the accompanying measurement error. When a regression line is based on only two data points, the line is a perfect fit and the residual term is equal to zero, erroneously suggesting that there is no error in the measurement (i.e., that true status = observed status). Multiwave data eliminate this problem inherent in two-wave data, as can be seen graphically in regressions lines x and y which represent trajectories ABD and ACD, respectively.

FIGURE 8.1. STUDENT ACHIEVEMENT OVER TIME: THE NEED TO ADDRESS THE DYNAMIC NATURE OF EDUCATION

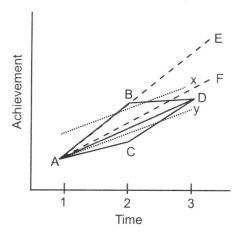

A second potential problem with basing an individual's growth model on only two observation points is that important policy-relevant information is lost. Only the trajectories based on three data points reveal two distinct segments of growth, one lagged and the other accelerated. Knowledge that such a pattern exists leads to a number of policy relevant questions. For instance, what happened at time 2 to stunt the achievement growth of the student represented by

ABD? Similarly, what happened at that point to bolster the achievement growth of the student modeled by ACD?

Furthermore, the three-point trajectories offer information regarding the rate at which a student is capable of growing in achievement. For instance, the student modeled by ABD evidences rapid growth (maximum slope) in segment AB. If that rate of growth could be maintained, the student could reach the potential outcome point E by time 3. Likewise, if the student modeled by the ACD trajectory was able to achieve initially his/her rate of growth in segment CD, he/she could potentially reach point F by time 3. The key to approaching these maximum achievement points at time 3 might lie in identifying the cause of the growth change at time 2. Although both individuals end at the same point D at time 3, this outcome is the result of very different processes. Consequently the use of multiwave data, which includes numerous data collection points over time, should be used whenever possible in place of more conventional single-point or two-wave data to model education productivity (Willett, 1988).

Since the education process extends over many years, analysts trying to explain the academic achievement of a particular student must look to earlier stages in that student's educational development. (See, for example, Gameron, 1992.) Although multiple regression equations common in productivity research generally control for family background, the most common control for previous educational experiences of the student is a pretest score, which has been criticized as inadequate for this purpose (Krueger, 1998). This approach fails to consider the dynamic nature of the educational process: inputs of one level of education produce outputs, which often become inputs for the next level of the education process. Recall, status at any point in time depends on the cumulative effect of many inputs. Gameron's study of high school course assignments in English illustrates the importance of looking to earlier stages in a student's educational career. Further, by concentrating resources at particular points in the education process, a variety of interventions (e.g., Head Start, Success for All, Upward Bound) reflect the awareness that outputs of one level of education become inputs for another.

APPRAISING THE FUTURE UTILITY OF EDUCATION PRODUCTIVITY RESEARCH

With the sorts of ongoing improvements discussed in the previous section, the education production function can become a more useful tool for policy makers looking for information on the relationship between educational inputs and outcomes. Coupling productivity information with data on costs can guide decision makers seeking to identify the most efficient policy alternative. Clearly, this approach can be a valuable tool in the current policy environment that prizes accountability and efficiency. Information on the properties of the education production process is key to the current emphasis on education adequacy, as well. However, questions remain as to the proper role of this kind of information in the decision-making process. What does this method allow us to say about the production of education? Which educational issues are amenable to this sort of analysis and which are not? What sorts of decisions can be made based on the findings of productivity research? What additional information is needed? The answers to these questions suggest that education productivity research is important, but incomplete in informing education policy decisions.

Recognizing the bounds of the productivity research is a first step to better understanding its utility. In other words, how comprehensive is the education production function? Which factors fall within this framework and which do not? While the conceptual specification of the education production function presented earlier in this chapter is quite comprehensive, operationalizing it is undermined by data and methodological limitations. The result is a body of production function research that includes only those factors that can be readily specified and measured. So, while the production function can reveal information on the ways in which some inputs translate into some outcomes, acting exclusively on the findings of production function research could neglect other important inputs and outcomes that may not be easily measured or agreed upon. One promising direction is to recognize the broader set of disciplines (and their methodological approaches) that have explored input-outcome relationships and the complexities of the education production process. Lessons learned from psychology, sociology, and anthropology, for example, could expand the range of inputs and outcomes beyond what more traditional econometrics have allowed.

A second issue relates to the certainty of the findings. As reported earlier, education production function studies, taken together, have been quite inconsistent in their findings to date. For instance, Hanushek (1996) identified 227 estimates of the impact of teacher-pupil ratio on student achievement. Of these, he reports that 15 percent were significantly positive, 13 percent significantly negative, and 72 percent insignificant. One response may be to assume that this particular input is not amenable to the production function framework. However, determining what makes sense to include is a complex matter. Some inconsistent findings may be the result of poor variable specification (e.g., class size versus student-teacher ratio) or design issues (e.g., experimental versus quasi-experimental, level of analysis issues). Indeed, a more consistent set of findings is emerging from recent research on the impact of class size that is based on demonstration programs or experiments. (See Finn & Achilles, 1999; Molnar et al., 1999; Nye, Hedges, & Konstantopoulos, 1999.) It is important not to exclude factors that may be reasonable to model but have not yet yielded definitive results; rather these matters need greater attention in future research.

Information on the comprehensiveness of the education production function and on the certainty of findings regarding particular inputs reveals insight about the breadth of this approach's contribution to policy discussions. Serious attention should be devoted to defining these bounds and identifying what we can say with confidence based on education productivity research. For example, a recent review of the literature examining the impact of various indicators of teacher quality reveals some consistent findings on the relationship between several teacher characteristics and student achievement (Monk & Rice, 1999). The point is that education production function research is not a panacea; its current utility is limited in scope to those factors that (1) can be specified and measured using this sort of framework, and (2) have consistently been found to be related to educational outcomes in one way or another. Future studies that synthesize what we know based on productivity studies could be instrumental in helping to make the findings of this tradition of research more useful to policy makers.

Knowledge about what falls inside/outside of this framework is also potentially useful in defining levels of decision making over education. For example, suppose we have clear and consistent findings that class size of 20 students or less is positively related to the reading achievement of low-income students in grades K-3. Information on the cost and effect of class size reduction policy could be compared with similar information on other policy alternatives (e.g., extended day program) to make efficiency-based judgments. In contrast, suppose no consistent relationship can be found between principal leadership style and student outcomes. Suppose further that, after careful consideration, researchers agree that this lack of consistency is not simply an artifact of data and methodological limitations. Rather, they argue, the impact of leadership style depends on a host of factors at the school, community, and personal levels and is not systematically linked with outcomes. This would suggest that principal leadership style should not, on efficiency grounds, be mandated by more central levels of authority.[14] The point here is that knowing more about the scope of the production function can have implications for the roles of different levels of administration. For example, more central-level administrators may want to exercise control over those inputs whose productivities are well understood. At the very least, they should have an interest in disseminating information about the relative productivities of those inputs to local decision makers. On the other hand, those matters that are not, by nature, systematically linked with education outcomes should be in the domain of more micro-levels (e.g., schools and classrooms).

Finally, normative judgments are part of any education policy decision. Education production function research provides no insight on normative matters. Rather, the production function paradigm is steeped in efficiency that is measured primarily in terms of student test scores. Policy makers must utilize other types of analysis that help them weigh competing values to balance efficiency with other sorts of social goods, such as equity and liberty. Normative analysis is also needed to mediate the priority that production function research gives to certain outcomes like student achievement and labor market success. These sorts of outcomes need to be balanced with studies that consider other educational goals like civic responsibility and cultural awareness.

This discussion suggests that the production function is a useful, but incomplete tool for education decision making. This argument has implications for research, including the use of less traditional methods from a variety of disciplines that examine input-output relationships, as well as for policy as we move into the 21st century. Education policies that assume the existence of a production function, or at least some regularity or predictability in the education process, should be tempered by the limits in our knowledge. We must identify and disseminate what we know with confidence, continue researching those matters about which we can learn more but have been thus far unable to secure consistent

---

14 However, one could imagine non-efficiency-based reasons for central levels to disallow some leadership styles (e.g., those relying on corporal punishment or mental abuse).

findings, and leave those matters that do not lend themselves to systematic relationships to more focused levels of decision making. By recognizing the limits of the education production function, it becomes an even more useful tool for informing education policy.

On a final note, as can be gleaned from the extensive citations, this chapter stands on the shoulders of scholars who have devoted decades to thinking about and studying the education production process. The work of Hanushek, Levin, Monk, and Murnane is particularly noteworthy. As we move ahead, attention to matters of education productivity will continue to build upon the progress already made. This overview of where we've been and where we're headed suggests that this is an important and evolving tradition of research. We continue to learn more about the productivity of various combinations of educational inputs, in part because the effort is growing more inclusive, recognizing the contributions of a variety of disciplines and the methods they use. This sort of broad-based investigation of the relationships between inputs and outcomes is the most promising direction for the future of this work.

REFERENCES

American Institutes for Research. (1999). *An educator's guide to schoolwide reform.* Arlington, VA: Education Research Service.

Becker, Gary S. (1976). *The economic approach to human behavior.* Chicago: The University of Chicago Press.

Bohrnstad, George W., Stecher, Brian M., & Wiley Edward W. (2000). The California class size reduction evaluations; Lessons learned. In Wang, M. L. and J. D. Finn (Eds.), *How small classes help teachers do their best.* Philadelphia, PA: Temple University Center for Research in Human Development and Education.

Brown, Byron W., & Saks, Daniel H. (1987). The micro-economics of the allocation of teachers' time and student learning. *Economics of Education Review,* 319–332.

Brown, Byron W., & Saks, Daniel H. (1986). Measuring the effects of instructional time on student learning. *American Journal of Education, 94,* 480–500.

Bryk, Anthony S., & Raudenbush, Stephen W. (1992). *Hierarchical linear models* (Newbury Park, CA: Sage.

Bryk, Anthony S., & Raudenbush, Stephen W. (1987). Applications of hierarchical linear models to assessing change. *Psychological Bulletin, 101* (1), 147–158.

Burkhead, J., Fox, Thomas G., & Holland, John W. (1967). *Input and output in large-city high schools.* Syracuse, NY: Syracuse University Press.

Burstein, Leigh, & Miller, M. David. (1981). Regression-based analysis of multilevel educational data. In Borsch, R. F., P. M. Wortman, D. S. Corday, et al. (Eds.), *Reanalyzing program evaluations.* San Francisco: Jossey-Bass.

Center for Research on Effective Schooling for Disadvantaged Students. (1992). *Information to schools considering the adoption of Success for All.* Baltimore: Center for Research on Effective Schooling for Disadvantaged Students.

Cohn, Elchanan, & Geske, Terry G. (1990). *The economics of education* (3rd ed.). Oxford: Pergamon.

Education Commission of the States. (1998). *Identifying effective models for comprehensive school reform*. Denver, CO: Education Commission of the States.

Educational Research Service, Inc. (1983). *Organization of the middle grades: A summary of research*. Arlington, VA: Educational Research Service.

Finn, Jeremy D., & Achilles, Charles M. (1999). Tennessee's class size study: Findings, implications, and misconceptions. *Educational Evaluation and Policy Analysis, 21* (2), 97–110.

Fowler, William J. (1993, April 2). *How important are school size effects on successful secondary school student outcomes?* Paper presented at the annual meeting of the American Educational Research Association, Atlanta, GA.

Gameron, Adam. (1992). Access to excellence: Assignment to honors English classes in the transition from middle to high school. *Educational Evaluation and Policy Analysis, 14* (3), 185–204.

Geary, Sue. (1988). *Class size: Issues and implications for policymaking in Utah*. An occasional policy paper sponsored by the FOCUS Project. Salt Lake City: University of Utah, Graduate School of Education.

Hanushek, Eric A. (1996a). Outcomes, costs and incentives in schools. In E. A. Hanushek and D. W. Jorgenson (Eds.), *Improving America's schools: The role of incentives* (pp. 29–52). Washington, DC: National Academy Press.

Hanushek, Eric A. (1996b). The quest for equalized mediocrity: School finance reform without consideration of school performance. In Picus, L., and J. Wattenbarger (Eds.), *Where does the money go? Resource allocation in elementary and secondary schools* (pp. 20–43). Thousand Oaks, CA: Corwin.

Hanushek, Eric A. (1986). The economics of schooling: Production and efficiency in the public schools. *Journal of Economic Literature, 24* (3), 1141–78.

Hanushek, Eric A. (1972). *Education and race: An analysis of the education production process*. Lexington, MA: Lexington Books.

Hanushek, Eric A. (1971). Teacher characteristics and gains in student achievement: Estimation using micro data. *American Economic Review, 61*, 280–288

Hanushek, Eric A. et al. (1994). *Making schools work: Improving performance and controlling cost*. Washington DC: Brookings Insitute.

Huttenlocher, Janellen, Haight, Wendy, Bryk, Anthony, Seltzer, Michael, & Lyons, Thomas. (1991). Early vocabulary growth: Relation to language input and gender. *Developmental Psychology, 27* (2), 236–248.

Jones, Lyle V. (1988). School achievement trends in mathematics and science, and what can be done to improve them. In E. Z. Rothkopf (Ed.), *Review of Research in Education* (vol. 15). Washington DC: American Education Research Association.

Kiesling, H. J. (1984). Assignment practices and the relationship of instructional time to the reading performance of elementary school children. *Economics of Education Review, 3,* 341–350.

King, Jennifer A. (1994). Meeting the educational needs of at-risk students: A cost analysis of three models. *Educational Evaluation and Policy Analysis, 16* (1), 1–19.

Kohut, Sylvester, Jr. (1988). *The middle school: A bridge between elementary and high schools* (2nd ed.). Washington, DC: National Education Association.

Krueger, Alan B. (1998, March). *Experimental estimates of education production functions,* Working paper #379. Princeton, NJ: Princeton University, Industrial Relations Section.

Lancy, D. (1983). *Cross-cultural studies in cognition and mathematics.* New York: Academic Press.

Lee, Valerie, & Bryk, Anthony S. (1989, July). A multi-level model of the social distribution of high school achievement. *Sociology of Education, 62,* 172–192.

Levin, Henry M. (1987). Accelerated schools for disadvantaged students. *Educational Leadership, 44* (6), 19–21.

Levin, Henry M. (1976). Concepts of economic efficiency and education production. In J. T. Froomkin, D. T. Jamison, and R. Radner (eds.), *Education as an industry.* Cambridge, MA: Ballinger.

Malen, Betty, Theobald, Neil, & Bardzell, Jeffrey. (2000). Achieving a "just balance" between local control of schools and state responsibility for K-12 education: Summary observations and research agenda. In Theobald, N. D., and B. Malen (Eds.), *Balancing local control and state responsibility for K-12 education* (pp. 313–332). Larchmont, NY: Eye On Education.

Molnar, Alex, Smith, Philip, Zahorki, John, Palmer, Amanda, Halbach, Anke, & Ehrle, Karen. (1999). Evaluating the SAGE program: A pilot program in targeted pupil-teacher reduction in Wisconsin, *Educational Evaluation and Policy Analysis, 21* (2), 165–178.

Monk, David H. (1994). Subject area preparation of secondary mathematics and science teachers and student achievement. *Economics of Education Review, 13* (2), 125–145.

Monk, David H. (1992). Educational productivity research: An update and assessment of its role in education finance reform. *Educational Evaluation and Policy Analysis, 14* (4), 307–332.

Monk, David H. (1990). *Education finance: An economic approach.* New York: McGraw Hill Publishing Company.

Monk, David H., & Jennifer King Rice. (1999). Modern education productivity research: Emerging implications for the financing of education. In W. Fowler (Ed.), *Selected Papers in School Finance, 1999* (pp. 111–139).Washington, DC: U.S. Department of Education, Office of Educational Research and Improvement.

Murnane, Richard J. (1981). Interpreting the evidence on school effectiveness. *Teachers College Record, 83* (1), 19–35.

Murnane, Richard J. (1975). *The impact of school resources on the learning of inner city children.* Cambridge, MA: Ballinger.

Nye, Barbara, Hedges, Larry V., & Konstantopoulos, Spyros. (1999). The long-term effects of small classes: A five-year follow-up of the tennessee class size experiment. *Educational Evaluation and Policy Analysis, 21* (2), 127–142.

Rice, Jennifer K. (1999). The impact of class size on instructional strategies and the use of time in high school mathematics and science courses. *Educational Evaluation and Policy Analysis, 21* (2), 215–130.

Rice, Jennifer K. (1995). *The effects of systemic transitions from middle to high school levels of education on student performance in mathematics and science: a longitudinal education production function analysis.* Unpublished dissertation, Cornell University.

Rice, Jennifer K., & Roellke, Christopher F. (1998, March 12–14). *The effects of block scheduled mathematics classes on student achievement and instructional practices: Some preliminary results.* Paper presented at the annual meeting of the American Education Finance Association, Mobile, AL.

Ross, S. M., Smith, L., Slavin, R. E., & Madden, N. A. (1997). Improving the academic success of disadvantaged children: An examination of Success for All. *Psychology in the Schools, 34* (2), 171–180

Stigler, James W., & Barnes, Ruth. (1988). Culture and mathematics learning. In E. Z. Rothkopf (Ed.), *Review of research in education* (vol. 15). Washington, DC: American Educational Research Association.

Summers, Anita A., & Wolfe, Barbara L. (1977). Do schools make a difference? *The American Economic Review, 67* (4), 639–652.

Taylor, William, & Piche, Dianne M. (1991). *Shortchanging children: The impact of fiscal inequity on the education of students at risk.* Report prepared for the Committee on Education and Labor, U.S. House of Representatives 102nd Congress, First Session.

Wehlage, Gary. (1991). School reform for at-risk students. *Equity and excellence, 25* (1), 15–24.

Willett, John B. (1988). Questions and answers in the measurement of change. In Rothkopf E. Z. (Ed.), *Review of research in education* (vol. 15). Washington, DC: American Education Research Association.

9

RESEARCH DIRECTIONS FOR UNDERSTANDING THE RELATIONSHIP OF EDUCATIONAL RESOURCES TO EDUCATIONAL OUTCOMES

David Grissmer
RAND

At the beginning of the new millennium, answers to the long running debate about whether additional educational resources can and have improved educational outcomes are increasingly being settled by new literature reviews, new experimental evidence, and reinterpretation of the historical trends linking changing educational resources to achievement. The counterintuitive view that "money doesn't matter" was supported primarily by one set of reviews of the nonexperimental literature, and by the apparent stability of historical achievement trends despite an apparent substantial infusion of educational resources. More recent evidence, however, from the experimental as well as the nonexperimental literature and from historical trend data appears to be converging on the hypothesis that certain kinds of targeted expenditures can raise achievement, particularly for disadvantaged students, but additional resources above current levels may not matter much for more advantaged students.

This chapter postulates that future research on this topic will be characterized by increasingly turning to experimentation, not only to provide "benchmark" results, but, perhaps more importantly, to test and improve our analysis of nonexperimental data. In the long run, we will be dependent primarily on nonexperimental analysis to guide educational policy, but major improvements are needed in specifications, assumptions, and in our understanding of bias in nonexperimental measurements before reliable results can be expected. Moreover, increasingly we need to develop theories of educational processes that explain *why resources affect outcomes.* In the end, theories that tell us how and why resources lead to better outcomes will provide the most compelling evidence.

This chapter provides a foundation for future analysis by tracing the changing debate about the effectiveness of additional resources in education, and about the effects of specific uses of resources on educational outcomes. This debate has mainly revolved around different interpretations from literature reviews of nonexperimental studies, and from different conclusions about how educational resources have changed nationally from 1970 to 1996 and whether these changes are reflected in achievement scores. However, future research must integrate the evidence from experimental data, explain why experimental and nonexperimental evidence differ, and build theories consistent with the empirical evidence that explain why resources affect achievement.

EVIDENCE FROM NATIONAL EDUCATIONAL RESOURCE GROWTH AND ACHIEVEMENT TRENDS

Measured in constant dollars using the Consumer Price Index (CPI) to adjust for inflation, real expenditures per pupil doubled between the late 1960s and the early 1990s. Hanushek (1994, 1996a, 1999) cites an apparent lack of achievement gains in this period as support for the ineffectiveness of additional resources. The most visible measure of achievement, SAT scores, declined in this period. While SAT scores can be easily discounted as valid measures of school achievement trends because of self-selection, Hanushek also cites NAEP scores of representative samples of 9-, 13-, and 17-year-old students as showing no clear positive trends.[1]

Other studies, however, provide a different interpretation of this evidence (Rothstein & Miles, 1995; Ladd, 1996a). Rothstein and Miles (1995), for example, suggest that using the CPI to adjust educational expenditures overstates their growth rate because education is highly labor intensive. Use of more appropriate price indices for adjustment of educational expenditures would indicate much lower estimates of real growth—approximately 60 percent rather than 100 percent from 1967 to 1992.

Even this smaller real increase appears to overestimate the additional resources available to boost achievement scores. A significant part of the smaller estimated increase went for students with disabilities, many of whom are not tested.[2] Some resources also went for other socially desirable objectives that are

---

1 See Grissmer et al. (1994) and Grissmer (forthcoming) for comparisons of SAT and NAEP scores and discussions of the flaws in the SAT scores.

2 There is agreement that a disproportionate fraction of the expenditure increase during the NAEP period was directed toward special education (Lankford & Wyckoff, 1996; Hanuskek & Rivkin, 1997). Hanushek and Rivkin estimate that about a third of the increase between 1980 and 1990 was related to special education. NAEP typically excludes about 5 percent of all students, mostly special education students. However, special education counts increased from about 8 percent of all public school students in 1976–77 to about 12 percent in 1993–94. These figures imply that 7 percent of students taking the NAEP tests were receiving special education resources in 1994, compared to 3 percent in 1976–77. This percentage is too small to have much effect on NAEP trends.

only indirectly related to academic achievement. However, taking into account better cost indices and including only spending judged to have been directed at increasing achievement scores for tested students, Rothstein and Miles (1995) concluded that the actual increase in real per-pupil spending available for improving achievement was approximately 35 percent over the period, rather than 100 percent.

This increase was disproportionately spent on compensatory programs directed toward minority and lower income students, or to programs that might have disproportionate effects on their scores (Rothstein & Miles, 1995). In addition, pupil-teacher ratios were significantly reduced nationwide in this period, and experimental evidence now suggests that achievement for minority and low income students is affected to a greater extent from such reductions than for other student groups (Finn & Achilles, 1999; Krueger, 1999a). Hence, if resources matter, then their effects on outcomes should be disproportionately seen in the scores of minority and lower income students.

Aggregate NAEP scores show small to modest gains from 1971 to 1996. Gains occurred in all three NAEP-tested subject areas (math, reading, and science) for 9- and 13-year-old students, and in math and reading for 17-year-old students (Digest of Educational Statistics, 1998). Only science scores for 17-year-old students show declines. The science and reading gains were small—approximately 0.10 standard deviation (three percentile points) or less for all age groups. However, math gains were larger for 9- and 13-year-old students—between 0.20 and 0.30 standard deviations. However, these aggregate results mask important differences by racial/ethnic groups.

During this period, substantial gains occurred for both Hispanic and black students and for lower scoring white students (Hauser, 1998; Grissmer et al., 1994; Grissmer et al., 1998a; Grissmer et al., 1998b; Hedges & Nowell, 1998). For instance, black gains between 0.30 and 0.80 standard deviations occurred for almost all subjects for each age group. Hispanic gains were also much larger than white gains. NAEP scores show flat or minor gains only for white students not classified as disadvantaged, who comprise the majority of students.

Analysis of the cause of these gains suggests that changes in family characteristics could explain the smaller white score gains, but could not explain most of the large minority gains (Grissmer et al., 1994; Cook & Evans, 1997; Grissmer et al., 1998b; Hedges & Nowell, 1998). Grissmer et al. (1998b) suggest that the timing and regional pattern of black score gains in the 1970s and 1980s are consistent with two explanations: changes in schools, such as falling pupil-teacher ratios and desegregation, and/or changing attitudes and motivations of black parents and students and their teachers. This shift in motivation and teacher attitudes might be expected with the expanding economic and educational opportunity for blacks arising from the implementation of civil rights, affirmative action, and war on poverty programs. Such a shift could have significantly altered the schooling experience for black students.

Pupil-teacher ratios fell nationally in this period of rising minority NAEP scores by approximately 8 students per teacher—a decline similar to reductions seen in the Tennessee experiment on class size, discussed below.[3] The national black score gains that would be predicted by the Tennessee experimental results are not inconsistent with explaining part of these national gains (Krueger, 1998; Grissmer et al., 1998b; Ferguson, 1998a).[4] This evidence suggests an alternative explanation to Hanushek's; namely, that additional resources matter more for minority and disadvantaged students, but may matter much less, if at all, for more advantaged families (Grissmer et al., 1998b; Grissmer et al., 1998c).

CHANGING INTERPRETATIONS FROM REVIEWS OF NONEXPERIMENTAL STUDIES

As noted, until the early 1990s, the empirical evidence was widely interpreted as showing that providing schools with additional resources would have little impact on student achievement, the so-called "money doesn't matter" thesis. This counterintuitive view dated from the "Coleman Report" that found family influences strong and school resources weak in explaining achievement differences across schools (Coleman et al., 1966).

Influential reviews by Eric Hanushek (1986, 1989, 1994) argued that evidence from the literature published prior to approximately 1990 provided no strong or systematic relationship between school expenditures and student performance. The reviews found that only a small proportion of previous studies had statistically significant results indicating a positive effect of resources. It was suggested that a reason for this was the lack of appropriate incentives within the public education system to utilize resources effectively and efficiently (Hanushek & Jorgenson, 1996; Hanushek, 1994; Hanushek, 1996b). This conclusion implied that the measurements reflected real differences in the effectiveness of resources across schools and school districts, rather than flaws in the measurement process itself.

Subsequent literature reviews questioned the criteria to choose studies for inclusion used in these reviews, and the decision to assign equal weight to all measurements from the included studies. Two subsequent literature reviews used the same studies as Hanushek did, but came to different conclusions. One study used meta-analytic statistical techniques for combining data that do not weigh each measurement equally (Hedges et al., 1994). Explicit statistical tests were made to see if the mean coefficients of resource variables are in fact positively related to achievement. The results concluded that for most resource variables, a positive relationship between resources and outcomes was supported. In particular, per-pupil expenditures and teacher experience provided the most consistent positive effects, with pupil-teacher ratios, teacher salaries, and teacher education having much weaker effects.

---

3 There is some evidence, however, that actual class size may not have declined in proportion with pupil/teacher ratio (Boozer et al., 1992). We also do not know whether class size differentially changed for black and white students.

4 Further research is needed on the NAEP trends to better determine the role of reduced class size and other changing factors that could have impacted minority and white scores. For instance, the Tennessee results seem to predict higher white gains than can be attributed to nonfamily factors (Grissmer et al., 1998b).

A more recent literature review using the same studies as Hanushek also concludes that a positive relationship exists between resources and outcomes (Krueger, 1999b). This review criticizes the inclusion and equal weighting of multiple measurements from single published studies, given that some studies provided as many as 24 separate measurements. Because many of these measurements simply divided the sample into subgroups, the average sample size for measurements will decline. As sample size declines, the statistical power to detect policy-significant effects also declines, and thus many insignificant relationships might be expected. Because the presentation of results for subgroups is not done uniformly across studies, some studies will effectively receive more weight. Krueger (1999b) reanalyzes the studies and concludes that the inclusion of equally weighted multiple measurements is a significant factor in explaining the original conclusions, and that less weight placed on these multiple measurements would lead to support for a positive relationship between resources and outcomes.

Another more comprehensive review of the literature prior to 1990 used meta-analytic statistical comparison techniques, but searched a wider literature than Hanushek, and imposed different quality controls (Greenwald et al., 1996). In this review, all studies used achievement as the dependent variable and measurements only at the individual or school level. The resulting set of measurements utilized in the study included many not included in Hanushek's studies, and rejected about two-thirds of measurements included in Hanushek's reviews. Thus, using better screening criteria and statistical tests than previous studies, this review supported the hypothesis that median coefficients were positively related to resources for six resource variables (per-pupil expenditure, teacher ability, teacher education, teacher experience, teacher-pupil ratio, school size). However, there was large variance in coefficients for each variable across the included studies, possibly due to extreme outliers, alternate specifications, or the presence of differential bias.[5]

These large variances and the sensitivity of the median coefficients to which set of studies were included provided little confidence, though, that the literature could be used to estimate reliable coefficients. In particular, models thought to have superior specifications provided no more-consistent results, and sometimes

---

5   This review also reported results for measurements using different model specifications (longitudinal, quasi-longitudinal, and cross-sectional). Longitudinal studies were defined as those having a pretest control score, and quasi-longitudinal defined as having some earlier performance based measure as a control. Cross sectional studies merely had SES type variables included as controls. The results showed that median coefficients changed dramatically for most variables across specifications, with no recognizable pattern. Although few studies had what were considered to have superior specification (longitudinal studies), the median coefficients for these models were negative for per-pupil expenditure, teacher education, teacher-pupil ratio, and school size. When the median coefficients of studies having quasi-longitudinal studies were compared to coefficients from the entire sample, results were similar for four variables, but differed for the remaining two variables by factors ranging from 2 to 20.

provided untrustworthy estimates. While some recent studies using better and more current data did show positive effects from resources (Ferguson, 1991; Ferguson and Ladd, 1996; Raudenbush, 2000), newer reviews by Hanushek (1996a, 1999) that included more recent studies (over 90 studies and about 300 measurements) still showed similarly inconsistent results when results are equally weighted. Further, two books published in 1996 addressing the questions of the effect of school resources on both short-term educational outcomes and longer-term labor force outcomes were also unable to reconcile the apparent diverse results from the literature (Ladd, 1996b; Burtless, 1996). While unable to explain the diverse results, these works focused attention on more specific and testable questions ("which uses of money matters"), and on the critical methodological assumptions underlying much of the literature.

Hanushek's newer reviews also attempted to determine if results differed when studies were grouped according to achievement outcomes, model specifications, grade level, and level of aggregation. Studies focusing on achievement showed no evidence of consistent effect, whether focusing on secondary or elementary levels or when using the "best" specification (production functions with pre- and post-test data). However, the level of aggregation did show a marked difference in the pattern of results.

Figure 9.1 summarizes the results of previous measurements by level of aggregation for the two reported input variables: per-pupil expenditures and teacher-pupil ratio (Hanushek et al., 1996). The data show that the percentages of both positive, and positive and significant coefficients increase with level of aggregation, but shift dramatically upward at the state level. Almost all coefficients are positive at the state level, and about two-thirds are positive and statistically significant, compared to less than 20 percent at the school/classroom level. These data are particularly surprising because sample sizes of studies are much smaller at the state level.

The presumption among researchers has usually been that data at lower levels of aggregation provide superior estimates, whereas results at higher levels of aggregation are more prone to bias (Bryk & Raudenbush 1988; Greenwald et al., 1996; Hanushek et al., 1996). Thus, the explanation of these results has generally been that aggregate measurements have an unidentified, upward bias. One analysis has suggested that the source of this bias is unobserved variables at the state level that are positively correlated with observed state-level variables (Hanushek et al., 1996). The unobserved variables suggested involve regulation of schools and teachers, but no empirical support is provided that these variables have significant effects.[6]

---

6   This analysis maintains that resource variables at the state level have little effect, but positively correlated regulatory variables have strong, significant effects. Given that both state resource and regulatory policies arise from a somewhat similar political process, it is hard to see how one set of policies could be effective and the other not. There is also little empirical evidence to suggest a strong effect for regulatory policies in effect during the period of previous measurements. Recent research has suggested that one area of state regulation—teacher certification—has no effect on achievement, leading some to suggest a deregulation of

FIGURE 9.1. PERCENTAGE OF SELECTED INPUT VARIABLE COEFFICIENTS FROM PREVIOUS STUDIES WITH POSITIVE OR POSITIVE AND STATISTICALLY SIGNIFICANT SIGNS ON OUTCOME MEASURES BY VARIOUS AGGREGATION LEVELS

Aggregation level	All Educational Outcomes				Achievement Only	
	Per-pupil expenditures		Teacher-pupil ratio		Per-pupil expenditures	
	Percent positive	Percent positive and significant	Percent positive	Percent positive and significant	Percent positive	Percent positive and significant
School/Class	63.4	16.2	45.2	10.8	61.0	17.8
District	65.1	25.1	61.6	19.3	61.4	24.7
State	96.0	64.0	91.0	64.0	88.0	75.0

SOURCE: Data taken from Hanushek et al. (1996).

THE ROLE OF EXPERIMENTATION IN IMPROVING NONEXPERIMENTAL MEASUREMENTS

While reviews of past studies would now support a conclusion that a generally positive relationship exists between resources and achievement, the results are so inconsistent and unstable that no reliable estimates are available to guide policy in the future. The source of this instability may be in the actual differences in effects across schools and school districts or from flaws in the measurement process. Ferguson and Ladd (1996) and Heckman et al. (1996) direct attention to the number and fragility of assumptions underlying model specification and estimation, implying that a key source of variation across previous studies might come from differences in model specifications, estimation and assumptions, and/or differential bias in measurements, rather than real differences in resource effectiveness. These differences make previous studies incomparable.

The question needing an answer is how results compare if previous studies used similar specifications and assumptions while focusing analysis on similar types of students at similar grade levels. If such a study could be carried out, it would not be surprising to see more-consistent results emerge from past measurements. However, this still leaves the question of what specification should be used in such an exercise.

There is no agreement among researchers concerning specification and estimation methods, or about the extent of bias across different measurements. Production function approaches have received much support, especially when used at lower levels of aggregation (Greenwald et al., 1996; Meyer, 1996; Hanushek et

---

teacher certification (Goldhaber & Brewer, 1999; Kanstoroom & Finn, 1999).

al., 1996). Others have suggested that hierarchical linear models (HLM) that incorporate data from several levels of aggregation (individual, class, school, district) come closest to producing unbiased results (Bryk & Raudenbush, 1988). Longitudinal data that would support modeling of achievement growth, rather than depend on cross sectional differences, has also been suggested. Singer (1998) has suggested that there may be far less difference in these approaches than commonly believed.

One consensus that seems to exist is that regardless of the specific specification and estimation techniques used, measurements at lower levels of aggregation always dominate measurements at higher levels of aggregation. Partly, this preference arises because individual-level data are usually collected with special surveys, allowing a more diverse set of variables, usually having much larger sample sizes and wider variance in both independent and dependent variables. But this preference does not address the possibility that some forms of bias may be greater for less-aggregate measurements. For example, the larger sample sizes usually present with data at lower levels of aggregation cannot compensate for bias. Thus, it is possible that more-aggregate measurements, even with significantly smaller sample sizes, may produce more accurate measurements than analysis with individual-level data with significantly larger sample sizes.

A possible alternate explanation of the difference in effect-sizes at different levels of aggregation in the nonexperimental literature is that measurements at lower levels of aggregation are biased downward, in contrast to more-aggregate measurements, which are biased upward. However, distinguishing between these hypotheses requires benchmark or "gold standard" measurements that establish whether more- or less-aggregate measurements are accurate. Such benchmark measurements can only come from expanding experimental or quasi-experimental measurements in the future.

The argument presented here is that well-designed, implemented, and analyzed experimental data that can be replicated remain as close as one can come to causal evidence in social science. The basic premise of experimentation—choosing two groups of subjects through randomization or preselection, such that the only difference between them is the variable of interest—remains the ideal method of building social science knowledge. However, while experiments are potentially capable of providing the most compelling evidence, they can fall far short of achieving this objective (Boruch, 1994; Heckman & Smith, 1995; Manski, 1996). To be effective in guiding future policy and research, experimentation needs to be carefully planned, implemented, and analytically tested to determine if inevitable flaws undermine the results.

EXPERIMENTAL DATA ON CLASS SIZE

The first experimental evidence on the effect of major educational variables came from a Tennessee study on the effects of class size (Word et al., 1990; Finn & Achilles, 1990; Mosteller, 1995). About 79 schools in Tennessee randomly assigned about 6,000 kindergarten students to class sizes of approximately 15 or 23 students, and largely maintained these class sizes through the third grade. Additional students entering grades 1 to 3 were also randomly assigned to these classes, making the entire experimental sample approximately 12,000. After grade 3, all students were returned to standard, large size classes through grade

8. The students in the experiment were disproportionately minority and disadvantaged, with 33 percent minority and over 50 percent eligible for free lunches.

Analysis of the experimental data shows statistically significant, positive effects from smaller classes at the end of each grade from kindergarten through grade 8 in every subject tested (Finn & Achilles, 1999; Krueger, 1999a; Nye et al., 1999a; Nye et al., 1999b). The magnitude of results varies depending on student characteristics and the number of grades in small classes. Results at third grade show students who were in small classes all four years have higher achievement of from 0.25 to 0.4 standard deviations (Krueger, 1999a; Nye at al., 1999). Current measurement of the long term effects at grade 8 show sustained effects at similar levels as at the third grade for those having three or four years in small classes, but little sustained effect for those in smaller classes one or two years (Nye et al., 1999a). Short-term effects are significantly larger for black students, and somewhat larger for those receiving free lunches.[7]

However, questions were raised whether the inevitable departures from experimental design that occur in implementing the experiment biased the results (Krueger, 1999a; Hanushek, 1999). These problems included attrition from the samples, leakage of students between small and large classes, possible nonrandomness of teacher assignments, and schooling effects. Subsequent analysis has addressed these problems without finding any significant bias in the results (Krueger, 1999a; Nye et al., 1999a; Nye et al., 1999b, Grissmer, 1999). It is possible for further analysis to find a flaw in the experiment that significantly affects the results, but extensive analysis to date has eliminated most of the potential problems.

Another quasi-experimental study on class size, the Wisconsin SAGE study, differed in several important ways from the Tennessee STAR experiment (Molnar et al., 1999). In the SAGE study, only schools with very high proportions of free-lunch students were eligible for inclusion. Assignments were not randomized within schools, but rather a preselected control group of students from different schools was matched as a group to the students in treatment schools. The treatment is characterized as pupil/teacher ratio reduction rather than class size, because a significant number of schools chose two teachers in a large class rather than one teacher in a small class. The size of the reduction in the pupil/teacher ratio was slightly larger than class size reductions in Tennessee.

There were about 1,600 students in the small pupil/teacher treatment group in Wisconsin, compared to approximately 2,000 students in small classes in Tennessee. However, the size of control groups differed markedly, with approximately 1,300 students in Wisconsin and around 4,000 in Tennessee, if both regular classes and regular classes with teacher aides are combined. The SAGE sam-

---

7 Long-term effects have not been reported by student characteristics. Following the experiment, Tennessee also cut class sizes to about 14 students per class in 17 school districts with the lowest family income. Comparisons with other districts and within districts before and after the change showed even larger gains of 0.35 to 0.5 standard deviations (Word et al., 1994; Mosteller, 1995). Thus, the evidence here suggests that class-size effects may grow for the most disadvantaged students.

ple had approximately 50 percent minority students, with almost 70 percent eligible for free or reduced price lunches.

The results from the Wisconsin study for two consecutive first grade classes show statistically significant effects on achievement in all subjects (Molnar et al., 1999). The effect sizes in the first grade are in the range of 0.1–0.3 standard deviations.[8] While the estimates seem consistent with the Tennessee study at first grade, more analysis is needed before the results can be compared.

DERIVING SPECIFICATION IMPLICATIONS
FROM EXPERIMENTAL STUDIES

The main value of good experimental data is generally seen as providing benchmark measurements for the effects of given variables. However, experimental data can serve a far broader, and perhaps more important purpose, that of testing assumptions, bias, and specifications used with nonexperimental data.

The results from experimental data on class size are more consistent with nonexperimental studies at the state level than the studies using less-aggregate data. This consistency at the state level may suggest that state-level measurements are not biased, and that measurements at less-aggregate levels are biased downward. We suggest below that the Tennessee experimental data point to flaws in model specification that would introduce more bias into individual level than state-level measurements with nonexperimental data. Grissmer et al. (2000) also discuss other forms of bias known to be present in educational data that can plausibly produce greater bias in less-aggregate measurements.

The Tennessee results suggest several specification implications. First, schooling variables in one grade can influence achievement at *all* later grades, so conditions in all previous years of schooling need to be present in specifications. Second, a pretest score cannot control for previous schooling characteristics. The Tennessee results suggest that two students can have similar pretest scores and similar schooling conditions during a grade and emerge with different post-test grades influenced by different earlier schooling conditions. For instance, despite having similar schooling conditions in grades 4 to 8, relative changes in achievement occurring in those grades might differ for those having one to two or three to four years in small classes during grades K-3. Another way of stating this analytically is that effect sizes at a given grade can depend on interactions between this year's schooling characteristics and all previous characteristics.

The production function framework using pretest controls assumes that any differences in pre- and post-tests are captured by changed inputs during the period. The Tennessee results suggest that coefficients of such specifications are *not interpretable from a policy perspective* because the effect of a change in resources during a period cannot fully be known until past and future schooling conditions are specified. Thus the answer to the question of whether a smaller class size in second grade had an effect cannot be known until later grades, and the answer will depend on what class sizes were in previous and higher grades.

---

8 The lower estimates between 0.1–0.2 occur in regression estimates, while the raw effects and hierarchical linear modeling (HLM) estimates are in the 0.2–0.3 range.

Conceptually this makes the effect of class-size reductions resemble a human "capital" input that can change output over all future periods, and models specifying the effects of capital investments may be more appropriate. Production functions generally assume constant levels of capital, but children's human "capital" is probably constantly changing and growing.

From the standpoint of child development, these results are consistent with the concepts of risk and resiliency in children (Masten, 1994; Rutter, 1988). Children carry different levels of risk and resiliency into a given grade that appear to interact with the schooling conditions in that grade to produce gains or losses. For instance, four years of small classes appear to provide resiliency against later larger class sizes, whereas one or two years do not.

Among commonly used model specification, cross-sectional models that incorporate all previous year's schooling characteristics come closest to being able to estimate the Tennessee results at each grade. Use of a simple average class size in all previous years would be able to estimate with reasonable accuracy the Tennessee effects at the fourth and eighth grades for students with different numbers of years in small classes.

Few, if any previous studies have included variables for elementary school characteristics in prior years. At the individual level, virtually no longitudinal data from kindergarten were available. At more-aggregate district and state levels, data are usually available describing average characteristics for earlier years, but were probably seldom used.

RECONCILING EXPERIMENTAL AND NONEXPERIMENTAL RESULTS

Grissmer and Flanagan (2000) and Grissmer (1999) have suggested that the issue of future model specification and estimation for nonexperimental studies must be addressed through three approaches that could eventually generate scientific consensus, or the "gold standard" model. They are:

1. Focusing on empirical research that can validate or invalidate the assumptions underlying model specifications with nonexperimental data

2. Directing research toward understanding *why* changes in resources affect achievement and developing theories of educational processes

3. Using experimentation and the resulting data to test specifications and assumptions used with nonexperimental data

Heckman et al. (1996) provide an example of testing assumptions underlying model specifications. It is possible to undertake a wide range of research directed toward verifying assumptions made in nonexperimental educational analysis. For example: Why do students in large and small classes have different characteristics? How important are parent and teacher selection processes in determining class size? Do more-senior teachers choose smaller classes? Are assumptions more valid in some kinds of schools than in others? Are class sizes in rural areas mainly randomly determined, whereas more selection occurs in cities? There are many empirical approaches to address these kinds of questions that would give us a better idea whether assumptions made in specifications are reasonable.

The second approach is to examine the assumptions made in nonexperimental specifications. Such assumptions include production functions concerning the nature of the mechanism inside the classroom that produces achievement effects. Previous studies have generally treated the classroom as a black box, and regarded the transforming processes inside as unnecessary to understand to measure accurate effects. Grissmer (1999) suggests that it may be an understanding of these processes that will guide the search for better specifications and assumptions to obtain accurate measurements in the future.

For example, we need to understand why changes in variables such as class size cause achievement gains. An understanding of what changes inside classrooms when class size is reduced, and how these changes cause short- and long-term achievement gains can inform the model specification process. Some studies have suggested that teachers have more instructional time in small classes due to less time spent in discipline and administrative tasks, and that teachers shift to more individualized instruction in small classes (Molnar et al., 1999; Betts & Shkolnik, 1999; Shkolnik & Betts, 1999; Rice 1999). Students also exhibit more on-task behavior in such classes, which continues even after being returned to larger classes in later grades (Finn & Achilles, 1999). Such shifts appear to be more dramatic in classes with more-disadvantaged students.

Such research can lead to development of theories that explain why achievement might increase in small classes based on changed teacher and student behavior and the developmental path of students. For instance, Betts and Shkolnick (1999) and Shkolnik and Betts (1999) develop an economic framework for teacher time allocation in classes and its relationship with achievement. Grissmer (1999) suggests an expanded theory that includes the substitution of parental individual time for teacher individual time in the classroom, leading to different time allocation and styles of teaching in classes where students have high or low levels of parental support. This type of analysis can suggest what variables should be in specifications and how they should be specified. It can also suggest interactions that need to be present in specifications.

Finally, experimental data can be designed to test the assumptions inherent in nonexperimental analysis. The Tennessee experiment, although not by design, has provided such information. In the long run, confidence in nonexperimental analysis is still needed for policy guidance, because there will be only a limited number of experiments possible, and contextual effects will be important influences in education limiting the generalizability of experimental results.

CONCLUSION

The key questions that future research on the relationship between educational resources and outcomes must answer include:

- ◆ Why are results from nonexperimental studies so inconsistent, and how can the variance be narrowed?
- ◆ Do experimental and nonexperimental measurements agree?

◆ If experimental and nonexperimental do not agree, what is the source of the disagreement?

◆ What theories of educational processes explain the pattern of experimental and nonexperimental measurements?

Although the evidence from literature reviews, experimental measurements, and historical trends in resources and achievement now tend to be more consistent with the hypothesis that additional resources matter most for disadvantaged students, the inconsistency of nonexperimental measurements still prevents accurate estimation of the size of such effects. A good part of the variation in nonexperimental measurements may be due to different specifications, assumptions, context, student populations, and sources of bias across measurements. Future research directed toward sorting out the precise source of the variance is needed.

Once the source of such variance is understood, it will be possible to compare experimental and nonexperimental measurements. Even with reduced variance in nonexperimental measurements, it is possible for well-done experimental and nonexperimental measurements to differ due to misspecification and bias in nonexperimental studies. Appropriately designed experimental data can help to identify the source of these misspecifications.

Future experimentation needs to be directed toward establishing benchmark measurements for major resource variables such as teacher salary, class size at all grades, teacher professional development, and preschool, summer school and after-school programs. However, the design of such experimentation should also be directed to discovering the source of differences between experimental and nonexperimental measurements.

Once experimental and nonexperimental measurements can be made to agree, or at least the sources of the differences are known, then theories need to be developed that explain how or why resources affect achievement. Such theories need to explain what changes in the classroom when resources are changed, and how those changes affect achievement for particular types of students. In the end, resource effects can be predicted from theories, and it is the theories that generate scientific and policy consensus.

REFERENCES

Betts, Julian, & Shkolnik, J. (1999, Summer). Estimated effects of class size on teacher time allocation in middle and high school math classes. *Educational Evaluation and Policy Analysis, 20* (2).

Boozer, Michael A., Krueger, A., & Wolkon, S. (1992). *Race and school quality since Brown v. Board of Education.* Washington, DC: Brookings Papers on Economic Activity (Microeconomic) 269–326.

Boruch, R. F. (1994). *Randomized experiments for planning and evaluation.* Thousand Oaks, CA: Sage Publications.

Bryk, Anthony S., & Raudenbush, S. (1988, November). Toward a more appropriate conceptualization of research on school effects: A three-level hierarchical linear model. *American Journal of Education.*

Burtless, Gary. (1966). *Does money matter?* Washington, DC: The Brookings Institution.

Coleman, James S., Campbell, Ernest Q., Hobson, Carol J., McPartland, James, Mood, Alexander M., Weinfeld, Frederic D., & York, Robert L. (1966). *Equality of educational opportunity*. Washington, DC: U.S. Government Printing Office.

Cook, Michael, & Evans, William N. (1997). Families or schools? Explaining the convergence in white and black academic performance. Working paper.

Digest of Educational Statistics. (1995). National Center for Educational Statistics, NCES 1995-036, Washington, DC: U.S. Department of Education.

Ferguson, Ronald F. (1998). Can schools narrow the black-white score gap. In C. Jencks & M. Phillips (Eds.), *The black-white test score gap*. Washington, DC: The Brookings Institution.

Ferguson, Ronald F. (1991). Paying for public education: New evidence on how and why money matters. *Harvard Journal on Legislation, 28,* 465–497.

Ferguson, Ronald F., & Ladd, Helen F. (1996). How and why money matters: An analysis of Alabama schools. In Helen F. Ladd (Ed.), *Holding schools accountable*. Washington, DC: The Brookings Institution.

Finn, Jeremy D., & Achilles, Charles. (1999, Summer). Tennessee's class size study: Findings, implications and misconceptions. *Educational Evaluation and Policy Analysis, 20* (2).

Finn, Jeremy D., & Achilles, Charles M. (1990, Fall). Answers and questions about class size: A statewide experiment. *American Educational Research Journal, 27* (3), 557–577.

Greenwald, Rob, Hedges, L. V., and Laine, R. (1996, Fall). The effect of school resources on student achievement. *Review of Educational Research, 66* (3), 361–396.

Grissmer, David. (forthcoming). The use and misuse of SAT scores. *Journal of Psychology, Law and Public Policy.*

Grissmer, David W., & Flanagan, Ann. (2000). Moving educational research toward scientific consensus. In David Grissmer & Michael Ross (Eds.), *Analytic issues in analytic issues in the assessment of student achievement*. Washington, DC: National Center for Educational Statistics, Department of Education.

Grissmer, David, Flanagan, A., Kawata, J., & Williamson, S. (2000). *Improving student achievement: What do state NAEP scores tell us?* Santa Monica CA: RAND (MR-924).

Grissmer, David. (1999, Summer). Assessing the evidence on class size: Policy implications and future research agenda. *Educational Evaluation and Policy Analysis, Summer, 20* (2).

Grissmer, David, Williamson, S., Kirby, S. N., & Berends, M.. (1998a). Exploring the rapid rise in black achievement scores in the United States (1970–1990). In

U. Neisser (Ed.), *The rising curve: Long-term changes in IQ and related measures.* Washington, DC: American Psychological Association.

Grissmer, David, Flanagan, A., & Williamson, S. (1998b). Why did black test scores rise rapidly in the 1970s and 1980s? In C. Jencks & M. Phillips (Eds.), *The black-white test score gap.* Washington, DC: The Brookings Institution.

Grissmer, David, Flanagan, A., & Williamson, S. (1998c). Does money matter for minority and disadvantaged students? Assessing the new empirical evidence. In William Fowler (Ed.), *Developments in school finance: 1997.* Washington, DC: U.S. Department of Education, NCES 98-212.

Grissmer, D. W., Kirby, S. N., Berends, M., & Williamson, S. (1994). *Student achievement and the changing American family.* Santa Monica, CA: RAND.

Hanushek, E. A. (1999, Summer). Assessing the empirical evidence on class size reductions from Tennessee and non-experimental research. *Educational Evaluation and Policy Analysis, 20* (2).

Hanushek, E. A. (1996a). School resources and student performance. In G. Burtless (Ed.), *Does money matter? The effect of school resources on student achievement and adult success.* Washington, DC: The Brookings Institution.

Hanushek, E. A. (1996b). Outcomes, costs and incentives in schools. In Eric Hanushek & Dale Jorgenson (Eds.), *Improving America's schools: The role of incentives.* Washington DC: National Academy Press.

Hanushek, E. A. (1994). *Making schools work: Improving performance and controlling costs.* Washington, DC: The Brookings Institution.

Hanushek, E. A. (1989). The impact of differential expenditures on school performance. *Educational Researcher, 18* (4), 45–51.

Hanushek, E. A. (1986). The economics of schooling: Production and efficiency in public schools. *Journal of Economic Literature, 24,* 1141–76.

Hanushek, E. A., & Jorgenson, Dale. (1996). Improving America's schools: The role of incentives. Washington, DC: National Academy Press.

Hanuskek, E. A., & Rivkin, Steven G. (1997, Winter). Understanding the twentieth-century growth in U.S. school spending. *Journal of Human Resources, 32* (1).

Hanushek, E. A., Rivkin, Steven G., & Taylor, Lori L. (1996, Fall). Aggregation and the estimated effects of school resources. *The Review of Economics and Statistics,* 611–627.

Hauser, R. M. (1998). Trends in black-white test score differentials: Uses and misuses of NAEP/SAT data. In U. Neisser (Ed.), The rising curve: Long-term changes in IQ and related measures. Washington, DC: American Psychological Association.

Heckman, James, Layne-Farrar, A., & Todd, P. (1996). Does measured school quality really matter? In Helen Ladd (Ed.), *Does Money Matter?* Washington, DC: The Brookings Insitution.

Heckman, J. J., & Smith, J. (1995, Spring). Assessing the case for social experiments. *Journal of Economic Perspectives, 9* (2).

Hedges, Larry V., Laine, Richard D., & Greenwald, Rob. (1994). Does Monday matter: Meta-analysis of studies of the effects of differential school inputs on student outcomes. *Educational Researcher, 23*, (3) 5–14.

Hedges, Larry V., & Nowell, Amy. (1998). Group differences in mental test scores: Mean differences variability, and talent. In C. Jencks & M. Phillips (Eds.), *The black-white test score gap*. Washington, DC: The Brookings Institution.

Krueger, Alan B. (1999a). Experimental estimates of education production functions. *Quarterly Journal of Economics, 114*, 497–532.

Krueger, Alan B. (1999b). *An economist view of class size reductions*. Mimeo, Princeton University.

Krueger, Alan B. (1998, March). Reassessing the view that american schools are broken, *Economic Policy Review*, 29–43.

Ladd, Helen F. (1996a). Introduction. In H. F. Ladd (Ed.), Holding schools accountable. Washington, DC: The Brookings Institution.

Ladd, Helen F., ed. (1996b). *Holding schools accountable*. Washington, DC: The Brookings Institution.

Lankford, Hamilton, & Wyckoff, James. (1996). The allocation of resources to special education and regular instruction. In Helen F. Ladd (Ed.), Holding schools accountable. Washington, DC: The Brookings Institution.

Manski, C. F. (1996). Learning about treatment effects from experiments with random assignment of treatments. *Journal of Human Resources, 31* (4), 709–733.

Masten, A. S. (1994). Resilience in individual development: Successful adaptation despite risk and adversity. In M. C. Wang & E. W. Gordon (Eds.), *Educational resilience in inner city america: Challenges and prospects*. Hillsdale: Lawrence Erbblaum Associates.

Meyer, Robert H. (1996). Value-added indicators of school performance. In Eric Hanushek & Dale Jorgenson (Eds.), *Improving America's schools: The role of incentives*. Washington, DC: National Academy Press.

Molnar, Alex et al. (1999, Summer). Estimated achievement and teacher time allocation effects from a quasi-experimental class size reduction in Wisconsin. *Educational Evaluation and Policy Analysis, 20* (2).

Mosteller, F. (1995). The Tennessee study of class size in the early school grades. *The Future of Children*, 5 (2), 113–127,

Nye, Barbara A., Hedges, Larry, & Konstantopoulos, Spyros. (1999a). The effects of small class size on academic achievement: The results of the Tennessee class size experiment. Manuscript under review, Department of Education, University of Chicago.

Nye, Barbara A., Hedges, Larry, & Konstantopoulos, Spyros. (1999b, Summer). The long term effects of small classes: A five-year follow-up of the Tennessee class size experiment. *Educational Evaluation and Policy Analysis, 20* (2).

Raudenbush, Stephen W. (2000). Synthesizing results from the trial state assessment. In David Grissmer & Michael Ross (Eds.), *Analytic issues in the assessment of student achievement.* Washington, DC: National Center for Educational Statistics, Department of Education.

Rice, Jennifer K. (1999, Summer). Estimated effects of class size on teacher's time allocation in high school mathematics and science courses. *Educational Evaluation and Policy Analysis.*

Rothstein, Richard, & Miles, K. H. (1995). *Where's the money gone? Changes in the level and composition of education spending.* Washington, DC: Economic Policy Institute.

Rutter, M., (Ed.). (1988). Studies in psychosocial risk: The power of longitudinal data. Cambridge, UK: Cambridge University Press.

Shkolnik, J., & Betts, J. R. (1998). *The effects of class size on teacher time allocation and student achievement.* Unpublished manuscript, Department of Economics, University of California-San Diego.

Singer, Judith D. (1998, Winter). Using SAS PROC MIXED to fit multilevel models, hierarchical models and individual growth models. *Journal of Educational and Behavioral Statistics, 24* (4), 323–355

Word, E. R., Johnston, J., and Bain, H. P. (1994). *The State of Tennessee's student/teacher achievement ratio (STAR) project: Technical report 1985–1990.* Nashville: The Tennessee State Department of Education,

Word, E., Johnston, J., & Bain, H. P. (1990). *Student teacher achievement ratio (STAR): Tennessee's K-3 class size study. Final summary report 1985–1990.* Nashville: Tennessee Department of Education.

PUBLIC AND PRIVATE FUNDS FOR PUBLIC AND PRIVATE SCHOOLS

10

NEW REVENUES FOR PUBLIC SCHOOLS: BLURRING THE LINE BETWEEN PUBLIC AND PRIVATE FINANCE

Michael F. Addonizio
Wayne State University

Public school finance at the start of the millennium is characterized by slowing revenue growth from traditional, broad-based state and local taxes (e.g., income, sales, and property taxes), and rising levels of revenue from nontraditional sources (Addonizio, 1998; Brunner & Sonstelie, 1997). These new, nontax sources of revenue are a testament to the creativity, and occasional desperation, of public education leaders who face at once flagging taxpayer support, rising enrollments, heightened expectations for academic achievement, and increasing competition for students and revenue arising from market-based changes in our public school system. Indeed, these market-based reforms, which typically involve increased school choice within and across local districts and, more recently, for-profit public schools, often trigger both a redistribution of traditional tax revenues across schools and the generation of new revenue from local sources.

These nontraditional revenue sources include user fees, developer fees, partnerships with private businesses, postsecondary schools and government agencies, direct donations from benefactors, indirect donations through local school foundations, booster clubs, parent-teacher organizations (including, most recently, fundraising through the Internet), volunteer services, and interest earnings on the investment of school resources. The growth in these revenue sources has raised concerns about their potentially disequalizing effects (Addonizio, 1998). Moreover, the distributional impacts of market-based reforms could be far greater, as families choose from intra- and interdistrict options, charter schools, and, increasingly, for-profit public schools and private schools involved in publicly or privately financed voucher programs.

This chapter first briefly reviews these nontraditional revenues, and then looks at the implications of these evolving changes in public school finance for educational outcomes and the equality of educational opportunities across local communities. More specifically, this chapter will explore the ways in which these new financial arrangements have been prompted by concern for educational quality and the pursuit of profit, and how they may be constrained by these same motivations.

NONTRADITIONAL REVENUE
SOURCES FOR PUBLIC SCHOOLS

Public elementary and secondary education in the U.S. has enjoyed remarkably steady revenue growth. Real expenditures per pupil increased 3.5 percent per year over the entire period of 1890–1990 (Hanushek & Rivkin 1997).[1] However, since 1990, the growth rate in real per-pupil expenditures appears to have slowed, due, in part, to increasing school enrollments. At the same time, fiscal pressures on public schools arising from this slowed revenue growth were exacerbated by a steady increase in the special education population, which continues to grow more rapidly than the general student population (Parrish & Wolman 1999) and by stringent tax and spending limits imposed on local districts in many states (Mullins & Joyce, 1996; Mullins & Cox, 1995).

The principal effect of these enrollment trends and tax and expenditure limitations (TELs) has been the increased dependence on nontraditional revenue sources by public schools and school districts. In general, three types of activities are used to supplement traditional revenues: donor activities, enterprise activities, and shared or cooperative activities, which pool functions with other agencies or organizations to lower costs (Meno, 1984). Other nontraditional initiatives include the investment of school resources and the pursuit of new government funds through grant writing (Pijanowski & Monk, 1996). These efforts have been productive, with potential budget impacts of 7 percent to 9 percent reported for public schools in regional studies of alternative revenues (Meno, 1984; Picus, Tetreault, & Hertert, 1995; Salloum, 1985). At the same time, some evidence suggests that relatively wealthy school districts enjoy greater success in tapping into these revenue sources than do their less affluent counterparts (Addonizio 1998). A detailed discussion of these activities appears in Addonizio (2000); a brief review is presented below.

DONOR ACTIVITIES

Direct or indirect donor activities raise funds, goods, or services from nongovernmental sources. These activities may consist of direct district fund raising appeals to individuals or corporations, either for a specific purpose or for the

---

1 This section is adapted from "Salvaging Fiscal Control: New Sources of Local Revenues for Public Schools" in the *2000 AEFA Yearbook* (Addonizio, 2000).

enrichment of educational programs. Such funds are generally given directly to a public school or district. Alternatively, they may involve the indirect donation of funds through local district educational foundations or booster clubs.

Educational foundations are nonprofit organizations created to receive donations for the district for a wide variety of school activities.[2] These activities have been reported elsewhere and, in most cases, the revenue raised by these foundations has been modest (Addonizio, 1998). Their potential, however, has yet to be tapped. A lucrative and path-breaking model is under consideration in Cary, North Carolina, where the town council has established the nonprofit Cary Education Foundation. Beginning in 2000–01, the council would donate a portion of its property tax revenue to the foundation. The size of the gift would depend upon school enrollment. The town plans to donate $200 for each of the district's 18,500 pupils in the first year, for a total contribution of $3.7 million. Such a transfer from a municipality to local schools is unprecedented in North Carolina and may include support for private, parochial, and home-schooled students. Program supporters face a possible legal challenge from local taxpayers but view the initiative as an efficient strategy for local economic development (Coles, 2000).

Foundation activity has been found to be more prevalent in relatively wealthy communities (Addonizio, 1998). A noteworthy exception to this trend, however, is the Public Education Network (PEN), an organization of local foundations established to help public school districts serve low income families and involve community organizations in school improvement efforts. Founded in 1983 with seed money from the Ford Foundation, PEN had 47 member Local Education Funds (LEFS) in 26 states and the District of Columbia, and were serving over 5.1 million students in 272 local school districts by 1999 (Public Education Network, 1999).

While local education foundations raise funds for school districts, funds for individual schools are often raised by booster clubs to support specific activities. For example, booster clubs and parent-teacher associations (PTAs) have relied for years on direct sales to raise revenue for school activities, staff development, computers, software, and other purposes. Participating schools often retain 30 to 50 percent of the retail price of a product, such as magazines, candy, or gift wrap. In 1997–98, public schools raised approximately $1.5 billion from product fundraising, fully 88 percent of the total net profit for this industry (Coles, 1998). Recently, however, concerns have arisen regarding the propriety of this fundraising emphasis by PTAs and the safety of students involved in door-to-door selling (Coles, 1998).

At the same time, some schools have turned to the Internet for revenue through product sales. Since fall 1999, more than a dozen Web sites have been launched that allow shoppers to have a portion of their payment sent to the school of their choice. Amounts range from 3 to 30 percent of the purchase price, with most in the 5 to 15 percent range (Thomas, 2000). Instead of going directly to an online merchant's site, users who want a rebate must go through a school-related site. These sites are virtual malls, with up to 200 retailers linked to

---

2 For an analysis of local education foundations in Michigan, see Addonizio (1998).

each one. If a shopper accesses one of these merchants through the site, a portion of the purchase is rebated to the referring site, which then forwards the money to the shopper's designated school. Typically, the site forwards about 75 percent of the rebate to the school and retains the balance.

These online fundraising firms are quite new and their profitability for schools is yet unproven. The largest online fundraising service, Schoolpop.com, has about 17,000 participating schools nationwide and reports rebating about $900,000 to participating schools between May 1999 and May 2000 (Trejos, 2000). Nevertheless, in view of the rapidly rising volume of Web-based commerce, this revenue source holds promise for participating schools.

ENTERPRISE ACTIVITIES

Enterprise activities include the imposition of user fees for school-provided programs or services, such as driver education, athletics, and pupil transportation; developer fees to help support public facilities necessary as the result of new development, such as roads, parks, police, fire, sewer, water, libraries, and, most recently, schools (Siemon & Zimet, 1992); and the sale of access to school property, including advertising on school buses and homework handouts, and, more recently (and dramatically), the sale of a school building name to a corporate sponsor (Garrett 2000). Other enterprise activities undertaken by public schools include the leasing of school facilities and services (Meno, 1984; Pijanowski & Monk, 1996) and the sale of personal seat licenses to finance the construction of athletic facilities (Blair, 1998). This latter initiative, undertaken by officials at Ravenna High School in Ohio in 1998, had been used in the past by a few colleges and universities, but may now become popular with public high schools.

The growing popularity of such enterprise activities, however, may pose constitutional or other legal issues in the future. For example, as more schools consider the use of fees for educational services, these fees will likely continue to be challenged on constitutional and statutory grounds.[3] Restrictions on user fees are largely a matter of state law, with federal courts generally deferring to state authorities (Dayton & McCarthy, 1992).

Further, impact fees raise a constitutional issue not associated with other public services or facilities. Specifically, case law provides that impact fees must be imposed on the basis of actual use. At the same time, virtually every state constitution requires "free" (i.e., tax supported) public schools, presumably making any payment of fees for the use of public schools unconstitutional. Although the authority of local governments to impose school impact fees was upheld by the Florida Supreme Court in 1991 in *St. Johns County, Florida v. Northeast Florida Builders Ass'n*,[4] their use is not widespread and has not been endorsed by the American Planning Association (American Planning Association, 1996).

---

3 For an analysis of the constitutional challenges to school fee policies, see Dayton and McCarthy (1992).

4 583 So. 2d 635 (Fla. 1991), 43 ZD 266.

SHARED OR COOPERATIVE ACTIVITIES

Sharing operating costs with other governmental agencies, private nonprofit or community organizations, colleges or universities, or businesses also serves to increase public school budget resources. These cooperative programs might include, for example, the shared use of public buildings for instruction, of recreational facilities (e.g., pools, gymnasiums), and transportation vehicles (Pijanowski & Monk 1996). Partnerships with institutions of higher education include opportunities for high school students to take courses tuition-free at local community colleges or four-year institutions in lieu of high school courses and school district participation in graduate student internship programs with local universities.[5]

Since at least the 1960s, schools often have relied on business partnerships to share school costs and gain access to the expertise of business officials who help shape educational programs to meet business needs (Monk & Brent, 1997). Partnerships between public education and business likely will become more prevalent in the future as schools seek to prepare students for a society increasingly driven by new technologies. The form of these partnerships, however, may be changing. Corporations are moving away from school adoption models focused on a single site and toward the funding of programs at multiple sites that are more closely aligned with the mission of the contributor (Blair, 2000). For example, Texas Instruments, Inc., cited by the Conference Board of New York City for the quality of their school partnerships, packages their donations of technology with extensive teacher training in the use of the hardware. Although such a hands-on approach on the part of business may not be welcomed in some schools, the accelerating pace of technological change and the growing focus on educational outcomes are likely to increase business presence in public schools in the coming years.

REVENUE IMPLICATIONS OF
MARKET-BASED REFORMS

Efforts to inject market competition into public education also have implications for school revenues as schools compete for students and investors finance the operations of for-profit firms that manage public schools. These market reforms arise from two principal motivations: the desire for improved academic outcomes and the pursuit of economic profit. This competition entails enhanced educational choice. Systems of educational choice seek a balance between parents' right to choose the influences and values to which their children will be exposed and the right of a democratic society to use the educational system to foster its most essential political, economic, and social institutions. Generally, two alternative approaches have emerged from efforts to preserve a common

---

5 Such arrangements, of course, may also be competitive. In Michigan, for example, high school students may enroll in courses at community colleges and public universities with tuition paid from a pro rata share of state school aid, in effect, a transfer from the local school district to the postsecondary institution.

educational experience while providing some measure of choice: a market system of private choices provided through vouchers or tuition tax credits and a market of public choice among schools that are sponsored or operated by government (Levin, 1991). Both approaches have implications for public school finance. Moreover, the distinction between private and public choice is becoming increasingly blurred by the privatization of public schools; that is, the rise of for-profit companies that run publicly funded schools, including charter schools.

GENERAL ISSUES

The implications for revenue distribution arising from various forms of school choice are significant and have been discussed in more detail elsewhere (see, for example, Addonizio, 1994; Levin, 1991; Odden, 1991). In most states, public revenue for public schools is calculated by multiplying the number of pupils served by a district or charter school by a fixed per-pupil amount. This practice of paying for schooling by the pupil ignores some important realities about school costs. First, almost all instruction occurs in classroom groups and the marginal cost of accommodating an additional student in a classroom is virtually zero (and would certainly be so if choices are restricted by seat availability). Second, the addition or subtraction of a few students does not appreciably change overhead costs for such things as buildings, administration, and transportation.

Thus, a choice program that allows movement across local district boundaries (e.g., interdistrict public school choice, charter schools, vouchers, etc.) provides a windfall for the receiving school or district and an arguably unfair loss to the sending district that will likely exacerbate the quality differences between districts, possibly encouraging further transfers of students and revenue.[6] At the same time, however, a failure to reward or penalize schools financially according to the choices families make may give schools little incentive to improve their programs to meet parents' demands. In view of the growing interest in various forms of school choice, including charter schools and interdistrict choice, revenue levels for individual public schools will become increasingly dependent upon the movement of students across district boundaries.

Further, the rise of market-based reforms, including interdistrict choice and charter schools, can be expected to elicit more aggressive fundraising activities by individual schools as they compete for students in the new public education marketplace. A glimpse into our future may be provided by New Zealand, where aggressive market-based education reforms, including individual school autonomy and full parental choice of public school, not only allow but encourage schools to supplement their traditional public operating revenue by raising additional resources on their own (Fiske & Ladd, 2000).

---

6 Eventually, of course, a sufficient accumulation of transfer students would require additional revenue for the receiving district if program quality is to be maintained.

FOR-PROFIT SCHOOLS

In the coming years, public school revenues may be increasingly impacted by the rise of for-profit public schools that are financed through a combination of public revenue and the resources of investors lured to public education by the prospect of long-run profit. Since 1992, more than a dozen school management companies have been created, each promising to turn a profit while raising student achievement. At the time of this writing, for-profit schools enroll approximately 100,000 students in about 200 schools, a miniscule share of our nation's 53 million elementary and secondary school children. Their rate of growth, however, has been substantial. For example, in two years, revenues for Boston-based Advantage Schools rose from $4 million to $60 million, while revenues for the more well-known Edison Schools, Inc. have grown from $12 million to $217 million in five years (Symonds, 2000).[7] Further, financial analysts predict explosive growth in the future, with for-profits capturing as much as 10 percent of the $360 billion K-12 market by 2009 (Symonds, 2000).

Investor interest is driven by the enormity of the potential market in public education and the public's apparently growing impatience with the slow pace and meager results of more-conventional education reforms. For example, the National Education Goals Report issued in December 1999 conceded that U.S. public schools had fallen far short of the goals established by governors a decade earlier. In response to parents' concerns about the quality of traditional public schools, particularly in urban districts, and their demand for more educational choice, 36 states have passed charter school legislation and the number of charter schools has risen from fewer than 100 in 1994 to approximately 1,700 in 1999. These new public schools, along with local districts seeking to rescue traditional schools beset with chronic educational and financial failure, comprise the demand side of the market for profit-seeking educational management firms.

The growth of for-profit public schools holds several implications for public school revenues. First, to the extent that these schools remain attractive to families, they can be expected to attract students from private schools, thereby exerting upward pressure on public school revenues. Second, this movement could accelerate the flow of private funds into public schools, particularly for capital spending. Typically, charter schools receive the same per-pupil operating revenue as local school districts. However, because they lack a local tax base, they cannot sell bonds to finance capital projects or raise any local matching revenue required for state aid. Consequently, the schools are forced to pledge operating revenue to borrow for capital projects.

One innovative approach to capital funding is being taken by Charter Schools USA, an educational management company based in Florida. The company negotiated an agreement with Ryder Systems, Inc. by which the trucking company paid $4 million to build Charter's new elementary school. In consideration, the children of Ryder employees are given preference for admission to the school. Such an arrangement whereby private parties in effect purchase the right to attend a public school, however, would not be permitted under some state

---

7 Edison Schools, Inc. raised $122 million in an initial public offering in 1999.

charter school statutes (Symonds, 2000). Eventually, if the charter school movement continues to grow at anywhere near its current rate, state legislatures may
allow these schools access to taxpayer-backed bonds and state capital aid in the
manner of traditional public school districts.

THE FUTURE OF FOR-PROFIT SCHOOLS

Despite the optimistic projections of some Wall Street analysts, the long-run
success of commercial operations in public education is far from assured. First,
creating a sustainable and profitable business in any industry is not easy. Studies
indicate that more than 70 percent of new businesses fail within eight years of
their inception (Dees, 1998). Substantial profits are rare. Indeed, in perfectly competitive markets companies make only enough to cover costs and compensate
investors with an adequate return.[8] Although early entrants into this market may
seek to take advantage of excess demand for alternatives to traditional public
schools, their financial performance to date has been poor. For example, The Tesseract Group, Inc., the education management company formerly known as Education Alternatives, Inc., has endured a series of financial setbacks since its
founding in 1986. A contract to manage public schools in Dade County, Florida,
was not renewed and the company was dismissed from Baltimore and Hartford.
In 2000, the company sold two Arizona charter schools and a for-profit business
college in response to mounting financial losses (Walsh, 2000). The company's
stock, which was removed from the Nasdaq exchange in February 2000 because
of declining asset value, fell from a high of $48.50 per share in 1993 to 37.5 cents
by early June 2000 in over-the-counter trading (Walsh, 2000).

One company's financial problems, of course, may not be indicative of the
potential profitability of an entire market. Tesseract's Arizona charter schools
were bought by Nobel Learning Communities, Inc. of Media, Pennsylvania,
which operates 151 private schools and public charter schools in 16 states. As a
state with a particularly aggressive charter school program, Arizona may be
viewed as a potentially lucrative market by for-profit education suppliers. Nevertheless, profit has proven elusive for businesses venturing into public education and may continue to elude investors unless for-profit operations attain sufficient scale. Moreover, the quest for profits by these firms may undercut the public education mission of their schools. That is, such cost control measures as
hiring inexperienced teachers, avoiding disabled students, and focusing largely
on the relatively inexpensive elementary grades may disqualify these schools as
truly public institutions that pass constitutional muster. Equally important, pub-

---

8 In competitive markets, economic profits become zero in the long run. Economic
   profit must be distinguished from accounting profit. Accounting profit is measured by the difference between a firm's revenue and costs, including actual outlays and depreciation expenses. Economic profit takes account of opportunity
   cost, including the return that the owners of the firm could make if their capital
   were used elsewhere. Of course, investors would like to earn a positive economic
   profit; that is what encourages entrepreneurs to develop and commercialize new
   ideas. However, as entrepreneurs enter a competitive market in search of such
   profits, competition drives economic profits to zero.

lic perception of such a failure by these schools to fulfill their responsibilities could dampen taxpayer support. For now, the enduring impact of for-profit public schools on school revenue and school outcomes is difficult to discern. Nevertheless, the unavoidable conflict between the interests of for-profit firms and their investors on the one hand and the public interest on the other could weaken the schools' claim to public funds in the future.

IMPLICATIONS FOR EQUITY
IN PUBLIC SCHOOL FINANCE

The scope and equity effects of nontraditional revenues have yet to be accurately determined, largely because of inconsistent, incomplete, and nonexistent reporting. The proliferation of these activities, however, has not been viewed with universal approval. Some of the concern has focused on the possible disequalizing effects of these revenues. Virtually every state allocates school aid to local districts by means of equalizing formulas designed to offset disparities in local fiscal capacity, generally measured in terms of taxable property wealth per pupil. States, however, are generally unaware of local revenues raised through foundations, booster clubs, and some commercial enterprises. To the extent that such activities are more prevalent in relatively affluent school districts, the equity effects of state school aid programs could be compromised.

Such disequalizing effects have been observed with respect to local education foundations. Addonizio (1998) found that the 153 local districts in Michigan that had formed foundations enjoy higher unrestricted public revenue per pupil, higher household income, and higher student achievement, on the average, than their nonfoundation counterparts. The foundation districts were also found to have a lower percentage of children eligible for free and reduced price lunch under the National School Lunch Act, and to enroll a student population that is overwhelmingly white, with an unweighted average of 91 percent across these districts (Addonizio, 1998). Although these equity concerns are mitigated somewhat by the relatively small financial contributions of the foundations, disequalizing effects may become evident in Michigan and elsewhere as local schools and districts, responding to the competitive pressures of the new education market, continue to pursue new revenues and evade state reporting systems and fiscal controls. The point at which these local "off-shore accounts" jeopardize state policy goals is difficult to gauge. Nevertheless, states would do well to strengthen local financial reporting requirements and establish threshold levels at which local revenue growth would trigger state aid offsets in the interest of statewide equity goals. Such offsets could be less than dollar-for-dollar, so as not to discourage local fundraising, but sufficient to allow some redistribution of state revenues to low-spending districts.

SUMMARY AND CONCLUSIONS

The public schoolhouse has entered the market square. Faced with slowing per-pupil revenue growth from traditional, broad-based taxes, rising expectations for academic achievement, and new forms of educational choice (e.g., charter schools, interdistrict choice), a growing number of public schools are aggressively pursuing new sources of funds. These sources include direct donations, business enterprises, booster clubs, local education foundations, and the sale of school access to private businesses. More recently, public schools have turned to the Internet to raise revenue through product sales and the governing boards of public school districts and charter schools have contracted with for-profit companies to run schools, sometimes supplementing public funds with private capital in the short run.

These entrepreneurial activities, though not unexpected in the increasingly competitive climate of public education, have raised concerns about fairness in school finance. Evidence suggests that communities that are more affluent are more successful in these revenue-raising efforts, thereby undoing, to some extent, the equalizing effects of public aid formulas. And, to the extent these new revenues are not recorded in standard school district financial reports, their perverse equity effects may go unnoticed and unchecked by policy makers.

Further, the infusion of private money into for-profit public schools, though quite modest at present, could accelerate in the coming years as educational choices for families continue to expand. The rapid growth of charter schools, public concern over the slow pace of more traditional educational reforms, and the lure of a huge potential market for school management services can be expected to attract private capital into public education, at least in the short run. Long-run prospects for these commercial enterprises will depend, of course, on their profitability and the degree to which political and educational leaders see them as contributing to the goals of public education. Whether these two objectives are compatible remains to be seen. The interests of investors and students may often collide, with short-run efforts to cut costs compromising the quality and breadth of educational programs in our public schools.

Finally, the pursuit of private money by public schools, particularly through commercial activities and the increasing presence of for-profit enterprises in traditional and charter public schools, may undermine taxpayer support for public education. As these commercial ventures proliferate, voters may overestimate their fiscal impacts and feel less need to support local tax referendums. Moreover, the increasing commercialization of public schools may obscure the social benefits of common and universal public education, thereby weakening rather than reinforcing community bonds and public school support. As we begin the new millennium, policy makers should examine closely these nontraditional activities and their compatibility with the purposes of universal public education and, at the same time, reevaluate the fairness and adequacy of traditional public support for our public schools.

REFERENCES

Addonizio, M. F. (2000). Salvaging fiscal control: New sources of local revenues for public schools. In Neil D. Theobald & Betty Malen (Eds.), *Balancing local control and state responsibility for K-12 education* (pp. 245–278). Larchmont, NY: Eye on Education.

Addonizio, M. F. (1998). Private funding of public schools: Local education foundations in Michigan. *Educational Considerations, 24* (1), 1–7.

Addonizio, M. F. (1994). *School choice: Economic and fiscal perspectives.* Bloomington, IN: Education Policy Center, Indiana University.

Addonizio, M. F. (1991). Intergovernmental grants and the demand for local educational expenditures. *Public Finance Quarterly, 19* (2), 209–232.

Addonizio, M. F., Kearney, C. P., & Prince, H. J. (1995, Winter). Michigan's high wire act. *Journal of Education Finance, 20,* 235–269.

American Planning Association. (1996). *Modernizing state planning statutes.* Chicago: Author.

Anderson, N. (1997, December 2). Going beyond the bake sale. *Los Angeles Times.*

Blair, J. (2000). Corporations, educators work on strategic giving. *Education Week, 19* (36), 12.

Blair, J. (1998). Ohio district takes sports fund raising to new level. *Education Week, 28* (12), 6.

Brunner, E., & Sonstelie, J. (1997). Coping with *Serrano:* Voluntary contributions to California's local public schools. *Proceedings: National Tax Association 89ᵗʰ Annual Conference* (pp. 372–381).

Chaikind, S., Danielson, L. C., & Brauen, M. L. (1993). What do we know about the costs of special education? A selected review. *Journal of Special Education, 26* (4), 344–370.

Coles, A. D. (2000, May 17). N.C. town forms foundation to give more to schools. *Education Week,* 13.

Coles, A. D. (1998, December 9). Season of selling has its fans, but some just say no. *Education Week,* 1,13.

Dayton, J., & McCarthy, M. (1992). User fees in public schools: Are they legal? *Journal of Education Finance, 18* (2), 127–141.

Dees, J. G. (1998). Enterprising nonprofits. *Harvard Business Review, 76* (1), 55–67.

Fiske, E. B., & Ladd, H. F. (2000). *When schools compete.* Washington, DC: The Brookings Institution.

Garrett, C. (2000, January 13). Officials may sell names of schools. *Detroit News,* p. 1B.

Gold, S., Smith, D., & Lawton, S. (Eds.). (1995). *Public school finance programs of the United States and Canada, 1993–94.* Albany, NY: The American Education Finance Association and The Nelson A. Rockefeller Institute of Government.

Governmental Accounting Standards Board. (1994). *Proposed statement: The financial reporting entity -affiliated organizations; exposure draft.* Norwalk, CT: Author.

Guthrie, J. W. (1997). School finance: Fifty years of expansion. *The Future of Children, 7* (3), 24–38.

Hamm, R. W., & Crosser, S. (1991, June). School fees: Whatever happened to the notion of a free public education? *The American School Board Journal,* 29–31.

Hanushek, E. A., & Rivkin, S. G. (1997). Understanding the twentieth-century growth in U.S. school spending. *Journal of Human Resources, 32* (1), 35–68.

Howell, P. L., & Miller, B. B. (1997). Sources of funding for schools. *The Future of Children, 7* (3), 39–50.

Johnston, J. (1995). Channel One: The dilemma of teaching and selling. *Phi Delta Kappan, 2*, 437–442.

Joyce, P. G., & Mullins, D. R. (1991). The changing fiscal structure of the state and local public sector: The impact of tax and expenditure limitations. *Public Administration Review, 51* (3), 240–253.

Kearney, C. P. (1994). *A primer on Michigan school finance* (3rd ed.). Ann Arbor: Educational Studies Program, School of Education, The University of Michigan.

Kelejian, H. H., & Oates, W. E. (1981). *Introduction to econometrics.* New York: Harper & Row.

Levin, H. M. (1991). The economics of educational choice. *Economics of Education Review, 10* (2), 137–158.

Maeroff, G. (1982, November 9). Schools seek private funds. *New York Times*, p. C1.

Meno, L. R. (1984). Sources of alternative revenue. In L. D. Webb & V. D. Mueller (Eds.), *Managing limited resources: New demands on public school management* (pp. 129–146). Cambridge, MA: Ballenger.

Meredith, B., & Underwood, J. (1995). Irreconcilable differences? Defining the rising conflict between regular and special education. *Journal of Law and Education, 24* (2), 195–226.

Monk, D. H., & Brent, B. O. (1997). *Raising money for education.* Thousand Oaks, CA: Corwin Press.

Mullins, D., & Cox, K. (1995). *Tax and expenditure limits on local governments.* Washington, DC: Advisory Commission on Intergovernmental Relations.

Mullins, D., & Joyce, P. (1996, Spring). Tax and expenditure limitations and state and local fiscal structure: An empirical assessment. *Public Budgeting and Finance*, 75–101.

National Association of Educational Foundations. (1994, Summer). *Educational foundations focus, 1.*

National Center for Education Statistics. (1995). *Digest of education statistics, 1995.* Washington, DC: Author.

Odden, A. (1991). *A new school finance for public schools.* Unpublished manuscript, University of Southern California, Center for Research in Education Finance.

Parrish, T. B., & Wolman, J. (1999). Trends and new developments in special education funding: What the states report. In T. B. Parrish, J. G. Chambers, & C. M. Guarino (Eds.), *Funding special education* (pp. 203–229). Thousand Oaks, CA.

Picus, L. O., Tetreault, D. R., & Hertert, L. (1995). *The allocation and use of educational resources in California.* Paper presented at the Annual Meeting of the American Education Finance Association, Savannah, GA.

Pijanowski, J. C., & Monk, D. H. (1996, July). Alternative school revenue sources: There are many fish in the sea. *School Business Affairs*, 4–10.

Pollack, A. (1992, May 17). "With Budgets Cut, Public Officials Seek Private Money." *New York Times*, p. L40.

Public Education Network (1999). *Findings from the annual members survey 1999.* Washington, DC: Public Education Network.

Salloum, K. (1985). *Private funding for elementary and secondary public education in British Columbia.* Unpublished master's thesis, Simon Fraser University.

Siemon, C. L., & Zimet, M. J. (1992, July). School funding in the 1992: Impact fees or bake sales? *Land Use Law*, 3–9.

Symonds, W. C. (2000, Feb. 7). For-profit schools. *Business Week*, pp. 64–76.

Thomas, K. (2000, Feb. 3). Schools go online to cash in on a treasury of fund-raising shopping sites. *Detroit News*, p. 3F.

Trejos, N. (2000, May 23). Schools turning to no-fuss fundraising online. *The Washington Post*, p. A01.

Walsh, M. (2000, May 17). Losing money, Tesseract sells charters, college. *Education Week*, 13.

Wassmer, R. W., & Fisher, R. C. (1997). *User charges and the financing of K-12 public education in the United States.* Working Paper 96–03. Sacramento, CA: Graduate Program in Public Policy and Administration, California State University.

Wassmer, R. W., & Fisher, R. C. (1996, Fall). An evaluation of the recent move to centralize the finance of public schools in Michigan. *Public Finance and Budgeting, 16* (3), 90–112.

11

PUBLIC MONEY AND PRIVATIZATION IN K-12 EDUCATION

F. Howard Nelson
Rachel Drown
Ed Muir
Nancy Van Meter
American Federation of Teachers

Fueled by a growing sentiment to privatize government functions, privatization in education will remain an important topic in the first decade of the new millennium. So far, however, privatization is more sound and fury than a force actually reshaping public education. Traditional providers of products and services, such as textbook companies, still dominate the for-profit education industry, but vouchers and charter schools may presage the future of privatization in K-12 education.

This chapter first describes the current education industry. The subsequent section sets the stage for looking at the future of private involvement in public education by examining the development of private management companies in charter schools over the past few years. Then, this chapter concludes by postulating four hypothetical alternative ideas about the direction public schools and privatization might take over the next ten years.

THE EDUCATION INDUSTRY

The education industry is enormous, accounting for nearly 10 percent of the U.S. Gross Domestic Product (GDP). As shown in Figure 11.1, tax-supported public K-12 and higher education comprise the bulk of the sector, although private providers dominate the childcare, training and development, and educational products sectors. A vigorous nonprofit private sector contributes about 7 percent to K-12 spending, and a somewhat larger percentage of postsecondary education.

**FIGURE 11.1 PROFILE OF VARIOUS ASPECTS
OF THE EDUCATION INDUSTRY, 1998**

Industry Segment	Childcare/ Preschool	K-12	Post-secondary	Training/ Develop-ment	Products/ Services	Total
Market size (in billions of dollars)	$35	$340	$225	$60	$30	$690
Schools/ providers (in thousands)	90.0	111.5	10.0	3.0	12.3	226.8
Students (in millions)	10	52	14	55	N/A	131
Publicly traded companies (revenues in billions of dollars)	$0.3	$1.0	$2.0	$1.9	$18.0	$23.2
Publicly traded companies (number)	3	5	16	15	33	72
Aggregate market capitalization for publicly traded compa-nies (in billions of dollars)	$0.3	$2.2	$4.9	$1.9	$28.7	$38.0

SOURCE: U.S. Department of Education (1999); Evereen Securities (1999).

Publicly traded companies represent only 3 percent of the entire education "market," and in the K-12 sector the fraction is one-third of 1 percent.[1] Together, the publicly traded companies have an aggregate market capitalization ($38 billion) about half the size of that of the Walt Disney Company (Evereen Securities, p.7). Although the impacts of private providers on the debate over public education overshadow their current financial impacts, rapid growth of private providers in the K-12 sector is possible—even if these companies never gain a double-digit market share.

---

1 Publicly traded companies sell stock to the public, which is then traded on stock exchanges. In order to sell and trade stock, these companies must comply with the public reporting requirements of the Securities and Exchange Commission.

Since 1980, childcare, K-12, and postsecondary education's share of national income grew from 6.5 to 7.2 percent of GDP (NCES, 1999, p. 34). K-12 education represents a $340 billion market, with 52 million students and about 110,000 schools. Nonprofit schools, most of them with religious affiliation, dominate private K-12 education. While private school enrollment grew by nearly one million students over the 1990s, public schools grew equally fast; hence the proportion of students in private schools remained at about 11 percent of the K-12 sector over the past decade.

Highlighting seemingly low tuition, some analysts often compare existing private schools to public schools, and look to these comparisons for cost-effective solutions to contain ever-increasing public school costs. However, private education has struggled with cost containment as much as public education. In fact, the cost of private education has escalated at a higher rate than the cost of public education during the past three decades. After adjusting for inflation, public school spending increased 155 percent since 1964, and private K-12 education costs rose by 242 percent (Nelson, 1998a). From 1987 to 1994, private school tuition escalated at rates double the rate of public school expenditures (NCES, 1996, p. 72; NCES, 1991, p. 70).

Despite legal limitations on public spending for private education, some public money has flowed to private schools for decades. Private school students are eligible for federal Title I services for low-income children, and also for special education services provided on site by public school systems. Some states provide financial assistance directly to private schools—as much as $600 per student in Ohio.[2] Additionally, many states require school districts to provide transportation for private school children.

Voucher programs are usually at the center of the debate over public money and private schooling. Flowing public money through families, rather than directly to schools, often circumvents legal restrictions on public money supporting religious institutions. Furthermore, not all students are eligible for vouchers in the three extant publicly funded voucher programs for students attending private schools. The programs in Cleveland and Milwaukee are designed for low-income students, whereas Florida's statewide program applies to students from failing schools.

In Cleveland, the 3,000-student program costs about $7.5 million for the vouchers, and about $12 million after accounting for all costs, including $2 million for transportation.[3] Most assistance went to students attending religious schools, or kindergarten students who had never been in school. Only about 200 students from public schools received vouchers. The only two for-profit schools in the Cleveland voucher program enrolled a disproportionate share of former

---

2 A report on the Cleveland voucher program (Murphy, Rosenberg, & Nelson, 1997) contains a description of state aid for private schools in Ohio, the state with the most generous public support of private schools.

3 The $12 million estimate is based on a cost of $4,000 per voucher student as calculated in Murphy et al. (1997). Other details of the Cleveland program are in the state auditor's report (Petro, 1998).

public school students (Metcalf et al., 1998). The for-profit Hope Schools, for example, converted to charter schools under Ohio's new charter school law for financial reasons.

Though the federal courts may dismantle the Cleveland voucher program, Milwaukee's voucher program survived a challenge before the Wisconsin Supreme Court. The program costs up to $5,100 per voucher student in 1999–2000, or $38 million across 4,200 students in religious schools and 2,300 students in secular schools (Bezruki et al., 2000, p. 17). The prominent management companies described in the next section do not operate any of these secular schools, in part because Milwaukee's charter schools get better funding.

In addition to voucher programs, which receive the bulk of public attention, several states also have legislation to provide a tax benefit for families paying private school tuition. Forms of tax credit already exist in Iowa, Illinois, Arizona, and Minnesota. The programs involve no school accountability. The laws hold the church-state relationship at arm's length, making them a preferred option for the support of parochial schools in many states.

Public funding also has been instrumental in stimulating the growth of for-profit companies in K-12 education. Education management companies made their first foray into public schools by contracting directly with school districts to manage existing public schools. The experiment with these "contract" schools was dealt a near fatal blow with the termination of several contracts. For example, from 1991 to 1995, Education Alternative Incorporated (EAI) managed one public school in Dade County, Florida; nine public schools in Baltimore, Maryland; and all of the public schools in Hartford, Connecticut. After numerous controversies, the Baltimore contract was canceled, Hartford terminated its contract, and Dade County chose not to renew their contract (Ascher et al., 1996). Other experiments with private education management companies include a contract with Alternative Public Schools to run a school in Wilkinsburg, Pennsylvania, and a Minneapolis contract with Public Strategies, Inc. Neither contract was renewed. As the new millennium began, the only company that contracts directly with school districts to operate public schools is Edison Schools, Inc.[4]

PRIVATIZATION IN CHARTER SCHOOLS

Distinct from contract schools, the charter school movement gave new life to the concept of privately managed public schools. These new or converted schools are "chartered" by agents of the state, offering families options in addition to their neighborhood public school or other choices that may be available through their school district. Charter school legislation generally grants greater fiscal and educational autonomy from school district and state regulations. Typically, a charter school is organized as a nonprofit institution. Its governing board, how-

---

4 This generalization ignores dozens of small private and nonprofit specialty schools serving special education and at-risk students that contract with school districts. Typically, these schools are considered private schools rather than privately managed public schools.

ever, may contract with a private education management company, an increasingly common practice.

Except for some schools managed under contract with school districts by Edison Schools, Inc., management companies operate almost exclusively in the charter school arena. The initial charter school concept envisioned small groups of teachers and parents starting innovative, experimental schools. However, charter school laws have also created an attractive environment for management companies, because charter schools face fewer regulations and are often free from the supervision of elected bodies such as school and state boards of education.

By the 1999–2000 school year, 36 states and the District of Columbia had enacted charter school legislation. For-profit companies managed approximately 200 for-profit schools—about 13 percent of 1,500 charter schools.[5] Because most companies operate larger charter schools than nonprofit operators, the percentage of charter school enrollment in management company schools is much higher than 13 percent. In 1998–99, for example, charter schools averaged 137 students compared to 475 for all public schools in the U.S. (RPP International, 2000. p. 20). In 1997–98, the average size of a management company school was approximately 400 students, as shown in Figure 11.2. Horn and Miron (1999) estimate that at least 70 percent of charter schools in Michigan during the 1998–99 school year were those involved with private education management companies.

The major education management companies involved with charter schools include Edison Schools, Inc., SABIS, Advantage Schools, Tesseract Group (formerly EAI), the Leona Group, Nobel Learning Communities, Beacon School Management (formerly APS), Mosaica, National Heritage Academies, White Hat Management Company and others.[6] They have successfully raised start-up money from wealthy individuals and venture capital firms. All are small companies. Few are publicly traded.

The remainder of this section profiles management company charter schools. This profile provides background for the scenarios presented in the section of this chapter that follows. Figure 11.2 presents demographic and staffing data for several management company schools operating in 1997–98.[7] The table also contains comparable information for school districts in which the charter schools are physically located.

---

5   The for-profit school estimate is from "For-profit schools" (2000, February 7) *Business Week*, p 65. The charter school data are from RPP International (2000).

6   Five of the first 15 charter schools in Ohio were run by White Hat Management Company. Two of the five were the Hope Schools that had started as voucher schools in Cleveland.

7   See note to Figure 11.2 for details.

FIGURE 11.2 SELECTED CHARACTERISTICS OF
MANAGEMENT COMPANY SCHOOLS, 1997–98*

	Surrounding District	Management Companies	N	Management Companies	
				Minimum	Maximum
School size (number of students)	†	397	36	60	1077
Percent enrolled who are special education students	10.2%	3.8%	29	0%	15.8%
Percent enrolled who are economically disadvantaged	47.9%	32.8%	34	0%	81.9%
Distribution of FTE teachers					
Kindergarten	4.7%	10.3%	25	0%	62%
Elementary	39.9%	46.4%	25	0%	90%
Secondary	42.3%	38.4%	25	0%	100%
Ungraded	13.1%	5.0%	25	0%	20%
Pupil to teacher ratio	16.9	16.8	29	9.8	28.5
FTE staff per 100 students					
Teachers	5.9	6.0	25	3.5	10.2
Instructional aids	1.4	1.2	25	0.0	5.0
Instructional supervisors	0.1	0.1	25	0.0	0.3
Guidance counselors	0.2	0.0	25	0.0	0.5
Library/media	0.2	0.1	25	0.0	0.6
Administrators	0.4	0.8	25	0.3	2.9
Administrative support staff	0.7	0.6	25	0.0	1.5
Student support staff	0.8	0.3	25	0.0	1.7
All other support staff	2.9	1.4	25	0.0	5.9

NOTES: * Most comparisons include five Leona schools, four Edison schools, one SABIS schools, nine Beacon schools, one Mossaica school and five National Heritage Academy schools. School size, pupil-to-teacher ratio, and enrollments for special education and economically disadvantaged students are available for nine Edison schools operating under contracts with school districts. Many schools, however, were excluded from the analysis because they did not provide information to the Common Core Data Survey.

† Public schools in the United States average 475 students and charter schools average 137 students (RPP International, 2000).

SOURCE: National Center for Education Statistics (U.S. Department of Education); Common Core of Data Survey; 1997–98; and state department of education Web pages.

SCHOOL SIZE AND PUPIL-TO-TEACHER RATIOS

The average public elementary school has about 475 students. The average charter school enrolled fewer than 140 students in 1997–98 (RPP International, 2000). Perhaps seeking economies of scale, the school sizes of management company schools look more like conventional public schools. In 1997–98, the average size for management company schools was nearly 400 students, as shown in Figure 11.2. The typical Edison Schools, Inc. elementary school serves approximately 600 students, if the facility is large enough. The pupil to teacher ratio for the schools shown in Figure 11.2 was 16.8, essentially the same as the 16.9 ratio in the surrounding school district. In contrast, RPP International (2000) reports that the median pupil-to-teacher ratio for all types of charter schools of 16.0 was less than the national average for all public schools of 17.2.

ADMINISTRATIVE COSTS AND ECONOMIES OF SCALE

The perception of administrative bloat in public schools proves an easy target, but management companies may not provide a solution. In the aggregate, management companies overlap rather than replace existing school district administration and support services. In addition to the obvious costs of travel and administrative overlap, multistate school management companies also spend resources to acquire specific knowledge of each state and school district's regulations, reporting requirements, and student assessments programs. For example, EAI cut instructional staff and redirected the resources to non-instructional costs, including lawyers, accountants, project administration, corporate travel, improvement of the physical plant, and profit.[8] Scale is also a problem for administrative efficiency. Highlighting the relationship between size and administrative efficiency, Edison Schools, Inc. 1999's Securities and Exchange Commission (SEC) filing indicates that the company believes it will achieve profitability if it can open 200 schools. At this scale, Edison's virtual school district would rank as one of the 20 largest in the U.S.

The prospect of management companies improving administrative efficiency may be brighter in the charter school arena, though, where diseconomies of small scale always present financial problems. Management companies provide assistance with time-consuming state reporting requirements and "running the business." Companies can apply experience in reporting and administration to multiple schools. The provision of education services, however, is not essential to management efficiency. Some companies provide only administrative and financial services. Arizona Benefits Solutions, for example, provides reporting and business services to more than 100 charter schools in Arizona, but leaves the educational and day-to-day operations to the charter schools.

Despite all of the reasons that management companies should be able to improve administrative efficiency in charter schools, some evidence indicates that full service management companies may be less effective than other charter schools in keeping administrative costs down. The PSC/MAXIMUS (1999) study

---

8 Arthur Anderson audit of EAI schools in Baltimore, 1993–94. Breakdown also presented in Nelson (1997, p. 69).

of Michigan charter schools, for example, revealed that administrative costs were considerably higher in schools operated by multischool "chain" management companies, such as National Heritage Academies or the Leona Group.[9] The analysis of staffing patterns shown in Figure 11.2 (p. 178) finds more administrators in management company schools (0.8 per 100 students) than in surrounding school districts (0.4 per 100 students). However, administrative support staff levels are practically the same as in school districts.

SPECIAL EDUCATION AND DISADVANTAGED CHILDREN

The major national management companies profiled in Figure 11.2 (p. 178) serve an average of 3.8 percent of students in special education (defined as students with Individualized Education Program required by federal law), compared to 10.2 percent in the average surrounding district. Generally, management companies seek to provide services only for special needs students who can be taught in regular classroom settings (KPMG-Peat Marwick, 1998; Wood, 1999, Zollers & Ramanathan, 1998).[10]

Management companies enroll children from economically disadvantaged families at a rate equivalent to the national average. Low-income students comprised 32.8 percent of enrollment in the management company schools profiled in Figure 11.2 (p. 178). In districts surrounding the management company schools, however, low-income students make up 47.9 percent of enrollment. Management companies tend to concentrate in urban areas where dense populations make it easier to operate large schools, transport students, and find facilities.

INNOVATION

Charter schools were envisioned as a way for teachers and parents to try innovative practices unlikely or impossible in traditional public schools. Like their school district counterparts, companies standardize to improve efficiency.

---

9 Chain schools spend a much larger percentage on administrative expenses than other schools (33 percent compared to 22 percent in single-entity charter schools, and 11 percent in host school districts). They spend much less on instruction (35 percent compared to 51 percent in single-entity charter schools, and 54 percent in host public school districts). However, these figures overstate administration costs for both chain and single-entity charter schools because facilities leases and payments to private contractors for instructional support are misleadingly classified as business and administration expenditures by the state uniform accounting system.

10 These investigations focused primarily on Massachusetts. A preliminary analysis of Arizona, Massachusetts, Michigan, North Carolina, and Texas indicates that the Massachusetts findings may extend to other states (Muir, Drown, & Nelson, 2000). Using the Common Core of Data, the study finds that company-run charter schools have significantly less special education enrollment than other charter schools, and that charter schools in general have less special education enrollment than surrounding districts.

Edison Schools, Inc. utilizes Success For All in its elementary schools.[11] Advantage Schools, Inc. offers Direct Instruction[12] and National Heritage Academies uses a "back-to-basics" approach with a strong emphasis on moral values. Management contracts also restrict the innovative mission of charter schools, though, because many contracts may restrict the dissemination of company innovations and the intellectual property developed at company charter schools (Hassel & Lin, 1999; Ceresoli, 1999).

PERFORMANCE CONTRACTING

Performance-based contracting logically should be at the core of private sector involvement in education. So far, this has not been the case. According to one study (Hassel & Lin, 1999), management companies generally make money simply by spending less than the revenue they collect, rather than by improving student achievement.[13] Hassel and Lin, as well as the Massachusetts inspector general (Ceresoli, 1999), also identify problems with monitoring contract performance when companies play a strong role in selecting members of the nonprofit board governing the school or in financing school operations and facilities.

COST CONTAINMENT

Though it is possible that management companies compete against each other based on price in order to get contracts with the nonprofit governing boards, the schools themselves do not compete based on price for the charter itself. Furthermore, because all charter schools receive approximately the same funding, successful charter schools are unable to charge a higher price for their successful product. With no way to raise the price for successful schools, and the diseconomies of small scale that plague charter school efforts to improve efficiency, cost cutting appears to be the primary way to make money for investors.

The cost-cutting formula for most management companies seem to focus primarily on reducing payroll costs, which is accomplished by increasing class size,

---

11 Success for All (SFA) is a widely admired reading program designed to raise student achievement in low-performing schools that have high concentrations of disadvantaged children. SFA was developed by researchers at Johns Hopkins University and is also used in approximately 500 traditional public schools throughout the U.S.

12 Direct Instruction is a highly proscribed teaching technique in which students learn reading and math through recitation. This instructional method has been used in many traditional public schools nationwide, and like Success for All, was rated highly in a recent comprehensive study of school-wide reforms.

13 This review of management contracts by the Charter School Friends National Network reveals that some companies keep the surplus (i.e., the excess of revenues over expenditures) as their fee. Other contractors charge a percentage of revenues or expenditures, usually in the range of 7 to 12 percent, but many of these contracts allowed the contractor to keep a surplus anyway. Only a few contracts have incentive bonuses (in the 2.5 to 3.5 percent range) for improving student achievement or meeting other performance standards.

hiring less experienced and less qualified teachers, or reducing compensation costs in other ways,[14] although the average management company school has a pupil-to-teacher ratio matching the surrounding school district (see Figure 11.2, p. 178). Michigan, for example, where management companies run a majority of charter schools, demonstrates labor cost cutting by companies in charter schools. According to Horn and Miron (1999), 48 percent of charter school teachers outside the Detroit area were under age 30 in the 1997–98 school year. Teachers averaged 6.4 years of experience, compared to about 16 years nationally (NEA, 1997). In the Horn and Miron study, only about one teacher in five had earned at least a Masters degree or higher, compared to 50 percent nationally. In Ohio, where White Hat Management Company ran 5 of the first 15 charter schools, and teachers averaged 4.2 years of experience compared to 14.8 years in surrounding school districts (Marsh-Huggins, 2000).

ATTRACTING PRIVATE SECTOR CAPITAL

Management companies have been able to attract private resources. EAI (now the Tesseract Group) raised $36.7 million in a stock sale (Richards et al., 1996). Edison Schools, Inc. raised almost $230 million from private investors, and raised another $120 million in its stock offering.[15] Advantage Schools, Inc. has venture capital backing from Chase and Fidelity.[16] These companies use capital largely to finance their own start-up operations, but some of it is used for up-front investments in the schools they manage for facilities and technology. Company investments are repaid with interest over the life of the contract. Although school districts can borrow money from private investors by issuing tax-exempt securities at far more favorable rates than those charged by management companies, private capital raised by management companies is more appealing to charter schools, which usually have difficulty maintaining cash flow,

---

14 Companies running schools under contract with school districts face the same cost-cutting incentives as charter schools. During the first two years of EAI's contract in Baltimore, 56 of 205 teaching positions were cut (Ascher et al., 1996). Typically, half of the teachers in an Edison school have fewer than 5 years of experience (Nelson, 1998b) in contrast to the national average in public schools of 16 years of experience (NEA, 1997). High teacher turnover rates in Edison schools result, in part, from teacher inexperience. The company revealed a 23 percent turnover rate in 1997–98 (Edison Project, 1998), twice the national average for urban public schools in 1994–95 (NCES, 1997). Alternative Public Schools (now Beacon Education Management) replaced 24 school district teachers with only 15 teachers in Wilkinsburg, Pennsylvania (Clune, 1998; AFT, 1999).

15 See "Edison schools file to make initial public offering" (1999, August 23) *Wall Street Journal*, for information or private investors. See "Education pays off royally" (1999, November 17) *New York Times*, for information on proceeds of the public offering.

16 "For-profit schools" (2000, February 7) *Business Week*, p. 65.

securing start-up funding, and procuring tax-exempt financing for facilities.[17]

Management company capital raises other issues as well. Most contracts with management companies clearly state that property purchased through the contract with public funds belongs to the management company (Hassel & Lin, 1999). If charter schools change management companies, schools may be left with no physical assets. The Massachusetts inspector general (Cerasoli, 1999) found that loan agreements between charter schools and their management contractors could render the schools excessively dependent on their management contractors, while reducing schools' contracting leverage.

IMPROVING STUDENT ACHIEVEMENT

According to an analysis of the education industry by Montgomery Securities (1997, p. 15), improving academic achievement and the need for a more knowledgeable and better-trained workforce will drive the growth of management companies. The record of private managers with school district contracts, principally EAI and Edison Schools Inc., is, in our view, unimpressive.[18] Early evidence on the effectiveness of management companies in charter schools—including company-dominated Michigan—demonstrates mixed results at best.[19]

Given the poor or mixed track record of the few management companies in business long enough to have one, it is surprising that several states enacted legislation that makes private management one of the tools for the reconstitution of low-performing public schools. Maryland is using its existing laws and regulations to do so, for example, and legislation allowing for forced privatization recently passed in Pennsylvania and Colorado.

---

17 Charter schools in Colorado, Michigan, and Texas have secured tax-exempt financing to build or purchase facilities. Because the investments are viewed as risky, interest rates are higher than for school districts. Points, fees, and reserve requirements can add up to 20 percent of the amount borrowed.

18 Over the three years of EAI management in Baltimore, standardized achievement test scores for EAI schools decreased, and then increased to about the preprogram level (Williams & Leak, 1995). Edison Schools, Inc. has issued two glowing self-reports (Edison Project, 1997, 1998), but the few available independent studies show otherwise (see Nelson, 1998b; 2000).

19 In a state with a large number of private operators, Arizona showed few patterns, no consistency across grade and subject matter, and few statistically significant differences (Mulholland, 1999). In Massachusetts, newspapers generally carried negative stories about the performance of charter schools on statewide tests For example, see Jordana Hart, "MCAS score fail to met expectations" (1998, December 12) *Boston Globe*. The PSC/MAXIMUS (1999) study of Detroit area charter schools concluded that the average charter school performed lower than surrounding school districts. In another evaluation of charter schools in Michigan, evaluators found that charter schools scored lower than host districts and also gained less over a two- or three-year period (Horn & Miron 1999).

A LOOK BACKWARD FROM THE YEAR 2010
ON THE FIRST DECADE OF THE NEW MILLENNIUM

This section presents four alternative hypothetical scenarios about the direction of public funding for privatization in the future. The scenarios are written as a look back from the year 2010 on the first decade of the new millennium. These scenarios are (1) an abandonment of public financial support for privatization, (2) a continuation of privatization trends established in the 1990s, (3) the replacement of government schools with contract schools, and (4) the domination of K-12 education by a few large education companies under contract with state governments. These scenarios are then followed by a discussion and our conclusions concerning which are likely in the coming decades.

ALTERNATIVE HYPOTHETICAL SCENARIOS
FOR FUTURE PUBLICLY FUNDED PRIVATIZATION

SCENARIO 1: AN ABANDONMENT OF PUBLIC
FINANCIAL SUPPORT FOR PRIVATIZATION

The tech bubble that greeted the new millennium burst under pressure from high interest rates. States soon exhausted their rainy day funds. Fickle states quit awarding new charters and suspended funding of charter school facilities. Other financial loopholes gradually closed over time as states focused on "vertical equity"—funding students with different needs differently. Because it had not been able to operate at a profit in a good economy, the industry's largest management company, Lightbulb Schools, Inc., folded. Smaller, more efficiently managed companies persisted for years in niche markets. Charter schools continued to show lackluster achievement gains, so state legislatures enacted "low-performing charter school" legislation. About 1,000 of the best charter schools still survive—mostly in the big cities and the fast growing states least threatened by charter school competition. Most religious schools pulled out of voucher programs in Milwaukee, Florida, Chicago, and New York City under court-mandated open records requirements regarding both student testing, personal records, and finances.

SCENARIO 2: PRESENT TRENDS CONTINUE

During the first decade of the millennium, states continued to enact politically popular voucher programs for low-income or low-achieving children, but generally without political or economic consequence. State and federal courts either rejected or sharply constrained most voucher efforts. Religious support for Milwaukee's voucher program waned after a judge ruled that public support for church facilities must be limited to reasonable and annualized per-pupil facilities charges.

Charter school legislation was enacted in every state except one. Facilities funding for charter schools existed in all states. Three thousand charter schools had opened by 2004, greatly pleasing the new president at the start of the new administration. Under financial pressure from diseconomies of small scale and a continuing shortage of teachers, charter school size, pupil-teacher ratios, and teacher salaries increased. Growth proved fastest in large cities and fast growing states where charter schools had the least impact on school districts. Under continuing pressure to escape controversy, improve student achievement, and follow state laws, one university chartering authority in Michigan became the model for strict charter school monitoring and accountability. Fierce advocates complained that charter school growth slowed because they had become too much like other public schools.

Management companies dominated political action for charter school expansion. The companies had been singularly unsuccessful in contracting with school districts to run existing public schools because they needed a "low-wage" model to operate, and they also experienced continuing controversies over special education and services for at-risk students. Lightbulb Schools, Inc. was an exception. It prospered in a niche market for contract schools when school districts needed to fight encroaching charter schools. Most states provided financial support for facilities and the IRS ruled that charter schools could issue tax-exempt securities. The ruling spawned a boom in charter school construction for small investment banking firms. Typically, these companies charged 5 points, a 5 percent fee, and held a 10 percent reserve, all conveniently capitalized into a package that one inner-city charter school principal described as "usury."

SCENARIO 3: EVERY SCHOOL A CONTRACT SCHOOL

In the 1990s, New Zealand's decentralization of school authority started an international trend. In an unexpectedly short time, 23 states and two cities in the United States followed suit. During the first 10 years of the new millennium, every public school and most private schools became contract schools in these states and cities. Using public funds, local school boards selected private providers to operate individual schools under formal contracts specifying the type and quality of education. Freed from operating schools, local school boards concentrated on improving educational policy. Parents were free to choose the best school for their children, which made the new system work. Contractors had complete control over budgets and staffing. Each local school board was party to many different contracts. However, dozens of contracts with failing schools had already been terminated.

Not all went smoothly, according to the secretary of the U.S. Department of Education. Contracts had been difficult to terminate, he admitted. Contractors successfully argued that it would take years to show good progress. Failing private schools proved the most difficult to hold accountable. For a variety of reasons, schools did not have complete autonomy over staffing. Although traditional labor contracts became a thing of the past, teacher unions preserved a centralized wage scale and benefit structure just like the unions in New Zealand, The Netherlands, and other countries with extensive school choice. Most religious schools had been incorporated into the public funding system. Technically private—and thus allowed to teach religion—they nevertheless had to pay prevailing teacher wage rates to qualify for funding. Private "back office" companies rescued the system from a management talent shortage and sure failure. "Full-service" management companies specialized in the takeover of failing contract schools. The reforms had some unexpected results. Surprising some, the schools with the best reputations were rather conventional and multipurpose schools located in good neighborhoods. These schools were the exception. Education quality in poor urban areas declined even further as parents gravitated towards schools with higher socio-economic status.

SCENARIO 4: HUGE EDUCATION
COMPANIES DOMINATE EDUCATION

Charter school and voucher experiments in the late 1990s proved unsuccessful at improving education quality. The most significant educational change in the new millennium began in an unlikely place—Inkster, Michigan. Lightbulb Schools, Inc. won the first contract to manage all aspects of an entire school district. Washington, DC was the first major city to follow suit when a disappointed Congress replaced the extant charter school system with a single contract to Lightbulb Schools, Inc. Benefiting from the enormous economies of scale and its ability to select low-cost students, the company proved highly profitable. Within a year, the public school system dissolved and many of the best schools merged with the company. Public schools serving the neediest children survived on philanthropy and government programs dedicated to needy students.

Under contracts with state governments, huge companies dominated the education industry by the end of the decade. From humble beginnings as a fragmented cottage industry in the charter school movement, management companies merged and consolidated to reduce market fragmentation. Following the lead of Lightbulb Schools, Inc., management companies established "chains" of schools, in effect creating their own interstate districts. Funding for a parallel set of traditional public schools was eventually eliminated so that taxpayers would not have to pay the high costs of running two separate systems. The companies now provide all aspects of education—teacher services, school facilities, special education services, and after-school childcare.

Management companies promised efficiencies, but like health-care in the 1990s, the result from a consumer standpoint was degra-dation of the quality of education at the teacher-to-student level. As the millennium dawned, it was hoped that education reform would im-prove efficiency and that the savings could be used for those children most difficult to educate. Instead, the companies squeezed teacher salaries, reduced labor costs through use of less skilled personnel, closed small schools, and merged others. The "savings" were chan-neled into shareholder profits, marketing, and overhead. The much-diminished public school system now served only poor students.

CONCLUSION

Which scenario is most likely? Continuation of current trends (scenario 2) is the safest bet, although a sour economy (scenario 1) both inhibits public funding for privatization efforts and damages the allure of private sector solutions. The every-school-a-contract-school concept (scenario 3) probably underestimates administrative and monitoring costs, and ignores the very serious issue of ineffi-ciency caused by small-scale operations. Furthermore, current contracts with management companies demonstrate little concern with academic performance, which would have to change for scenario 3 to work. An industry run by big com-panies (scenario 4) is least likely for numerous reasons, primarily the tradition of local governmental control of education that is still firmly embedded in both rural and suburban areas.

For all the furor surrounding vouchers and management companies in public K-12 education, very little privatization currently exists, nor is likely to in the future. Voucher programs currently enroll only about 10,000 students nation-wide, and approximately 3 of 4 of those voucher students are served in tradi-tional nonprofit religious schools. The business of contracting with public school districts suffered after the initial failures of several efforts by management com-panies. Management companies multiplied only under the provisions of state charter school laws.

Despite early setbacks for privatization in K-12 public education, any look at education's future must include an assessment of the role of management com-panies. The potential attractiveness of public education for private investors remains. The public K-12 education system is a huge, stable industry. The virtual absence of private sector management allows for high growth rates. The compa-nies argue that they can bring much needed capital to the schools, contain run-away costs, reduce administrative overhead, and change academically dysfunc-tional schools into world-class learning institutions. Such arguments suggest that interest in privatizing K-12 public education will persist.

This chapter grounded the scenarios for the future of private sector involve-ment in K-12 public education on current practices of the private sector. The dis-economies of small scale work against the notion of management efficiency. The relatively big schools and standardized education programs of charter schools run by management companies duplicate the urban education models attacked by education reformers. Other evidence indicates few striking differences com-pared to other public schools. Most importantly, no independent evaluation of student achievement in schools managed by companies has shown superior student academic performance. These attributes of current attempts at privatization suggest that this movement will perform no differently in the millennium.

REFERENCES

Ascher, Carol, Fruchter, Norm, & Berne, Robert. (1996). *Hard lessons: Public Schools and Privatization.* New York: Twentieth Century Fund Press.

American Federation of Teachers. (1999). *Beacon educational management.* Washington, DC: Author.

American Federation of Teachers. (1995). *How private managers make money off public schools: Update on the EAI experience in Baltimore.* Washington DC: Author.

American Federation of Teachers. (1994). EAI's mismanagement of federal education programs: The special education and Chapter I track records in Baltimore. Washington, DC: Author.

Bezruki, Don, McKim, Karen, Holbert, Rachel, Lecoanet, Robin, Miller, David, & Smith, Joshua. (2000). *Milwaukee parental choice program.* Madison, WI: Legislative Audi Bureau.

Cerasoli, R. J. 1999. *A management review of commonwealth charter schools.* Boston: Office of the Inspector General. (Visited 3/30/00) Executive Summary: http://www.state.ma.us/ig/publ/chscx.htm; full text: http://www. state. ma.us/ig/publ/chscrpt.pdf.

Clune, Eleanor. (1998, June 29). Special report: Outcomes debated as school district resumes control of Turner Elementary. *Pittsburgh Gazette.*

Edison Project. (1998). *Second annual report on school performance.* New York: Edison Project. (Visited 3/30/00) http://www.edisonproject.com/annual frame.html.

Edison Project. (1998). *Response to the AFT report on student achievement in Edison schools.* (Visited 3/30/00) http://www.aft.org/research/edisonproject/edrespnd/edresp2.htm.

Edison Project. (1997). *Annual report on school performance.* New York: Edison Project.

Evereen Securities. (1999). *Educational services industry.* Chicago: Author.

Hassel, B., & Lin, M. (1999). *Contracting for charter school success: A resource guide for clear contracting with school management organizations.* St. Paul, MN: Charter School Friends National Network. (Visited 3/30/00) http://www. charterfriends.org/partnerships.html.

Horn, J., & Miron, G. (1999). *Evaluation of the Michigan public school academy initiative.* Kalamazoo, MI: Evaluation Center, Western Michigan University. (Visited 3/30/00) http://www.mde.state.mi.us/reports/psaeva19901/wmu_finalrpt.pdf.

KPMG-Peat Marwick. (1998). *Tuition rate study: Study of charter school tuition rate calculations*. Boston: Massachusetts Department of Education. (Visited 3/30/00) http://finance1.doe.mass.edu/charter/tuition_study.html.

Marsh-Huggins, A. (2000). Report: Ohio's charter schools get poor grades. The Associated Press.

Metcalf, Kim K., Muller, Pat, Boone, William, Tait, Polly, Stage, Frances, & Stacey, Nicole. (1998a). *A comparative evaluation of the Cleveland scholarship and tutoring grant program*. Bloomington, IN: Indiana Center for Education, Indiana University.

Metcalf, Kim K., Muller, Pat, Boone, William, Tait, Polly, Stage, Frances, & Stacey, Nicole. (1998b). *Evaluation of the Cleveland scholarship program: Second-year report (1997–98)*, Bloomington, IN: Indiana Center for Education, Indiana University.

Montgomery Securities. (1997). *The emerging investment opportunity in education*. New York: Montgomery Securities.

Muir, E, Drown, R., & Nelson, F. H. (2000, March 10). *Special education enrollment in charter schools: Implications for a market based education system*. Paper presented at the Annual Meeting of the American Education Finance Association, Austin Texas.

Mulholland, L. (1999). *Arizona charter school progress evaluation*. Tempe, AZ: Morrison Institute for Public Policy, Arizona State University. (Visited 3/30/00) http://www.ade.state.az.us/charterschools/info/CharterSchoolStatusMain Report3–15–99.pdf.

Murphy, Dan, Rosenberg, Bella, & Nelson, F. Howard. (1997, July). *The Cleveland voucher program: Who chooses? Who gets chosen? Who pays?* Washington, DC: American Federation of Teachers. (Visited 3/30/00) http://www.aft.org/research/reports/clev/contents.htm.

National Center for Education Statistics. (1999). *The Digest of Education Statistics, 1998*. Washington, DC: U.S. Department of Education. (Visited 3/30/00) <http://nces.ed.gov/pubs99/digest98/>.

National Center for Education Statistics. (1997). *Characteristics of stayers, movers and leavers: Results from the teacher follow-up survey: 1994–95*. Washington, DC: U.S. Department of Education. (Visited 3/30/00) http://nces.ed.gov/pubs 97/97450.html.

National Center for Education Statistics. (1996). *The digest of education statistics, 1995*. Washington, DC: U.S. Department of Education.

National Center for Education Statistics. (1991). *The digest of education statistics, 1990*. Washington, DC: U.S. Department of Education.

National Education Association. (1997). *Status of the American public school teacher, 1995–96*. Washington, DC: Author.

Nelson, F. Howard. (2000). *Setting the record straight: Trends in student achievement for Edison Schools, Inc*. Washington, DC: American Federation of Teachers.

Nelson, F. Howard. (1998a) *Trends in private school cost and tuition: No immunity from the cost disease.* Paper presented at American Educational Finance Association, Mobile, Alabama, March. (Visited 3/30/00) http://www.aft.org/research/reports/private/privcost/index.htm.

Nelson, F. Howard. (1998b). *Student achievement in Edison schools: Mixed results in an ongoing enterprise.* Washington, DC: American Federation of Teachers. (Visited 3/30/00) http://www.aft.org/research/edisonproject.

Nelson, F. Howard. (1997, Spring). How private management firms seek to make money in public schools. *Journal of School Business Management.* (Visited 3/30/00) http://www.aft.org/research/reports/private/jsbm/jsbm.htm.

Petro, Jim. (1998). *Cleveland scholarship and tutoring program: Special audit report. July 1, 1995 through June 30, 1998.* Columbus, OH: Auditor of the State of Ohio.

Prince H. (1999). Follow the money: An initial view of elementary charter school spending in Michigan. *Journal of Education Finance*, 175–194.

Public Sector Consultants, Inc., and MAXIMUS, Inc. (PSC/MAXIMUS) (1999). *Michigan's charter school initiative: From theory to practice.* East Lansing, MI: Michigan Department of Education. (Visited 3/30/00) http://www.mde.state.mi.us/reports/psaeva19901/pscfullreport.pdf.

RPP International, Nelson, B., Berman, P, Ericson, J., Perry, R., Perry, R., Silverman, D., & Soloman, D. (2000). *A national study of charter schools: Fourth-year report.* (Visited 3/30/00) http://www.ed.gov/pubs/charter4thyear/.

Richards, Craig E., Shore, Rima, & Sawicky, Max B. (1996). *Risky business: Private management of public schools.* Washington, DC: Economic Policy Institute.

Tyack, David. (1974). *The one best system: A history of American urban education.* Cambridge, MA: Harvard University Press.

Williams, Lois C., & Leak, Lawrence E. (1995). *The UMBC evaluation of the Tesseract program in Baltimore City.* Baltimore, MD: Center for Educational Research, University of Maryland Baltimore Campus.

Wood, Jennifer. (2000). *Early examination of the Massachusetts charter school initiative.* Dartmouth, MA: Donahue Institute, University of Massachusetts. (Visited 3/30/00) http://www.donahue.umassp.edu/.

Zollers, N., & Ramanathan, A. (1998). "For-profit charters and students with disabilities: The sordid side of the business of schooling." *Phi Delta Kappan, 79,* 297–304.

CONCLUSION

12

CONCLUSION

William J. Fowler, Jr.
National Center for Education Statistics

Stephen Chaikind
Gallaudet University

What will the new millennium mean for education finance? One assumption is that the future will be like the most recent past, although this common assumption has often proved erroneous. In this 2001 AEFA Yearbook, our learned contributors have sketched out a broad range of potential directions in education finance that they anticipate for the future. Much of this thinking diverges from previous paradigms. Rossmiller sagely notes this caveat:

> Projections of school enrollments and expenditures require one to assume that the trends that have been witnessed in the recent past will continue into the future. Whether these projections withstand the test of time will depend, in large part, on several emerging trends and factors that may alter in significant ways the amount of money devoted to support public education, and the way in which that money is allocated to districts, schools, and classrooms in coming years. Among these trends and factors are the outcomes of school finance litigation, whether the property tax is reduced or replaced as a source of school revenue, the implementation of new and emerging technologies to deliver educational programs and services, policy initiatives to reduce class size, changes in teacher compensation practices, the growth of charter schools and voucher programs, and almost certainly a number of other factors yet to be identified.

Remaining alert to such a variety of new and unique developments is crucial for future education finance research and policy.

In addition, Guthrie and Rothstein assert that in the future:

> American education finance may be entering a new era characterized by the challenging concept of adequacy. This concept directly links financial distributions with education arrangements, and thereby propels education finance from the periphery to the center of policy debate.

If Guthrie and Rothstein are prescient about funding adequacy being evaluated in terms of education arrangements, the millennium may bring about much more of a change in education finance than has even been suggested by our contributing authors.

Historically, through good economic times and bad, public support has continued to grow for education; and public revenues per student have grown almost continuously through the pervious century. However, this rate of growth has seemed to moderate in recent decades. In 1930, per-student revenue as a percentage of per capita personal income was 10.7. By 1970, it had risen to 19.8 (an 85 percent rise). In the 30 years since 1970, through periods of generally great affluence, it had risen to 23.7 by 1997 (a 20 percent rise). In other words, people are no longer willing to continue to increase the share of their per capita personal income going to elementary and secondary public revenue per student as much as they had in the past (National Center for Education Statistics, Table 62-1, p. 177).

However, while the growth rate in public revenues to education has necessarily slowed, robust individual support can be seen in other arenas. For example, the rise of alternative revenue sources described by Addonizio in this Yearbook, and the emergence of charter and public funding of private education entities described by Nelson et al., both suggest alternative financial arrangements may supplement public revenues for education in the future. In addition, there is the potential of giving poor and underachieving students and their families a direct choice over their learning environment, as noted by Moore, which also intimates a different direction for future public financial support for education.

Another change that is taking place is in the sources of public school financing. Traditionally, school districts have obtained the majority of their funding from local revenue, particularly in the Northeast and Midwest. In 1979, state governments contributed more, on average in the United States, for the first time than did local governments, but this pattern reverted back to a greater share of support from local government sources within a decade. By the late 1990s, the state share has again begun to exceed local share. In the Midwest, though, the level of local funding fell from 1992 to 1997, corresponding with the 1993–94 reduction of the property tax in Michigan (see Figure 12.1). Now, for the average public school district, state and local governments contribute about equally; the federal government share has never reached 10 percent of total revenues, and is now approximately 7 percent of all revenues for public elementary and secondary education (National Center for Education Statistics, 2000, March, Figure 11, p. 49; and 2000, June, Indicator 63, p. 102, and Table 63-1, p. 178). (These trends are shown in Figure 12.2.) In higher education, too, changes are occurring in the sources of funds to institutions and individuals, as noted by McKeown-Moak, with shifts occurring away from direct government expenditures to more reliance on payments from students and their families, coupled with additional financial aid. Will changes in public finance, budgeting, and taxation again alter these sources of funding in the future?

As noted in the overview to this Yearbook, one important trend for the future is the increasing emphasis on linkages between education finance and outcomes through accountability and testing. While the demand for improved outcomes

FIGURE 12.1 PUBLIC FINANCIAL SUPPORT: PERCENTAGE DISTRIBUTION OF REVENUES FOR PUBLIC ELEMENTARY AND SECONDARY SCHOOLS BY SOURCE OF FUNDS AND REGION: 1991–92 TO 1996–97

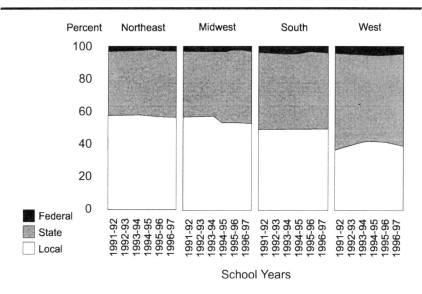

SOURCE: U.S. Department of Education (2000, June, Indicator 63, p. 102).

FIGURE 12.2 SOURCES OF REVENUE FOR PUBLIC ELEMENTARY AND SECONDARY SCHOOLS: 1970–1971 to 1996–1997

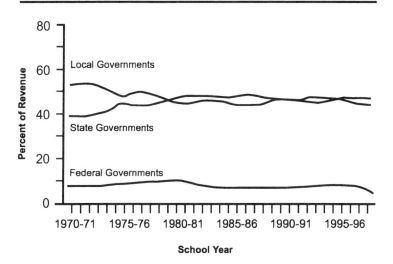

SOURCE: U.S. Department of Education (2000, March, Figure 11, p. 49).

may lead to increased funding for education, one must also be aware of the possibility that it may also have unanticipated consequences in the public's support for financing elementary and secondary education (as well as for higher education). In some states, for example, state testing has led to less than stellar results, and may also have led to instances of cheating by educators (Mathews & Argetsinger, 2000). High failure rates, if widespread, may sour public support for education as much as they may lead to increases in funding. Further, the use of adequacy for evaluating revenue in terms of education may instead result in the use of lower levels of revenue to define adequacy. This becomes apparent when one examines the greater equity in those states with lower levels of revenue:

> [M]any of the states ranking lowest from the perspective of the median revenue per student appear to be among the most equitable.... [T]he nine states with the lowest median revenue all reflect a relatively high degree of equity....Conversely, the five states with the highest actual median revenue per student show a broad range of variation in revenues, or inequities, across the districts within these states....As an extreme example,...students at the highest levels of revenue per student in Mississippi ($4,089 at the 95th percentile) receive less than even the lowest revenue students (5th percentile) in 29 states. Also students overall appear to receive more revenues in inequitable, high revenue states than in many of the more equitable, low revenue states. For example, students in New York at the lowest levels of spending (5th percentile) receive more revenues than the vast majority of students in other states where total educational spending is more equitable. Most New York students receive more than the median student in 45 of the 50 states. (National Center for Education Statistics, 1998, p. 102)

Guthrie and Rothstein argue that the role of state governments ascends in significance when adequacy is the policy objective. While it is still too early to tell how the states will react as they indeed begin to play more prominent roles in assuring adequacy, such ascendance may or may not in fact result in greater levels of revenues for public education. It may be that as the state becomes the primary revenue source, students will experience lower levels of revenue. When we examine the 100 largest school districts in the nation, the average state support is 48.7%. Detroit, Albuquerque, San Bernardino, and Newark are all above 75% state support (National Center for Education Statistics, 2000). As Monk and Brent (1997) observe, high-percentage state-supported school districts are more susceptible to economic downturns, because states tend to depend upon sales and income taxes for revenue, which are very responsive to such economic downturns. If adequacy and state funding become ascendant, districts with property-poor tax bases often become the most vulnerable, because they are more dependent upon state support, and hence, under certain scenarios, poor school districts in the millennium may be the poorer for it.

As Fowler notes in his chapter, financial reporting is beginning to move toward more "public-friendly" reporting that incorporates finances into school district "report cards," as well as other policy and publicly meaningful financial reporting. These school district report cards often now include student outcomes. To date, these report cards have not typically been used to assess the fiscal adequacy, effectiveness, or outcome productivity of a school or school district. In part, as noted by Rice, this is because there has been no agreement regarding the educational production function. The most recent evidence suggests that even the best "black-box" models are not sufficient to identify accurately and reliably those school districts that are the most "productive" (Bifulco & Duncombe, 1999).

If, as several of our authors suggest, the emphasis in the future becomes a stronger linking of finance and student outcomes, then the comparison of school districts on these characteristics might be described as comparisons of "relative efficiencies." If "relative efficiency" becomes the sole focus of education policy makers, there is the potential for dislocations in public elementary and secondary education to occur, as they have in health care. As we observe the attempts of policy makers in health care to contain costs and implement a version of "relative efficiency," it appears there that there are problematic results, particularly from the patient's perspective. Hospital stays have been shortened to reduce costs, for example, and many procedures previously thought to require hospital stays are now routinely performed as outpatient procedures. Further, nonprofit hospitals are increasingly being taken over by for-profit institutions Patients who require expensive interventions and long hospital stays are increasingly shunned by being discouraged from admittance. Patients who have only Medicare are increasingly being denied enrollment. If school finance is inextricably linked to efficiency, does a similar future await?

There is, of course, the real potential for the emphasis of elementary/secondary education assessment to reflect some definition of finance linked to adequacy—school districts may be held to some standard of performance, particularly in comparison to their peers. Relative efficiency may well be defined as the degree to which a school district can produce satisfactory student outcomes at the lowest cost. But if this occurs, public and policy makers alike must take care to avoid the pitfalls that have recently befallen the health care sector. Otherwise, if Grissmer is correct that different types of students are more sensitive to allocations of resources and smaller pupil-teacher ratios and compensatory intervention than others, then implementation of "relative efficiency" in education might have many of the detrimental effects observed with health care.

Chaikind explains how the U.S. Department of Education has developed a set of performance indicators for programs for students with disabilities. These indicators include "indicators measuring...reading, math and other academic proficiency gains; school completion rates; employment success; disciplinary actions undertaken; (and) parental satisfaction." Such indicators may already reflect an example of how outcomes are gaining focus among educators and policy makers. Since those who provide federal funding follow the accomplishment of these special education performance indicators, this might be cited as an already existing example of Guthrie and Rothstein's prognostication that the concept of adequacy will transmogrify into similar performance indicators related to funding. The flexibility that Moore describes in proposed federal legislative options that would permit states the authority to waive Title I requirements in the interests of achieving better student performance also maintains the linkage between funding and student outcomes.

One result of an increased emphasis on outcomes might be less satisfaction by students and their parents with the services provided by public schools. For example, one potential approach to achieving outcomes within this framework would place students without special or compensatory education needs in larger classes, with "less productive" teachers, receiving markedly fewer resources than other students. Or, "effective" (and better compensated?) teachers might be assigned to teach the students who are more sensitive to additional resources. We should not forget that a common practice of school districts in the past was to have schools that had selective admission, often on the basis of achievement testing. Would relative efficiency cause public schools to reimplement testing for admission to certain schools? And if selective admission becomes common, will the improvements in high school completion be reversed? If public education experiences any of the public dissatisfaction that is now felt with the provision of medical care, the public's willingness to fund public education might be severely harmed. As a result, the alternative funding mechanisms described by Addonizio, and the privatization of K-12 education and use of public money to support more private choice in education described by Nelson, might intensify. Nowhere might this be more prevalent than in poor school districts with poor student outcomes.

However, a more sanguine implementation of changes in education finance in the millennium might also be in our future. As Rice notes, "Policy makers must...weigh competing values to balance efficiency with other sorts of social goods, such as equity and liberty." State elementary/secondary education policy makers, placed in ascendancy, might well choose to define efficiency and equity as requiring additional resources for school districts with poor outcomes. There is no reason to assume that these education policy makers will not take into account, for example, the dislocations that have occurred in health care, and not respond to student and parent dissatisfaction when seeking to guarantee adequacy. Thus, lower levels of state support for more equitable education funding systems, any increased use of alternative funding sources, and the preference to use public funds for private or alternative education are not inevitable consequences of the linkage between funding adequacy and educational program adequacy. As Grissmer asserts,

> Future experimentation needs to be directed toward establishing benchmark measurements for major resource variables such as teacher salary, class size at all grades, teacher professional development and preschool, summer school and after-school programs.... [T]hen theories need to be developed that explain how or why resources affect achievement. Such theories need to explain what changes in the classroom when resources are changed, and how those changes affect achievement for particular types of students. In the end, resource effects can be predicted from theories, and it is the theories that generate scientific and policy consensus.

We do not know whether education finance in the millennium will reflect a persistence of current trends, heading in directions that are simple extensions of the recent past, or if, as has happened so often, the future will resemble something entirely unique. The evolution of concepts such as adequacy, the linkage of aspects of finance to outcomes, innovations in technology and classroom processes, flexibility in the use of funds both public and private, new models of public finance, budgeting, and taxation, and many other factors, all have the potential to transform education finance in the future in ways we are only beginning to envision.

REFERENCES

Bifulco, Robert, & Duncombe, William. (1999, March). *Evaluating school performance: Are we ready for prime time?* Paper presented at the American Education Finance Association Annual Conference, Seattle.

Mathews, Jay, & Argetsinger, Amy. (2000, June 2). Cheating on rise along with testing. *Washington Post*, p. A01.

Monk, D. H., & Brent, B. O. (1997). *Raising money for education*. Thousand Oaks, CA: Corwin Press.

National Center for Education Statistics. (2000). *Characteristics of the 100 largest public elementary and secondary school districts in the United States: 1998-1999* [excluding Puerto Rico, Hawaii, and Washington, DC], by Beth Aronstamm Young. Washington DC: U.S. Department of Education.

National Center for Education Statistics. (2000, June). *The Condition of Education, 2000*, U.S. Department of Education.

National Center for Education Statistics. (2000, March). *Digest of Education Statistics, 1999*. U.S. Department of Education.

National Center for Education Statistics. (1998) *Inequities in Public School District Revenues*, by Thomas B. Parrish & Christine S. Hikido. Washington, DC: U.S. Department of Education.

INDEX